VASSAL STATE

How America Runs Britain

ANGUS HANTON

Swift

SWIFT PRESS

First published in Great Britain by Swift Press 2024

1 3 5 7 9 8 6 4 2

Copyright © Angus Hanton 2024

Typeset by Tetragon, London
Printed and bound in Great Britain by CPI Group (UK) Ltd, Croydon, CR0 4YY

A CIP catalogue record for this book is available from the British Library

ISBN: 9781800753884
eISBN: 9781800753891

CONTENTS

Introduction

MY SEARCH FOR FACTS

Thirty years ago, I got lucky: I bought a single share in an investment and insurance business called Berkshire Hathaway. It cost me $3,000 and I did it just to get some information. In the foggy days before the internet, only those people listed on the Berkshire Hathaway share register received the accounts and the annual letter from chairman Warren Buffett. Half philosophical reflection, half market report, these letters have acquired a kind of mythical status in the business world, in part because Mr Buffett is an insightful man but also because, since I bought that single share, the value of Berkshire Hathaway stock has risen, not just a few times but by a factor of 170, so that, by the end of 2023, it had grown in value to half a million dollars. I have been passionate about understanding business and investment my whole life and my purchase was a welcome accident, really – I was just trying to understand how Berkshire Hathaway worked.

Mr Buffett's success is a stark illustration of US capital at work – taking calculated risks, buying businesses in profitable sectors and determinedly growing wealth. His approach has not changed in more than half a century, but the US economy has. In the past 15 years, it has been impossible to ignore how three great American commercial forces have become truly massive in their scale and riches: big tech, private equity and US-based multinational corporations. And a basic, obvious question has continued to press on my mind: how much of the UK's economy is now US-owned?

Originally, I believed such a simple question would be well understood by the British government, and so – because I am nosy – I filed a volley of Freedom of Information requests asking about US corporate muscle here. Simple stuff, but the answers were anything but straightforward.

I started with big state spenders – looking for the value of US contracts with the Ministry of Defence (MOD) and the NHS. Both admitted they do not analyse their vast spending by the nationality of the companies supplying them. I approached the Office for National Statistics (ONS) in Newport, South Wales, and asked how many UK workers are employed by US corporations. They said that they do not record even this basic data, but, without irony, they offered to put together a guesstimate for me based on figures from Dun & Bradstreet, a Florida-based information company. On the phone, the ONS official expressed with pride that he subscribes to this service – costing $40,000 a year – and said that other government departments cannot justify such cost. Even so, the ONS admitted its estimate of 'about 1 million' was too low, as it would not include the tens of thousands of 'self-employed' Uber and Amazon drivers, or the delivery workers on platforms supplying takeaway food. Conservative analysis, as we shall see, suggests the true figure is not 1, but 2 million Brits who are ultimately working for American bosses.

What I really wanted was trade data, total sales figures between the US and UK, and I recalled that Britain, along with other Western governments, had started to collect exactly that information. In order to protect tax revenues, the national tax authorities had required all multinationals in the Organisation for Economic Co-operation and Development (OECD) to reveal their accounts on a country-by-country basis. So, I wrote to HMRC's Freedom of Information department in Newcastle, asking for the turnover, profits and taxes paid by the larger US companies. Their team replied categorically, and somewhat puzzlingly, that they did not have that data. But a few months later, after my persistent questioning, they replied: 'Please accept our sincere apologies for the confusion caused by our first response. We confirm we do hold the requested information.' My excitement was short-lived, however, because they then stated that they would not be sharing what they knew, explaining that such secrecy 'ensures a safe place to consider policy options in private... There is a strong public interest in protecting against encroachment on the ability of ministers and officials to develop policy options freely and frankly.' I was shocked that, although officials at HMRC had, eventually, admitted that they do hold this basic information on US corporations, which had been gathered at taxpayers' expense, and which affects how much tax everyone else has to pay, they were still point-blank refusing to share it.

Then, in a fortunate break, one of the HMRC officials must have sensed the absurdity of this because he quietly gave me a vital tip-off: he pointed out an obscure page of the website of the US Internal Revenue Service (IRS) where the Americans themselves had already published all the information I was looking for, and that the British were at such pains to protect. It was, and is, a treasure trove of data and, for anyone who reads columns of numbers as a hobby, it is a full-blown, marmalade-dropping eyebrow-raiser. The IRS had listed the total sales made by the big US corporations to every country around the world, together with their profits and any tax they paid. And it included sales to the UK and how these compared with the American footprint in other

European countries. It also listed the enormous sums US multinationals were routing through tax havens such as Luxembourg, the Netherlands, Switzerland and Ireland.[1]

These revelations led me to the idea that other useful statistics might be 'Made in the USA', suggesting that it would be sensible to check a range of US sources to see if the UK has been singled out for economic capture. Sure enough, Washington's Bureau of Economic Analysis (BEA) showed something that the British statisticians cannot. The BEA proves that Britain has been overwhelmingly the preferred hunting ground for US multinationals buying up businesses abroad.[2] The figures imply that the US has placed 30 per cent of all its overseas investments into the UK. In summary, it is clear that the invitation to buy up Britain, first extended by Margaret Thatcher in the 1980s and reiterated by every prime minister since, has been enthusiastically accepted by Americans. What are the consequences?

One answer comes day by day from the British media. Much of the key writing has been done by journalists like Alex Brummer (the *Daily Mail*), Ben Marlow (the *Daily Telegraph*) and Phillip Inman (*The Guardian*), who describe the consequences of the sell-off of large UK companies. The *Financial Times* has been a close follower of the exploits of US private equity in Britain, with implicit warnings contained in articles by Daniel Thomas, Peggy Hollinger, Harriet Agnew and Kaye Wiggins. And Stephen Glover (the *Daily Mail*) has asked the essential question about what happens when critical authority over strategic assets is placed into the hands of billionaire tech titans – as is the case with Elon Musk's Starlink internet provision in Ukraine. What's striking is that the concerns about US economic power over the UK and the world cut right across many domestic political differences.

The rest of us can see the outlines of the problem: our high streets and small businesses are under pressure, crushed by slick,

US-dominated online competition and a tax regime which makes far greater claims on domestic businesses than on US corporations. Most of our digital infrastructure and even our principal system of exchange – card payments – are overwhelmingly US-owned. And, increasingly, British consumers are paying a royalty to US businesses on most transactions, moving from one-off purchasers to renters and subscribers, who slog away on payment treadmills for the benefit of shareholders on the other side of the Atlantic. The consequences could not be graver: impoverishment, loss of autonomy, and a drain on talent and treasure.

The shape and extent of US economic power in the UK is, for all this, something Britain avoids discussing in the round. The term 'big tech' is usually used to describe 'US tech'. When reference is made to 'private equity' there is a strong chance it really means US private equity. Talk of a 'multinational' means, more often than not, a US multinational. But we do not discuss the US hold over us in economic terms even if we sense we are constantly dealing with US companies. Politicians rarely discuss it save to talk about a 'special relationship' and a 'partnership', but, as we shall see, the facts are routinely misrepresented in British political statements about Anglo-US relations. There could be a reason for that: after all, what does a 'partnership' really look like when one side is the mightiest superpower in the history of the world and holds an overwhelming stake in the other's economy?

Perhaps the answer is not to look too closely – and Whitehall does not. There comes a point, though, when you have to. I think we are past that point, for obvious reasons: if the companies that control Britain's growth and success are ultimately accountable to a much greater authority than Parliament, the actions of London politicians will be increasingly irrelevant. A totally subordinate Britain will make a poorer and more irrelevant partner for the US, as well as Europe, something that will matter most of all in the coming century, when the challenges we face require global action, be they climate change or, more immediately, the defence of democracy against authoritarianism in Russia, China and elsewhere.

The essential case of this book is not a rejection of all American values or of democracy or of the carefully negotiated and sustained alliances that defeated fascism in the 1940s and secured peace in Europe and in many other places in the aftermath. It is not about a mythical 'evil empire'. On the contrary, the US state has defended many decent values that the UK took centuries to create. Instead, what matters most in this story is business, not politics. It is companies like Apple and Amazon, private equity ingenuity and corporate muscle that have conquered Britain through innovation, determination and sheer size. So what follows is a nuts-and-bolts examination of the choices that have set British businesses back while making the US richer, and an analysis of Britain's appalling failure to confront the reality of dealing with a superpower ally with a dynamic and innovative commercial approach that has outmanoeuvred and outperformed its junior partner. This is a call for a new conversation from the one led by politicians apparently obsessed with presenting a false prospectus about Britain's economic prowess, its role in the world and the path to prosperity. And it is also a call to action to stop further transfers of parts of the economy to powerful and unaccountable American owners and to reset Britain on a course for more economic independence.

Behind it all hangs the gravest risk, one that we rarely consider: what could happen to the UK if the US were ever to break with the values shared between our two countries for the past century? How robustly could British policy-makers respond, for example, to a second Trump presidency that turned its back on the rule of law, worked much harder to erect trade barriers, shrank NATO and promoted ever closer relations with the Russian dictator Vladimir Putin at the expense of Ukraine?

Consider this: there are two countries with close political, economic and military ties, founding members of a defensive military alliance; each is the other's principal trading partner and they share a common language, even if there are notable differences. The senior partner controls a significant percentage of the junior partner's domestic businesses, and while the junior partner is occasionally critical, it relies on the senior partner for much of its economic growth, its defence and its geopolitical muscle. I am, of course, describing the relationship between Belarus and Russia. Angela Merkel called Belarus a 'vassal state'; US Secretary of State Antony Blinken likened it to 'a client state'. The principal difference between that relationship and Britain's with America is that Britain still controls its own democracy. For how long will that matter if the bulk of British businesses and enterprises are owned by another country, while the bulk of products and services we buy are also supplied by that country?

This book collates evidence that numerous levers of control over Britain have already moved across the Atlantic. The UK, it turns out, chose to 'take back control' from Europe in 2016 while meekly passing ever more economic power to another continent entirely. Are the politicians Britain elected ready to address all this? Far from it. As we shall see, a tour of the economy suggests a thundering herd has just charged in...

1

THUNDERING HERD
CHARGING INTO ALL CORNERS OF THE KINGDOM

Like many expeditions this one starts in the supermarket. The smell of fresh bread is piped through the air conditioning and the lights are calibrated to raise appetites and lower inhibitions. Subconsciously, we shoppers are being manipulated to make quick choices and spend as much as possible. And, even in the age of online shopping, British enthusiasm for supermarkets is undimmed. We visit around 70 times a year, spending an average of 43 minutes on each shopping trip. Even though the number of products in the typical supermarket has grown from around 7,000 to more than 40,000, we think we have a pretty good idea about what is on sale.[1] We are proud of our cosmopolitan tastes for international cuisine, as well as valuing home-grown British staples. But inside these buildings that we depend on there is a hidden history, and secret origin stories for many of the goods we know so well. You won't always find the clues on the labels: on the contrary, those may give you a misleading impression. As for what you think you have always known about your favourite brands: things have almost certainly changed. To find the facts about the packages, tins and bottles, you have to look closely and ferret around.

Start with breakfast. The cereal shelves are stacked high with household names, brands that tell us how we should see ourselves at breakfast time: Ready Brek ('Get up and glow'), Alpen ('Breakfast at its peak') and Weetabix ('Incredible inside'), all feeling as British as they come. On the back of the Weetabix packet a statement declares it to be the most popular cereal in the UK and a royal warrant shows that it is 'by Appointment to HM the Queen' – an endorsement of good health and longevity, which will apply equally when the endorsement is changed to 'HM the King'. But there is no clue about who owns the brand. With the help of two of our American friends, an iPhone and Google, we can establish that all three of these brands are in fact owned by Post Holdings of Missouri. Next to them there are rows and rows of boxes from Kellogg's, of Battle Creek, Michigan. Their name is not hard to find – perhaps because the owners of the 'Special K' brand supply over a third of the UK cereal market. Then we spot some old favourites which we suspect are American: Cheerios and Honey Monster Puffs – and the tiny print on the back tells us they are owned by General Mills of Golden Valley, Minnesota. At least there is the reassuring sight of own-brand cereals, which are less expensive even if they do taste remarkably similar. That should not be surprising, because a bit more research reveals that they are often produced by the same companies. The Weetabix-owning Post Holdings, based in the US Midwest, reportedly also makes many of Tesco's and Asda's own-label brands.[2]

In the confectionery aisle there are chocolates and sweets from Cadbury of Bournville, the UK's market leader. An online search confirms it is fully owned by Mondelez of Chicago. That Illinois company also owns best-selling brands Milka, Oreo and Toblerone. Dozens more sweets come from Mars, Incorporated of Virginia, which owns Wrigley, Galaxy and Maltesers. Their products are also entrenched in other sections of the store, with Uncle

Ben's rice in the ready-to-cook food, and in pet food too Mars is the pack leader, owning both the Pedigree and Whiskas brands.

The soft drinks section is a head-high celebration of plastic and sugar, where Pepsi and Coca-Cola are way ahead of locally owned brands and sell far more than just colas – PepsiCo owns Tropicana and Quaker Oats, while Coca-Cola owns Fanta, Sprite, Dr Pepper and Innocent. Atlanta-based Coca-Cola also now owns the brand that itself makes a virtue of secrecy with its slogan 'Schhh… Schweppes'. Their advertising plays on a long-standing myth in which the 'housewife', or 'homemaker', and the US brands are in cahoots to present food as home-made rather than processed, just like the oven-ready croissants and cookies from the Pillsbury Company of Minnesota.

Next aisle: cleaning, washing and sanitary products. Although there are still some large UK suppliers, such as Unilever, this sector is dominated by Procter & Gamble (P&G) of Ohio and Colgate-Palmolive of New York. Some of their brands are upfront about their US connection, such as Colgate toothpaste, which is seemingly packaged in the American flag and even squeezes out in red, white and blue stripes. The ownership of others is kept obscure, perhaps allowing many shoppers to mistake Fairy Liquid for a British brand when it is really owned by P&G. Kimberly-Clark of Texas cleans up financially in toilet paper and paper tissues, with its market leaders Kleenex covering 60 per cent of its market, and Andrex taking 30 per cent of the toilet paper spend.[3] Millions of households spend over £1 each week on the product made famous by the Labrador puppy.[4] The nappies section is filled by Huggies and Pampers: only careful examination shows that these brands are from Kimberley-Clark and P&G, respectively.

While strong branding makes Kimberly-Clark tissues and nappies profitable through a combination of high margins and repeat business, there are dozens of other American-owned market leaders. For example, British women spend £3 billion every year on tampons. P&G stands out, with its Tampax Compak and Pearl brands being favoured by 6 million users. Boots UK Limited, formerly Boots the Chemists, whose ultimate headquarters are in Deerfield, Illinois, sells its own-brand tampons to another half a million customers, and together the US companies have 60 per cent market penetration in this sector.[5] In personal care and perfume, Estée Lauder of New York has a profitable niche, and Dr. Scholl's of Boston has a virtual monopoly in footcare products, allowing it to charge whatever price the market will bear.

Right across the supermarket, strong brands are a sure way to extract profits. The American businessman Charlie Munger, discussing the early days of the legendary US corporation Berkshire Hathaway, said: 'Originally we didn't know the power of a good brand. Over time we just discovered that we could raise prices 10 per cent a year and no one cared.'[6]

As we shop we look behind the labels and discover that companies like Mondelez and Kraft Heinz, both based in Chicago, are harnessing scale in marketing and distribution to keep out locals and, where necessary, buy up successful competitors. Many argue that this leads to higher prices, more limited choice and increased packaging.

The US food companies are well aware of the power of sugar, salt and fat, and are adept at harnessing the consumer's addiction to these. In October 2022 rules were introduced to stop large supermarkets strategically placing unhealthy items near checkouts to make a 'suggestive sell' to queueing customers. Mike Tattersfield, chief executive of Krispy Kreme, has said he will find other ways to promote his products and asserts that his customers can easily be trained to look for the doughnuts in different places. He knows that doughnuts sell: 'I don't see the world changing to kale cake for their break… it's not that much fun to share.'[7]

The dominance of big US food continues as we wander through the aisles: General Mills of Golden Valley, Minnesota, makes Green Giant products, Yoplait yogurt and Häagen-Dazs ice cream – which leads us on to the chilled- and frozen-food cabinets. Here we find plenty of chicken, the UK's favourite source of protein: research shows that half of it is produced by US-controlled agribusinesses. The biggest of these are Pilgrim's Pride of Colorado and Avara, largely owned by Cargill of Minnesota. Between them these two companies raise 550 million birds each year for the UK market, equivalent to an American-owned chicken for each UK household every 18 days.[8] Pilgrim's Pride is also the largest pork producer in the UK.[9]

Arriving at the checkout you might notice that your shopping is being scanned by machines from NCR Voyix, formerly National Cash Register, of Atlanta, Georgia. You will almost certainly pay through an American company – Visa, Mastercard, Amex, Google Pay or Apple Pay. Even if you are that rare shopper still using cash taken from a 'hole in the wall' or ATM, there is a two-thirds chance it came from a machine made by NCR.[10]

Punch-drunk with the pervasiveness of US businesses, we can't help wondering whether the rest of Britain is equally American-owned and, if so, how much it all adds up to – but to find out more we leave the comfort of the supermarket.

Step into the high street for a cup of coffee and the choice is limited: we spot three US chains – Starbucks, Caffè Nero and Costa, now a subsidiary of Coca-Cola.[11] Together these chains have more than 4,500 branches, selling hundreds of millions of drinks each year. It fits the pattern of much American commerce in Britain in being a high-margin business. Through bulk-buying, the cost of the ingredients and a paper cup for our coffee has been driven down to about 30p, while the product sells for £3 or more. Many outlets are selling for more than 12 hours a day and 7 days a week. Other high-street chains, such as Boots with its 1,900 branches, are highly profitable but, like Costa and Morrisons, are not widely recognised as US-owned. Whether hiding behind long-established British brands or openly American, US businesses have a direct relationship with the British shopper and they own dozens of chains now well established in the high street. Across the UK our high streets are hosting many American-owned chains, such as Pizza Hut, McDonald's, KFC, Gail's Bakery, Majestic Wine, Taco Bell, Nike, Gap, TK Maxx, Abercrombie & Fitch, Timberland, Foot Locker, Levi's, Costco, Subway, Hotel Chocolat, Waterstones, Ralph Lauren and Sweaty Betty. In other European countries, the US presence is far, far smaller.

Online shopping and delivery

Once home from shopping and realising we have forgotten something, we go online. Most likely we will be buying through Seattle-based Amazon, whose sales now make up more than 30 per cent of all UK online commerce. Of this total, 60 per cent of what is badged as being from Amazon is, in reality, from third parties using the 'Amazon marketplace'.[12] The US giants don't just build their own powerful market positions across the economy: they have become the controllers of the 'platforms' and 'pipes' through which everyone else's goods and services are delivered. Owning the route to market allows companies such as eBay or Taskrabbit, both based in the San Francisco Bay Area, to make chunky 'toll charges' year after year.

After we have placed our online order, we will expect speedy and reliable delivery, and very likely that will come from one of the US companies – FedEx, UPS or XPO – who together have more than 15,000 lorries and vans in the UK. All three enterprises have grown fast, turbo-charged by Covid-19, which prompted an upward lurch in home shopping. These three have expanded by buying up their rivals, taking over TNT, Lynx Express, ANC and Kuehne + Nagel's UK operations. They exploit economies of scale and are indispensable to the large corporations, which need a single, trusted supplier so that they can track their goods precisely. This demand for accurate and real-time data on deliveries is squeezing out smaller local companies, who cannot afford to set up such systems. Any remaining locals are mostly 'bottom feeders' picking up scraps of low-value business. During the Covid period, one of the few remaining independent carriers, Hermes, which delivers more than a tenth of all UK parcels, was snapped up by Advent, a private equity company from Massachusetts, and the carrier was renamed 'Evri'.[13] With all this extra stuff being shipped to us we might want to use self-storage, and maybe go to the world's biggest self-storage company, Public Storage of California, which controls Shurgard, a market leader in the UK. In other forms of storage, Iron Mountain of Massachusetts is easily the biggest UK supplier to the £1 billion-a-year paper-archive industry, but the most rapidly growing form of storage, data in the 'cloud', has no British suppliers – that market has been sewn up by the US tech giants.

Entertainment

After the business of shopping is finished, we watch an on-demand video service, most likely from one of the US media giants: Disney, Netflix, Amazon Prime, Apple TV or Now/Sky. The biggest, Netflix, has almost 17 million UK subscribers – historically invoiced every month from the Netherlands, taking advantage of low tax rates.[14] The others are all growing strongly too: during the Covid period 60 per cent of consumers signed up for a new streaming service. Alternatively, we might play computer games, along with two-thirds of the population. Gamers are almost equally likely to be men or women, and gaming is such big business (more than £7 billion a year) that in the UK it generates twice the revenue of the combined income from the music, movie and theatre industries.[15] On the other side of the screen from the gamers, the majority of suppliers are American, including Microsoft, Apple, Amazon and Epic Games of North Carolina. Their software engineers make games which are highly addictive, and players have to pay extra for 'in-app purchases', so although an initial purchase may be for only 60 per cent of a game, extra features will cost more. One outstanding company in the sector is Steam, based in Bellevue, Washington State, which created the best place to find new games. Thousands of creators add more than 14,000 new games each year and generate a handsome royalty for the company.[16] It is almost the perfect business model: with no physical delivery needed, no development costs and worldwide reach, the business produces a torrent of cash. So, like many other US companies in the UK, it has become the indispensable marketplace where buyers and sellers meet: the toll bridge over which all must cross. And, in common with hundreds of US companies operating in the UK, they pay minimal tax: historically Steam's sales have often been routed through Luxembourg.[17]

Or perhaps we are tired of games and want to go to a real event, for which we get out our laptop, probably made by Dell of Texas or Apple of California, and find we have received an email from Mailchimp of Georgia inviting us to sign up through Eventbrite of San Francisco. We get the confirmation email back via Google's Gmail or Microsoft's Outlook. Indeed, their programs have become so entrenched that many of the UK government's own online forms offer no option except to make submissions on Adobe or Microsoft products (from San Jose, California, and Redmond, Washington, respectively); signing of documents often demands the use of DocuSign (San Francisco) or one of the handful of its US competitors. This entrenchment of programs extends to complying with HMRC's ongoing paperless project, 'Making Tax Digital', with the result that there is no realistic alternative to using US software. In the larger market of business software, 90 per cent comes from the US West Coast and, to use it, UK companies spend more than £20 billion annually. Putting this in perspective, that equates to more than £700 a year for every British household.

Our whistle-stop tour of the consumer economy has shown us just how wide and deep US ownership has become. As we have seen, it is often well hidden behind traditional British brand names. The public may think of Arsenal FC, Liverpool FC, Everton FC, HP Sauce, Terry's and Trainline as being British, but in fact the owners of these companies are based in Missouri, Massachusetts, Florida, Pennsylvania, Illinois and New York, respectively.

A walk around the City of London

Ignore the big brands for a minute, though, and look at the fish. The atrium of an office block in Bishopsgate in London's financial district is overshadowed by a giant aquarium. The tank sits behind the concierge desk and measures 13 feet high and 65 feet wide, and holds 1,200 fish, all collected from the Great Barrier Reef in Australia.[18] Two permanent staff feed the fish and there are three part-time divers who clean the rocks and the inside of the glass tank. This gigantic immoderation is a picture of marine life but also a glimpse of how profoundly powerful US money has become at the centre of the City of London.

To proclaim their power and wealth, the owners, Salesforce (of San Francisco), also renamed the building 'Salesforce Tower', having bought the rights from the developer, a Massachusetts company, Boston Properties, Inc. Salesforce.com are leaders in 'big data' as well as having the biggest private aquarium in Europe. One of the many applications of Salesforce's software is for managing savers' funds – another industry being shaped by the American model. Until recently, investors entrusted their funds to money managers, who would pick which shares they thought might rise and charge an annual fee whether they succeeded or not, and on average their performance was, well, pretty average. In response, a pioneering organisation, Vanguard Group, of Pennsylvania, proved that most investors will do much better if fees are kept very low and the money is simply invested in 'tracker funds' which follow the market. This idea has triumphed, with the result that Vanguard, along with BlackRock (New York) and State Street (Massachusetts), has become a leading firm in the City of London, and by 2023 they were managing worldwide funds of more than $20 trillion. To put that number in context, it is much more than the value of all the assets in the UK, including all property, shares and businesses.[19]

Walking around the City we see the shiny headquarters of the US banks who have moved in: Goldman Sachs, JPMorgan, Morgan Stanley, Wells Fargo, Citigroup and Bank of America. They offer what UK banks cannot: a one-stop shop of banking services across the world and balance sheets to finance giant loans for multinationals. Such borrowing is the 'secret sauce' of US capitalism because it magnifies reasonable earnings into abundant profits. A company making a return on capital of 10 per cent a year can often use borrowing to double the return on the owner's capital to 20 per cent – or more. Indeed, borrowing, for most companies, is non-optional – if they don't borrow they are likely to be taken over by someone who will 'gear up' using borrowings to increase profits.

Another area where these US banks have taken control is simply looking after customers' assets, that is, being custodians. Whereas this was once mostly a matter of having a strongroom for share certificates and jewellery, it is now a highly profitable, multi-trillion-dollar industry with sophisticated record-keeping, and hundreds of nominee companies with clever security and encryption. Worldwide, the six biggest financial custodians are all US firms, led by Bank of New York Mellon – together these Wall Street institutions have custody of almost $100 trillion of assets (equivalent to $14,000 for every individual on the planet). UK banks have been sidelined by these corporations, who process documents more efficiently and whose fortress-like balance sheets inspire savers' confidence.

Not far from Salesforce Tower is Lloyd's of London, which once dominated the insurance market, with wealthy individuals acting as 'names' standing behind the underwriters, but it all went horribly wrong in the 1980s and 1990s. US courts held insurers fully responsible for the damage caused by asbestos, pollution and smoking. Lloyd's 'names' were required to pay up and Lloyd's of London was almost wiped out. Big insurance companies, many of them US-based, moved in. The American Insurance Group (New York), Aon (Chicago) and Berkshire Hathaway (Nebraska) have each taken big chunks of the London insurance and reinsurance markets.

Many of the offices we see around the City of London have been quietly rebadged after the occupants were taken over, such as Jardine Lloyd Thompson, a large insurance broker bought out by Marsh McLennan of Chicago in 2019. Another takeover, in late

2021, was of Vectura, a maker of inhalers, bought by the cigarette company Philip Morris International, and mostly owned by US shareholders. This acquisition was breathtaking: a company creating the biggest threat to pulmonary health bought out a company offering remedies.

Such deals are just the culmination of a 20-year period of transatlantic takeovers: between 2000 and 2018 US companies spent £56 billion more on buying UK firms than UK firms spent across the Atlantic.[20] In recent years this has been by far the biggest route of cross-border takeovers in the world – and this flow is in addition to the organic growth of the US companies.[21]

Moving away from Salesforce Tower to the heart of the City, we reach the offices of New York lawyers Kirkland & Ellis, Latham & Watkins and White & Case: there are 16 US legal firms in the UK with annual revenues of more than $100 million and much of their work is for US corporates who prefer to employ the same firm to work for them in different jurisdictions around the world. The US lawyers' determination and power is clear: in order to drive growth, they have been heavily outbidding local law firms to get the best talent. In 2023 they were offering some newly qualified lawyers starting salaries in excess of £160,000.[22]

We then leave the 'City' itself and move on to London's West End, where we find a cluster of large management-consultancy offices. US management consultants also pay top dollar to recruit the best graduates, the biggest three being Boston Consulting Group, Bain (also based in Boston, Massachusetts) and McKinsey, the oldest and largest of them all. Everyone knows that McKinsey's spiritual home is Boston, its birthplace, but in order to remind people of its size and worldwide reach its website claims: 'we do not have a "headquarters" in the traditional sense.'[23] Together, these three, nicknamed 'MBB', charge more than $30 billion a year for their advice and a good chunk of that is to the UK government and UK companies.

The West End is also home to the giant advertising agencies – including Omnicom and Interpublic (both of New York) – servicing the big US companies expanding in the UK, such as Apple, Ford and Marriott, who usually opt for single suppliers. In the West End we naturally move on to that most English of spots, Berkeley Square, where the US 'private equity houses' are centred: Blackstone is on the square, and the second-largest private equity company, KKR, is just next door in Bond Street, with its new 60,000 square feet of offices. Nearby, off Tottenham Court Road, a third US private equity giant, Apollo, has even bigger offices. These are the three leading companies buying up British industry, and for each of these New York firms the West End of London is just a place for their regional office. It is becoming clear that the true financial capital of the UK is located on Manhattan Island.

Our safari of businesses operating in the UK also confirms that 'data is the new oil' and US corporations are at the well heads.[24] This is most apparent in the enormous quantities of data collected by each of the 'big five' tech companies which are customer-facing (Meta/Facebook, Apple, Microsoft, Amazon and Alphabet/Google – collectively known as 'MAMAA'), but there is more to it than that. All the big US companies are gaining an advantage by amassing data, as never before, about their customers and their markets. Data capture is often commercially decisive, as shown by the market for information on genealogy, which is a very widespread UK hobby. The leading operator, Ancestry.com, sells access to its vast database of family trees, and sells kits for analysing DNA – using your saliva they can accurately locate where your ancestors lived and will link you up to relatives you didn't even know you had. Ancestry.com's business is a leading example of the power of 'network effects', because the more people their database captures the more essential it is for new researchers to use their system. Every new person who asks for a DNA test is not only paying £79 to spit into a plastic test tube, but handing over their data and reinforcing the company's market position.[25] As testing becomes cheaper, more effective and more popular, the value of the business increases and the company's iron grip over the UK's genetic data becomes ever stronger. Ancestry.com was taken over by New York's Blackstone in 2020 for $4.7 billion, and such takeovers are a key part of US corporate expansion. And, consistent with the way such companies usually behave, they sell their testing kits into the UK through Ireland, thereby avoiding UK corporation tax in the process.[26]

US firms control hundreds of business niches and often their biggest advantage over local firms is that, having developed a product in their large home market of mainland USA, extra sales to the UK are a very lucrative bonus. Apple has developed a smartphone which is sold in the US for $1,000 (dollars) but the same phone is sold in the UK for £1,000 (pounds), about 25 per cent more expensive and even more profitable.

A drive out to the countryside

You might think that US ownership ends at the city's edge, but as you travel out into the countryside with a careful eye, the situation does not change. The estate-agency boards on the M1 advertise sweeping new warehouse developments. These 'to let' signs carry the nondescript acronyms 'JLL' and 'CBRE', representing the UK's two biggest real-estate professionals, Jones Lang LaSalle of Illinois and Coldwell Banker Richard Ellis of Texas. Together, these two commercial agencies generate £2.5 billion in fees each year – mostly recurring income from revaluations, property management and rent reviews – and have the lion's share of the commercial property market. It leaves the locals, with their much smaller 'for sale' boards, mostly chasing domestic house sales for low, one off fees.

Once into rural Britain, we immediately find ourselves giving way to farm machinery, such as tractors being driven between fields. These are big machines, leaving us in no doubt that the countryside has been industrialised. Helpfully, we can track the manufacturers of Britain's 10,000 tractors through the government's long-established register, and we see that Massey Ferguson (Duluth, Georgia), John Deere (Moline, Illinois) and Case IH (Racine, Wisconsin) supply 50 per cent of the British farm machinery market.[27] However, this also demonstrates the patchy nature of Britain's data collection. Although tractor ownership is logged there is no central analysis of who owns the fields. When we pass a farm with 'Copella' signs on it a Land Registry look-up reveals that it is ultimately owned by PepsiCo. Although ownership of individual farms can be looked up, the Department for Environment, Food and Rural Affairs makes no record nationally of how much farmland is owned by, for example, the US drinks companies.

Similarly, American brands have big positions in the combine-harvester market and in earth-moving equipment through Caterpillar (Deerfield, Illinois). Most machinery deals, as with car sales, involve a finance element and US suppliers offer loans which drive sales as well as creating a profit stream of their own. They also lock the farmer into buying a single brand and usually having their machines serviced and insured through the same company. But equipment for farming is undergoing a new revolution: automated machinery controlled by satellite navigation, satnav, is combining with clever software and more productive seeds to change how the land is used. In some farms in East Anglia, for example, giant unmanned machines, using US-supplied satnav, work the fields day and night. The market leaders here are Trimble of Colorado and AGCO of Georgia. One farmer told me that combine harvesters clear the fields one day; other machines work the fields during the night, and by the time the sun rises the new crop is planted and growing: 'No drivers are needed, and no sunshine wasted because of the US technology we're using. Drones, AI, satnav and weather forecasting are all working together – there's nothing comparable being developed in Britain.'

What we can't see on our visit to the countryside is that parts of British farming are now under existential threat: young people are moving away from meat and more than 30 per cent of millennials are moving towards plant-based diets.[28] This has stimulated the development of factory-produced proteins, which are already being widely used for ingredients by US outlets McDonald's, Subway and Hard Rock Cafe. The new suppliers are led by two Californian companies: Beyond Meat of Los Angeles, and Impossible Foods of Redwood City. Both are well beyond the start-up phase, with investors betting that, despite a dip in the sector in 2023, creating proteins in factories will eventually take lumps of the food market away from the farmers altogether.

When farmers do sell their produce, they deal with one of the handful of low-profile commodity companies who process, store and sell on to the food industry. The international players dominating this sector are often referred to as 'ABCD': Archer-Daniels-Midland (ADM), based in Illinois, Bunge, based in Missouri, Cargill, based in Minnesota, and Louis Dreyfus of France. In the UK, it is two of the American firms who are in control, ADM and Cargill, with ADM annually buying about $2 billion worth of British farming output to sell on.[29] Processing and distributing has always been a steadier, more profitable business than being the actual grower, as it requires less capital, is less competitive and prospers through good harvests and bad. This particular duopoly, like other pairs of dominant actors, does not fight pointless price wars. The illusion of competition is there, but in reality it is a cosy, complementary and profitable coexistence that keeps out any new entrants. Let us indulge in a thought experiment in which two ice-cream vendors are deciding where to position their ice-cream vans on the beach. If the beach front is 100 metres long, the ideal outcome for customers is if each van is positioned 25 metres away from each end of the beach so the longest distance any buyer has to walk is 25 metres. But in a free market it doesn't work out quite like that. The space in the middle, between the vans, is attractive to each vendor and they will progressively move their ice-cream van towards the centre. By doing this they can capture more of the market, so that in the end they will be back-to-back in the centre of the beach – far from ideal for the customers near the edges. Cargill and ADM are not alone in making their offerings very similar, and represent just one of dozens of competitive partnerships dominating their markets – such as Coca-Cola and Pepsi, Burger King and McDonald's, Oracle and Salesforce, Android and IOS, Intel and AMD, Visa and Mastercard.

Lastly, when the farms we drive past need fertilisers, they will very likely be buying from CF Industries (Illinois), which holds a dominant position in UK fertiliser production.[30]

Into the industrial heartlands

Heading to the Midlands, we reach more territory where US companies have been rapidly expanding. In the last few years those firms whose offices we saw in London's West End – Blackstone, Apollo and KKR (all based in New York) – have swooped in and taken ownership of dozens of large warehouses and distribution centres to profit from the rise of online retailing. In 2021, Blackstone also spent more than £1 billion buying St Modwen Properties, the brownfield-land development company. The private equity pack is also colonising unglamorous industrial sectors: in waste management KKR spent more than £4 billion in 2020 buying Viridor, which has local council contracts across the UK, and in industrial gases Air Products (Michigan) and Praxair (Connecticut) are both dominant operators. Long-established US manufacturers have also been increasing their UK footprint, such as 3M, originally the Minnesota Mining & Manufacturing Company, which annually sells about £650 million worth of manufactured goods into the UK.[31]

Jetting off on holiday, and looking at the UK from above

The usual attempts to leave the UK will find more US operators. At the airport we have a 40 per cent chance of flying on an aeroplane made by Boeing (based in Seattle and Chicago), but even if we take a European-made Airbus the engines will most likely be made by Pratt & Whitney (Connecticut), General Electric (Massachusetts) or CFM (Cincinnati), who together produce 80 per cent of the world's commercial jet engines.[32] The aviation fuel will be supplied from Fawley, the UK's biggest refinery, owned by ExxonMobil. It turns out that three Texas-based refiners, ExxonMobil, Valero and Phillips 66, process more than 60 per cent of the UK's oil, making petrol, diesel, airline fuel, tarmac and feedstock for dozens of other markets.[33] One example from ExxonMobil's refinery at Fawley is the supply of raw materials for Dow Chemical Company (Michigan) to make antifreeze and agricultural fertiliser.

When you scratch the surface of almost any UK industry you find US ownership – but you also find US enterprises creating the toll bridges which consumers have to cross to find suppliers: Airbnb for accommodation, eBay for second-hand goods, Etsy for handmade products, Tinder or Bumble for dating, and Amazon Marketplace for everything else. As a result, the British constantly have to pay royalties to access their home market.

Raw numbers on the US

Official numbers quantify this brutal story. The combined effect of rapid US company growth and aggressive takeover activity is laid bare by those statistics from the IRS referred to in the Introduction. Collected as part of a larger project to protect US tax revenues, these figures reveal how Britain has been singled out. Of all the assets held by US corporations in Europe, over half of them are in the UK – and that is true even though the IRS defines 'Europe' widely: as the whole of the EU, Eastern Europe, Russia and Turkey. It is confirmed by the numbers of workers: US corporations have more employees in the UK than the number they have in Germany, France, Italy, Portugal and Sweden combined. Measured by sales, the largest US companies sell more than $700 billion of goods and services to the UK, which amounts to over a quarter of the UK's total GDP.[34] That total, from the latest IRS report, is 36 per cent greater than it was just four years previously. Considering how much of GDP is necessarily made up of labour costs and rental income, these numbers are eye-watering. But it is worse: the true amount of UK GDP dependent on US businesses will be even higher since US companies with less than $850 million of annual sales are not even included in the IRS figures.

The same IRS figures show that while Germany has over half a million workers directly paid by the big US companies, Britain has at least three times as many: almost 1.5 million workers are officially dependent on large US employers; if we count the indirect employees, such as Uber drivers and Amazon's agency workers, at least 2 million UK workers have ultimate bosses in the US (6–7 per cent of the UK workforce). By contrast, as Table 1 illustrates, Southern Europeans have kept the penetration rate much lower: Italy and Spain have just under 1 per cent of their workers taking instructions from the US.

Table 1. US penetration of the UK compared to other countries[35]

	SALES OF US MULTINATIONALS AS A PERCENTAGE OF GDP	PERCENTAGE OF WORKFORCE EMPLOYED BY US MULTINATIONALS
UK	25%	4.0%*
Italy	5%	0.8%
Spain	6%	0.9%
France	7%	1.2%
Germany	9%	1.2%
TAX HAVENS		
Ireland	207%	7.2%
Luxembourg	204%	4.0%
Switzerland	77%	1.8%
Netherlands	35%	2.0%

* These figures are understated, as described later. The second figure for the UK should be around 6%.

It is not the turnover or the employee numbers that most interest US corporations – it is the profit. The IRS data itemises just how much profit the larger US corporations are earning from the UK each year. In 2019 that was $88 billion, equivalent to £2,500 of US profit for every British household.[36] But this is an understatement of the US profits because there are billions of pounds' worth of US sales to the UK that are only recorded in the tax havens of Luxembourg, Holland and Ireland – for example, Apple's sales to the UK are mostly done through Ireland. While the US companies reinvest a small amount of their profits, figures from other US government sources for later years confirm that amounts of more than £2,100 for every British household are actually sent back to the 'homeland' each year.[37]

Even the largest British companies are now dwarfed by the US multinationals, as shown by the value of either Apple or Microsoft. Each of their valuations of over $3 trillion is, at the time of writing, greater than the combined value of all the UK's top 350 listed companies.[38] In addition, the US ownership share of British listed companies is itself growing steadily. According to the ONS, more than 25 per cent of these UK companies is owned by US shareholders.[39] This number has been rising since 1994 when it was only around 10 per cent, with the result that big domestic companies such as BP, Shell, GSK, Aviva and HSBC are already about a quarter US-owned.

And the US visitors have arrived en masse: by 2020 there were 1,256 US multinationals in the UK – based on the IRS definition of a multinational as an enterprise with more than $850 million of foreign sales.[40] And while Britain's new corporate owners have been rapidly expanding, just five of them, which are consumer-facing, represent an even more dominant force roaming the land: the US tech giants, known as 'MAMAA', whom we encountered earlier in this chapter. All five are based on the West Coast of the

US: Meta/Facebook effectively runs social media and messaging; Apple sells millions of devices; Microsoft supplies the bulk of the UK's software; Amazon organises shopping and website hosting; and Alphabet/Google is the leader in UK information. To give a sense of scale, the combined value of just these five tech companies, measured by market value (more than $10 trillion), is now four times that of the total of the UK companies in the FTSE 100.

In 1930, as Britain's empire weakened and the US's industrial supremacy grew, the American economist and historian Denny Ludwell wrote in *America Conquers Britain*:

> We were Britain's colony once, she will be our colony before she's done. Not in name, but in fact. But we shan't make Britain's mistake: too wise to govern the world we shall merely own it. Nothing can stop us, nothing… what chance has Britain got against America?[41]

Over 90 years on, has Ludwell's prediction been realised? Are the British retaining the illusion of independence while being ever more financially and functionally under the control of others? As we have seen, the full extent of US ownership has left most of British society in the dark or, in some quarters, in denial. This did not happen in a policy vacuum: the US corporations' rapid and deep penetration of the UK has only been made possible because these new owners have been welcomed with open arms.

2

GRIM AND GRIMMER
WELCOMING THE BUYERS

If you tell a lie that is big enough and keep repeating it, people will eventually come to believe it. The lie can be maintained only for such time as the State can shield people from the consequences of the lie.

– anon.

This encapsulates the theory of the 'big lie', the truth of which has been confirmed through many experiments. Oddly, it turns out that a repeated false statement will be believed regardless of the listener's prior knowledge as to its truth.[1] Such psychology is germane to the way politicians use the term 'FDI' – 'Foreign Direct Investment'.

For over 40 years Westminster politicians have been extolling the virtues of FDI, but there has always been a deep deception at the heart of their claims. Incoming investments can be in two forms: genuine new investment in physical plant and new building or – quite differently – foreign purchases of existing companies. These are chalk and cheese. By deliberately confusing these two ideas, politicians can imply they are drawing lots of foreigners into making new and creative investments in the UK while in reality they are encouraging a progressive sell-off of the UK's best businesses.

In his 2023 Autumn Statement to Parliament, the chancellor, Jeremy Hunt, boasted about how successful Britain has been at attracting FDI: 'We became the second country in the world to have a stock of Foreign Direct Investment worth 2 trillion dollars.'[2] This figure includes all foreign-owned businesses and properties. And Hunt also basked in the fact that, around the world, chief executives say that Britain is one of the best places to invest. Like other ministers, he repeatedly says he wants more FDI into the UK and that every effort should be made to promote it. The rhetoric and the deceptive numbers hide the fact that FDI figures measure the combination of selling off national treasures and the occasional building of new factories. It is as though they have lumped all their chalk and cheese together and are delighted that its weight adds up to 2 trillion tons.

Of course, there are a few cases of genuine new investment, and that is what makes the big lie believable. In 1986 Nissan opened a large new factory in Sunderland, an area of high unemployment, and the Japanese created hundreds of new, skilled jobs and installed new productive machinery. At its peak in 2016, the plant was making 500,000 cars each year, although by 2023 that had dropped by about half.[3] This was rightly celebrated as good FDI, and should not be confused with foreign financiers buying up existing UK businesses. But it almost always is.

Chancellors such as Jeremy Hunt deliberately conflate investments like Nissan's with the far bigger phenomenon of foreign purchases of existing companies, such as the purchase by Kraft of Cadbury in 2010 (which led to the closure of the UK factory), or the myriad company sales to US private equity buyers – what former prime minister Harold Macmillan might have described as 'selling off the family silver'.[4]

In the years since the 1970s this deliberate ambiguity about what counts as FDI has allowed government ministers to announce steadily rising numbers for 'inward investment' despite much of it being the sale of profitable companies. Britain's policy-makers appear uninterested in where decisions are made about the country's workers, where company profits go, who pays taxes or what culture dominates the lives of citizens. Speaking to two former chancellors, I found neither of them concerned about the level of US ownership, but both recognised structural failings in the UK economy. As one commentator, Walter Ellis, who writes for the UK economics site CapX, has put it:

> What we are seeing is the continuing flight of British capital from anything that requires long-term investment and a com-mitment over time to the technologies of the physical world. UK governments past and present, as well as a generation of British entrepreneurs... fell into a trap of their own making. It is one thing for Britain to attract inward investment, quite another simply to take the money and run.[5]

Grim and Grimstone

The government, too, took its money and ran, in the wave of privatisations. To make these happen in the 1980s, Margaret Thatcher worked with Treasury officials, including a young man named Gerry Grimstone, who has described himself as 'the gov-ernment's salesman'.[6] By his own account he was responsible for 20 privatisation deals. Even the Labour Party turned to him in 2008 for advice on selling assets, when Gordon Brown as prime minister asked him to help plug a hole in the government finances: Grimstone weighed up the selling off of BBC Worldwide, British Energy, Northern Ireland's water company and even the Commonwealth Development Corporation.[7] Probably the best person to do the job, he was well connected and a strong believer in privatisation. Having started his career at the Treasury in the 1980s, Grimstone knows his way around government and he has also been a 'salesman' for privatisations at Schroders, a cost-cutter for the MOD and deputy chairman of Barclays.

Wind forward to 2020, and Gerry Grimstone, by now 70, re-emerged when prime minister Boris Johnson invited him to set up a new 'Office for Investment' within the Department for International Trade. Even though it was an unpaid role, it came with a life peerage, so he joined the House of Lords as Lord Grimstone of Boscobel. His role as salesman continued with a scripted fireside chat in which he explained how the new office would give him the tools to pursue 'the success of Global Britain's future'. This would 'rest on our ability to remain open for business, open to innovation and open to global investment'.[8] And His Lordship believes deeply in foreign ownership, as shown by his view, given to BBC Radio 4's *Today* programme on 25 August 2021 and reported in the *Daily Mail* on the same day, that British firms perform better when they are owned by foreigners. The context was the pursuit of Morrisons by two different US private equity groups, each hungry to gobble up one of the UK's largest supermarket chains. According to Lord Grimstone, when British firms are bought out by foreign groups they are 'more productive', hire more staff and export more. He added, in relation to foreign takeovers, 'It would be a sad day for this country if we put the shutters up so that we weren't a mercantile entrepreneurial country.'[9]

Grimstone's opinion that British firms flourish best under foreign ownership is consistent with the way in which politicians have acted for the past 40 years. They constantly repeat the formula that foreign ownership is a 'good thing', so it is understandable that much of the public have gone along with endorsing ever-increasing FDI. In 1988, Thatcher claimed that Britain was attracting more inward investment than any other European country, and, in 2001, her admirer across the political divide, Tony Blair, boasted about attracting inward investment: 'Last year the UK was the third largest recipient of inward investment – over $130bn – in the world, and the leading location in Europe.'[10] As prime minister, Gordon Brown also sought more FDI, and his minister Lord Davies announced their success in 'attracting foreign direct investment'. He went on: 'There are over 75,000 foreign-owned companies in the UK and they account for around 40% of GDP.'[11] Jeremy Hunt's $2 trillion-stock-of-FDI boast is another repetition of the big lie, and it comes directly from statistics produced by the Office for National Statistics (ONS).

I spoke to Andrew Jowett, the statistician from the ONS in Newport who puts together the FDI statistics which the chancellor relies on. He told me about his difficulties in collecting reliable data: even though it is compulsory for companies to fill in his forms, many are returned late or only partially completed. To improve the data, he samples a lot of companies and the big ones are surveyed every year. He also works with Companies House and the Land Registry. His conclusion is that, while the UK still has a lot of investments in other countries, inward FDI has been increasing much faster. Andrew fully understands the ambiguity of the term FDI: the difference between real, new investments in new productive assets on one hand and the purchase of existing lucrative UK companies on the other. Despite this, he openly admits that his statistics put both in the same bucket. I asked him if he would be able to separate them out, and he replied sardonically: 'You aren't the first person to ask that.' Apparently the ONS does have plans to try to do that in the future. Meanwhile, it seems, politicians will also continue to lump together genuinely desirable inbound investments such as new factories along with, for example, a Russian oligarch's purchase of a mansion in Knightsbridge or the acquisition of a strategically important UK defence contractor.

Andrew Jowett confirmed that the dominant foreign owner is the US, representing about half of foreign ownership. In the three years to 2021, US ownership of UK assets increased sharply, and Americans now own more of the UK than all the EU countries combined. The ONS reports show a steady increase in US ownership: in the latest year that increased by about £90 billion.[12] To put this number in perspective, it is as though for every UK household £3,000 worth of the UK was bought by American companies in a single year.

The position turns out to be significantly worse than this because the ONS does not look at the ultimate owner but only the nationality of the company on the register as the owner of the asset. And we know from IRS statistics that the US multinationals mostly put ownership of their European assets into subsidiaries based in Luxembourg, Holland, Ireland and Switzerland. It allows them to pay rents and fees to those subsidiaries to reduce tax, but the effect is that hundreds of billions of pounds' worth of assets in the UK registered as European-owned are ultimately American-owned. Mr Jowett has done some work on this and unsurprisingly he finds that, when you strip out the intermediate country, the US share shoots up and amounts beneficially owned by Luxembourg and Holland drop away. He has yet to quantify that increase, but we can make an educated guess by using statistics from the US.

How much of the UK is now owned by the US?

According to the Washington-based Bureau of Economic Analysis (BEA), the US owns a far bigger chunk of Britain than Britain owns in the other direction. It says that the US owns $1,100 billion worth of British assets, while the UK owns only $660 billion worth of US assets. But a deeper dig shows that even this large difference is a serious underestimate because Americans may indirectly hold roughly a further $800 billion worth of UK assets hidden in European tax havens. This number needs some unpacking. According to the BEA, the US's biggest countries for investment – after the UK – are the European tax havens of the Netherlands, Luxembourg and Ireland, where together US corporations own a further $2.1 trillion of assets. Based on the fact that around 38 per cent of non-tax-haven US sales to Europe are with the UK, it seems reasonable to estimate that roughly a further $800 billion of US-owned assets in the UK are owned through these three countries for a total of almost $2 trillion.[13]

This really does indicate the extent to which the UK has been singled out for US takeover, and means that UK assets owned by the US probably represent about 30 per cent of all US overseas investments. That would be more than the total value of the FTSE 100 – the 100 biggest listed companies in the UK – or more than three times the total value of all of England's agricultural land, or the equivalent of £53,000 for each UK household.[14]

Why have British investors allowed their companies to be bought up?

Listed companies are particularly vulnerable to private equity because of the 'rules of the investment game', which mean that institutional investors have a very short-term focus and will sell out for a quick profit. As the late Lord Paul Myners said: 'It's quite difficult to give up the share price pop that comes with a bid because it could be the difference between a good quarter and a bad quarter.' Fund manager James Macpherson, formerly of the giant money manager BlackRock, agrees: 'When a big premium is offered for a company whose shares have gone nowhere for a few years, it's very tempting to take that rather than give the current management the benefit of the doubt.' He gives the example of the takeover of Arm Holdings in 2016, which went ahead despite the opposition of its largest shareholder, Baillie Gifford of Edinburgh, who believed the deal would deprive the UK of a national tech champion. But as Macpherson says: 'The Arm management were acquiescent [in the takeover] too,' and Baillie Gifford was unable to pull together enough support to help Arm remain independent. Arm was duly acquired by a Japanese private equity fund, SoftBank, and later relisted on NASDAQ in New York.[15]

The burden of regulation and investor demands reduces the price of quoted companies. As Macpherson says: 'By establishing this bifurcated world of highly regulated quoted companies and unregulated private companies we're creating the opportunity for US private equity groups to plunder these assets that are weighed down by regulations and expectation.'[16]

The availability of British assets to foreign takeover can be seen both as a product of an ideological predisposition for FDI and as the result of the influence of some powerful vested interests. Chief among those interests has been the financial sector, which has been keen to profit from delivering up companies to foreign takeover. Because such takeovers engorge chancellor Jeremy Hunt's FDI numbers, one can see why he would not object. In 2015, Viscount Hanworth expressed this eloquently in the House of Lords:

Our rules of corporate governance amount to a system of self-regulation by the financial sector. They create few impediments to mergers and acquisitions or to financial trading and do nothing to protect the national interest. They contrast markedly with the rules that prevail in Germany, for example, where there are statutory anti-takeover provisions and where the public and politicians are strongly opposed to hostile takeover bids. German firms that are listed on their stock market are governed both by a management board and by a supervisory board, which must by law comprise a large contingent of the firm's employees. The supervisory boards act as a restraint on financial activities that might be harmful to the company. It would be greatly to our advantage to adopt a continental model of corporate governance and to replace our unitary boards of directors by a two-tier system.[17]

Hanworth goes on to explain how

the failures of our industrial sector are to a great extent due to the power and the influence of our financial sector, whose activities are inimical to a long-term industrial strategy... sales of our assets to overseas buyers has raised the foreign exchange value of the pound, which has made our manufactured goods uncompetitive in world markets. Ideally, I should like to see the financial sector diminished and its activities restrained.[18]

Although, as Hanworth, Myners and Macpherson all say, the financial sector gets a short-term boost from such sell-offs, the consequences can take decades to work their way through the system. The sell-off of the UK's water sector has seen steady increases in water bills so that cash pours into the companies, while sewage pours onto British beaches. Privatised companies such as Thames Water have allowed the pipe network to become increasingly leaky, while they borrow money that gushes out to foreign owners via the Cayman Islands.[19] Accountability is lost, but still foreign owners continue to be ushered in.

UK welcomes the 'barbarians at the gate'[20]

Unlike Britain, most other countries do not welcome the purchase of their companies by foreigners, and many regulate with laws limiting foreign ownership to 49 per cent. This has been the case for many industries in China, India and Indonesia. Some countries, such as Iran and Saudi Arabia, limit ownership in oil, telecoms and media. This presumption against allowing foreign buyers extends to the US, where the Committee on Foreign Investment in the US (CFIUS) protects the national interest and decides whether national security issues are raised by foreign ownership. US presidents have authority under the Exon–Florio Amendment to block any takeovers which they regard as threatening national security, and there are even stronger rules to protect the defence and technology sectors.[21] As president, Bill Clinton was wary of relying on foreign investment, saying: 'If we don't act now… we'll be terribly dependent on foreign funds for a large portion of our investment.'[22]

Chancellors and prime ministers – deeply divided loyalties

The tone of British policy on FDI is set by the Chancellor of the Exchequer, so it is unsettling to see how intimate successive chancellors have been with the US. The strength of these connections is indicated by the jobs they took after, or before, their terms in office. In the 16 years between 2007 and 2022 there were nine different chancellors, almost all of whom, on retirement, embraced the Americans. Gordon Brown, on leaving office, joined the advisory panel of the giant US bond investor Pimco, and similarly Alistair Darling immediately joined Morgan Stanley.[23] George Osborne became a founding partner of 9Yards Capital of California.[24] Philip Hammond became active in private equity and bid for the government contractor Amey alongside a US firm, One Equity Partners. Before him, Sajid Javid took roles with JPMorgan and a US artificial intelligence group – each of them paying him £150,000 annually.[25] Kwasi Kwarteng was employed by JPMorgan before he went into politics.[26]

And it is no different with prime ministers – perhaps worse. After the Brexit vote David Cameron took well-paid positions at Illumina, a Californian Biotech company, and First Data Corp, a financial services business in Atlanta, and did consulting for Afiniti, an American AI company. He also linked up with a Washington advocacy firm and registered to be a highly paid speaker with the Washington Speakers Bureau. It is through the same bureau that Theresa May hired out her services and earned more than £500,000 of speaking fees in the first year after leaving office – largely lecturing to American audiences, including JPMorgan. That particular New York bank has followed a policy of engaging recently retired leaders: it employed Tony Blair once he left office. Liz Truss, too, found support for her economic views from the US Heritage Foundation, which is part of a global network of libertarian free-market think tanks. They promote tax cuts and deregulation, as she did in her infamous mini-budget. More recently, Boris Johnson, who only gave up his US citizenship in 2016, went on a well-paid 2023 US speaking tour, visiting Texas, Washington and Las Vegas. Before leaving office Johnson showed his commitment to the US by publicly offering this advice to his successor: 'Stay close to the Americans.'[27]

The current prime minister, Rishi Sunak, probably has the strongest loyalties to the US of all of them. After a degree at Oxford he went on to study for an MBA at Stanford University in California. Next he worked for American companies, first with Goldman Sachs of New York and then with the Theleme hedge fund in California, which for tax purposes is based in the Cayman Islands. The Sunaks retain ownership and use of a luxury apartment in Santa Monica, California, overlooking the Pacific. Even after he took ministerial office in London he retained his US Green Card, normally the first step towards becoming a US citizen. He only gave it up, following official advice, when he was visiting the US as UK chancellor.[28] His sister lives in New York. His wife is the daughter of the billionaire founder of Infosys, and, until 2022, she sheltered her income from UK tax by claiming non-dom status. In order to do this, she had to assert that the UK was not her main country of residence – an extraordinary position for the spouse of the then Chancellor of the Exchequer. Through this tax-exempt status she is estimated to have saved at least $20 million of personal tax.[29] The majority of foreign high-income earners residing in the UK claim non-dom status, a recognised form of efficient tax planning. On the back of the public criticism she announced she would pay tax on her future earnings.

Rishi Sunak is the wealthiest prime minister ever and much of that wealth is tied to the US.[30]

There can be no doubt about the allure of the US to current and former leaders: they have been co-opted into the American machinery of influence and have rarely, if ever, questioned its growing dominance. The recruiting of top UK politicians is a live issue: Nick Clegg, former deputy prime minister, now works full time for Meta/Facebook. He is their president of global affairs, earning at least £2.8 million annually for advancing the company's interests in Britain and Europe. And, in November 2023, when Rishi Sunak hosted a big conference on the safety of AI, the star guest was Elon Musk. Sunak's 40-minute interview with Mr Musk at Lancaster House was so gushing and unexpected that the prime minister was accused of angling for a job once he leaves office.[31]

Even in cases in which foreign companies do properly invest in new industry in Britain, they demand large financial inducements before committing. Indian-owned Jaguar Land Rover (JLR) made public that it was considering building a new electric-battery plant as part of its switch to electric vehicles. Chancellor Jeremy Hunt really wanted this genuine FDI, but had to offer incentives to JLR for them to build in the UK and apparently offered £500 million of government support – in hard cash, reduced energy costs, upgrading of the power network and the financing of new transport connections for the site in Bridgwater, Somerset.[32] This was an enormous inducement – but at least it brings the giga-factory to Somerset rather than Spain and secures 9,000 jobs. In other cases, the government has offered a subsidy just to keep plants open. Such subsidies have an addictive quality and they build expectations: most automotive factory investments in the UK get 10–20 per cent of their costs paid in subsidies.

In examining what could attract more genuine inward investment, the House of Commons International Trade Committee wrote a report on FDI in 2021.[33] It was damning: it found that the government's approach is piecemeal, overly political and skewed towards London and the south-east. Policy is based on poor data and the Department for International Trade fails to 'monitor closures of companies associated with inward investment, or downsizing by such companies'.[34] It suggested that Lord

Grimstone was working with the prime minister and chancellor in preference to the relevant departments and that some decisions might be politically motivated. He told the committee that he was offering a 'concierge service' for inward investors, that they needed a 'front door' and that there is no better front door than one with 'No. 10' painted on it. As soon as Boris Johnson resigned as prime minister in the summer of 2022, Grimstone left too. Within 15 months he had taken a job with the American consultants Bain & Company.[35]

As well as subsidies, companies can find that putting money into the UK neatly fits into a tax-planning strategy. When Google decided to build its headquarters in King's Cross it bought the land outright, which tax experts suggest was a tax-efficient move, since it allowed them to avoid taking their offshore profits back to the US, where it would have attracted an onshoring tax bill. The new building has been labelled a 'landscraper' and is longer – at 330 metres – than the height of the Shard.[36] The 1 million square feet building transmits a feeling of power and success: the sports hall will have views over London; there will be a 25-metre swimming pool for staff and, on the roof, a 200-metre running trail. This is all counted by the UK government as FDI, yet it feels like the control centre of a foreign power. Being in King's Cross it is in the heart of London and next to the arterial railway lines leading to the rest of the country. Google also wants a big foot in 'adland', which it now dominates, and it has made what chancellor Jeremy Hunt would classify as an FDI in Covent Garden – buying a series of buildings each brightly painted in Google's primary colours with views across the city, gyms and a dance studio (the new headquarters of Twitter/X also has a yoga studio). Google is said to have bought these offices outright for $1 billion – small change for a company with cash reserves of more than $100 billion and with money pouring in. It made sense tax-wise and is a declaration that they intend to remain a permanent Foreign Direct Investor.

The landscraper neatly demonstrates how official FDI figures are deeply flawed, fail to recognise what is happening on the ground and reflect confused thinking on the part of policymakers. A Land Registry search, which I submitted, shows that Google actually owns the building through a Luxembourg company, so it will not be counted as US-owned in the official figures. One advantage to Google is that the rent they pay to their Luxembourg subsidiary, which could be set at quite a high level, will reduce the company's UK tax bill and neatly move the money to Luxembourg, where the income will probably be taxed lightly, if at all.

The 'special relationship'

A big part of welcoming so-called 'inward investment' from the US into the UK has been the 'special relationship', which is a bit like the proverbial elephant described by a group of blind people. To one it is large and reassuring; to another it is trunk-like but moves all over the place, and to another it is hairy and stringy and dangling at the rear. To another it just feels menacing.

As the US Department of State explains: 'The United Kingdom (UK) is a popular destination for foreign direct investment (FDI) and imposes few impediments to foreign ownership.' It goes on: 'A Bilateral Tax Treaty specifically protects US and UK investors from double taxation.'[37]

Why has the UK been targeted? It cannot just be because of the English language or because the UK is geographically close. US investors say that the stability of the country helps, but the overwhelming reason must be because the British have welcomed these investors with open arms. There are few rules limiting what percentage of companies can be owned, and there is no restriction on foreign ownership of UK real estate. The US Department of State's website also recognises Britain's role as a beachhead: 'The UK also hosts more than half of the European, Middle Eastern, and African corporate headquarters of American-owned multinational firms.'[38] In what Lord Grimstone calls the 'globally competitive sport' of attracting inward investment – in other words, selling off a country's businesses – the British are winning hands-down.[39]

Sometimes the mask slips and Britain's 'partnership' narrative is undermined. When prime minister Gordon Brown made his first official visit to Washington following Barack Obama's election he received a chilly reception. It was March 2009, and Brown had just written a gushing piece in the *Sunday Times* about the 'special relationship' in which he said: 'there is no international partnership in recent history that has served the world better.'[40] He described himself as an 'Atlanticist' and made bombastic references to Churchill. The UK prime minister expected an official banquet, but it turned out Obama could only make time for a 'working lunch' and also cancelled the planned press conference. The *Daily Telegraph* described the treatment as what might be handed out to a 'minor African state' and the exchange of gifts seemed calculated to wound: while Brown gave Obama a first-edition biography of Churchill and a pen holder carved from the wood of HMS *Gannet*, the White House gave the prime minister a DVD box set of old Hollywood movies. Reportedly these were not playable in the UK because of the 'region lock' that US media companies use to protect their 'intellectual property' (IP). For the children, the Obamas gave plastic models of the presidential helicopter to the Brown boys, while Sarah Brown had carefully chosen outfits and British books for the Obama girls. By the end of the visit the British press was describing the special relationship as 'a joke' and the *Times* ran the headline 'Humiliated, hopeless, paralysed'.[41]

Something to laugh about

One senior Obama adviser, Jeremy Shapiro, admitted later that the US–UK bond 'was never really something that was very important to the United States'. He added: 'From my perspective it was very important for us to mention the special relationship in every press conference that we had when the UK people were here… but really we laughed about it behind the scenes.'[42] This is pursued to the point where it can sound like mockery. The new US ambassador to the UK, Jane Hartley, was interviewed soon after her appointment in 2022 by Times Radio, and she alluded to the 'special relationship' 24 times.

Britain is now tethered to the US in a world which is divided into three giant trading blocs, centring on three regions: Europe, China and the US. On leaving the EU, Britain was stepping semi-consciously into the US sphere of influence. Washington is fully aware of this, and rather than treat the UK as a junior partner it treats it in an offhand way: our membership of that bloc is on US terms. The US presidential election of 2020 did not change this: one of the candidates promised to put American workers first, to produce American goods to fulfil government orders and to take a tough stance on trade partners. That candidate was Joe Biden.[43]

In his first term as president, Biden chose not to conclude a trade deal with the UK despite Britain's near desperation to do so. The UK said in May 2020 that it wanted a deal to be an early priority given that the US is the UK's largest trading partner, but, by deferring it – perhaps indefinitely – the US can hold it over the

UK in numerous unrelated negotiations.[44] In any trade deal, US companies may want favourable terms on healthcare, drug pricing and IP. In agriculture, they will demand that the UK accept their chicken, hormone-treated beef, genetically modified food and lower regulation of pesticides. As Philip Hammond told me in 2020: 'The US is in an incredibly strong position to do a trade deal with the UK.'[45] As a supplicant, the UK can be repeatedly threatened with not being given a trade deal whenever a concession is needed on some other matter. All this makes it harder for the UK to resist foreign direct investment from the US – even if it wanted to. This sword of Damocles is also reassuring to the US companies who have bought up UK businesses – they know that Washington has this leverage with which to protect their interests.

Our survey of the UK economy suggests that these FDI investments are only rarely new job-creating factories. They are mostly investments in profitable existing businesses and rent-yielding properties. But, indiscriminate support for any FDI into the UK does not look as if it is about to be abandoned. In November 2023 Jeremy Hunt used his Autumn Statement to back the ideas of Gerry Grimstone, saying, 'We will put in place a concierge service for large international investors... and will increase funding for the Office for Investment to deliver it.'[46] Such pandering to foreign buyers has enabled a progressive takeover of UK businesses, particularly by those from the United States. But there is one group that has gained greater power than any other – the US tech giants – and they are roaming across the UK looking for more opportunities right now.

3

ISLAND OF THE TECH GIANTS

I want to thank every Amazon customer and every Amazon employee because you guys paid for all this.

— Jeff Bezos, founder of Amazon[1]

On 20 July 2021, an 18-metre rocket named *New Shepard* soared 63 miles above Culberson County, Texas. At 8.15 a.m. it entered outer space, slowed to a stop and began to plummet back to earth. On board: Jeff Bezos, the executive chair and founder of Amazon, his brother Mark, a private equity executive, and an 18-year-old Dutchman, Oliver Daemen, the son of another private equity executive who paid unspecified millions of dollars for the trip.

Next to them sat Wally Funk, a top-performing member of the US Mercury 13 programme, which worked to train female astronauts in the 1960s. Long abandoned, that initiative failed to take women into space but, aged 82, Funk finally achieved her dream that morning.

The first manned mission by the Bezos-led Blue Origin programme was an unprecedented media spectacular: or at least might have been if Britain's Richard Branson had not himself emerged from his own spaceship in New Mexico just nine days earlier.

It is estimated that Bezos spent at least $5.5 billion of his own money on the Blue Origin project, while Branson's Virgin group is reported to have invested far less – hundreds of millions – in the Virgin Galactic programme before raising further investment from private backers and, eventually, floating not through space, but on the New York Stock Exchange.

Both men remarked on how their journeys had provided them with a new perspective on the world. 'I was once a child with a dream looking up to the stars. Now I'm an adult in a spaceship… looking down to our beautiful, beautiful earth,' said Branson as he and his passengers achieved weightlessness.[2]

The view from his flight, said Jeff Bezos, was profound: 'Everybody who goes into space, they say this: that it changes them, that they look at it and are kind of amazed and awestruck by its beauty but also by its fragility.'[3]

After his capsule achieved zero gravity, Bezos and Daemen could be seen throwing sweets at each other's mouths in the flight recordings. Space is fashionable among billionaires, and perhaps the leader of the 'it crowd' is Elon Musk, the head of Tesla cars and founder of SpaceX, which, after receiving a slew of NASA contracts, is now the leading private spacecraft manufacturer. Microsoft co-founder Paul Allen also invested hundreds of millions into building the Stratolaunch space plane, used to ferry rockets to the edge of the atmosphere.[4]

Each investment in space by these men, taken in isolation, might be considered eccentricity or even smart business. Viewed collectively, however, their endeavours could also look like keeping up with the Joneses.

Space, in any case, is just the latest frontier of competition between the US tech titans for mastery of every conceivable sphere – including the oceans. In the first decade of this century, Paul Allen was locked in a battle with Oracle Corporation's Larry Ellison to see who could build the bigger yacht. After Allen had commissioned the 416-foot *Octopus*, Ellison asked the dockyard building his boat, *Rising Sun*, to add an extension, bringing it to 452 feet in length.[5]

The frontiers these tech titans seek to tame are not merely mechanical, however. Peter Thiel, who founded PayPal with Elon Musk, has invested millions to assess the viability of building new societies on the oceans, outside the jurisdiction of any government, a concept known as 'seasteading'. Thiel, Bezos and the Google founders Sergey Brin and Larry Page have each also pumped millions into technology ventures designed to combat ageing and to try to 'solve death'.

The rest of us can only watch these exploits in despair or admiration – seeing the vainglory of men made wealthy through narrow expertise, or further evidence of their gravity-defying drive, ambition and imagination. To what degree are we – as shareholders, employees and customers of the businesses these titans built, and as voters who elect the politicians who oversee them – complicit in all their extraordinary adventures and follies? After a safe touchdown in Texas, Bezos used the post-flight press conference to announce that this adventure had only been possible because of Amazon customers and employees.

How much of Amazon's profits from the UK fuelled that trip to space? Over the course of the past decade or so, the company's annual UK profits rose from around £1 million in 2011 to £204 million in 2021 – a drop in the ocean when compared with the investment in Blue Origin. Similarly, the UK corporation taxes that Amazon pays seem meagre – less than £15 million in 2019. But there is something striking about the UK profits and taxes of this company. They are dwarfed by its UK sales, which were

£12 billion in 2019. And as the pandemic gripped, and people turned to online shopping with ever more desperation, Amazon's net UK sales soared again: to more than £20 billion in 2020, yet they paid corporation tax of just £18 million. For the second year in a row, in 2022 Amazon paid no UK corporation tax. Instead it received a £7.7 million tax credit.[6]

Beneath that blunt headline, things get more complicated: Amazon operates in many sectors of the UK economy but not all of these are recorded in Britain. In the case of Amazon Web Services (AWS) the business has operated through Luxembourg, seemingly routing revenue across the world and finally to the US, where tax is finally paid and what is left feeds Amazon and its shareholders. Chief among these is Jeff Bezos and, eventually, some share of that money finds its way onto the launch pad in West Texas. But, across tax territories and continents, we cannot confidently follow the money.

Whatever the facts, that sense that taxes are deferred and profits are rerouted pervades the activities of the major US corporations we buy from. Microsoft, Starbucks and Apple are all companies with meagre tax bills in the UK. What is going on?

The answer is an avalanche of national policy choices, lobbying campaigns and regulations, but, in the first place, it is because the essential business practices of these firms demonstrate quite different priorities from those of the businesses most of us understand. Low tax bills do not represent failing or unsuccessful businesses, however. The priority isn't profit; it comes down to one word: scale. Each of these businesses is constantly seeking to increase revenue at a faster rate than costs, to avoid any so-called 'stall points' – when, to expand their supply, they have to take unreasonable risks – and to create consistent and dramatic revenue growth.

To achieve this, these businesses invest heavily in research and development (R & D). They use the cash they throw off to invest in their own infrastructure and, once proven, they sweat that infrastructure for maximum profit. Back on Blue Origin's Texas launch pad, Jeff Bezos himself described the scale-up principle at work:

> The architecture and the technology we have chosen is complete overkill for a suborbital tourism mission. We have chosen the vertical landing architecture. Why do we do that? Because it scales. It's an architecture that can grow to a very large size. So we want to have experience with architectures that can grow big to *New Glenn* [a future Blue Origin mission to enter orbit] and one day to *New Armstrong* [another future mission]. So to have the idea that you want to build big from the beginning, lets you choose an architecture, because the whole point of doing this is to get practice. Other kinds of architectures don't scale in the same way to very large size.[7]

In the aftermath of the *New Shepard* launch, many journalists joked that Bezos had spent $1.38 billion for every minute he spent on the mission. They missed the point: it is not the cost of the first flight that matters to Mr Bezos but the cost of the one hundredth. As well as the cost of every subsequent innovation and expansion.

Britain's Richard Branson cannot boast that his Virgin Galactic programme can scale in the same way. On the contrary, when Virgin announced it had minted an impressive-sounding deal with NASA to take astronauts to the International Space Station, you had to read the fine print to discover that they may not even be travelling on Virgin's spacecraft. And, if a comparison of approaches to 'scale' between Blue Origin and Virgin Galactic does not flatter Mr Branson, this issue – of US businesses outper-forming and outgrowing British competitors – undermines much of the UK economy.

How US businesses scale

Given the tools, the investment and the determination, tech businesses can scale with unprecedented speed. Having demon-strated rapid growth in the US, it can cost almost nothing to roll out apps across large new markets, increasing their user numbers for little more than some data-storage costs and a handful of new employees in each region.

Without their own fast-scaling giant corporations, techno-logical change means that British markets are left open for US businesses to exploit.

Just four years after the first guest had been registered, Airbnb was already in 89 countries and a million nights had been booked on the platform. By 2022 there were 70,000 Airbnb locations in London alone and about $6 billion each year was being spent on UK accommodation through this San Francisco-based platform.

Uber spent two years in development before the first customer used the app. Four years later it was operating in 100 cities – 'a global brand focused on helping move you towards opportunity out in the world', as the company immodestly claims.[8] Its rival Lyft followed the same path but, by 2023, despite billions in annual revenue, neither taxi app had turned a significant profit.

Large US investors continue to value these businesses in the billions, however, because they have already decided that scale matters more than immediate returns. They have seen what happened to MySpace – what happens when you 'Punch the Monkey'.

When Rupert Murdoch's News Corp purchased MySpace in 2005, it was the most popular social media platform in the world. And, although Facebook was growing quickly, News Corp pressured MySpace to 'monetise'. It did so – raising several billion in revenue in the years that followed.

But the cash was generated by besieging users with irritating ads, driving them to hand over personal data, complete surveys or enter credit card details – one of the most notorious, called 'Punch the Monkey', appeared to be a game but enticed users to give their contact details to third-party marketers.

Sean Percival, the former vice president of online marketing at MySpace, told a newspaper subsequently: 'It was one of the most annoying things you could do with an ad, but they just didn't care: they had no respect for the users. It was all about monetisation. Making money, squeezing every dollar out of it. And think about Facebook – the ultimate winner here. No focus on monetisation early on… They do more native, more inline advertising, things that feel a little more natural. Not Punch the Monkey.'[9]

News Corp had paid $580 million for MySpace. In 2011, they offloaded it for just $35 million. A year later Facebook floated on the NASDAQ at $104 billion. US investors realised that it pays to wait.

Long before all these examples emerged, Jeff Bezos coolly laid down how tech investment must work. In 1997 he wrote to Amazon investors:

We believe that a fundamental measure of our success will be the shareholder value we create over the long term… We will continue to make investment decisions in light of long-term market leadership considerations rather than short-term profitability considerations or short-term Wall Street reactions… We choose to prioritize growth because we believe that scale is central to achieving the potential of our business model.[10]

None of this means that US businesses are not ruthless in their drive for efficiency. Amazon's UK warehouses use mezzanine levels to fill as much as possible of the floor plan of their site with sale items – squeezing the most intense use from the smallest space possible.

And the same rationale is at work in Bezos's Blue Origin project, as he explained while sitting by his launch capsule:

> Right now we have a mission life, we think, somewhere between 25 and 100 flights for one of these vehicles. We'd like to make that closer to 100 than 25, and then once it's at 100 we'll push it past 100… This is a big vision, but big things start small and this is how it starts. We are going to build an infrastructure just like when I started Amazon.[11]

Britain's businesses do not 'scale up'

The UK government tells a confident story about Britain's tech business acumen. In one 2023 example, a press release from Rishi Sunak invited investment in the tech sector, calling the UK an 'island of innovation'. In it, he explained that the UK corporation tax rate was the lowest in the G7 and that the UK capital allowance for investors was 'one of the most generous' in the OECD. Even better, the UK Treasury offered 'full-expensing for qualifying business investments in more plant and machinery for three years – a tax cut worth £27 billion'.[12] This is generous, and notably so when in 2023 the UK spent more than £100 billion servicing the interest on state debts. And, viewed in a certain light, the generosity has got results. The PM also claimed that the UK has created 134 'tech unicorns' – companies with a valuation of more than $1 billion.

Sunak's wide-eyed enthusiasm is broadly shared by tech boost-erists in the UK. A 2021 report by UK start-up cheerleaders Tech Nation also boasted that Britain has launched more than 100 'unicorns'.[13] Even if nearly half of those were created between 1990 and the 2008 crash, the figures sound impressive – outstrip-ping every country in the world save China and the US. And Tech Nation claimed better news: 'The UK now has an incredible 132 futurecorns [companies likely to be worth $1 billion], more than France and Germany combined, which demonstrates the extent to which the UK is leading Europe.'[14]

But a focus on these numbers can be misleading, because Britain's new businesses do not tend to scale up to become global challengers. The country offers no rivals to the biggest US firms: Meta/Facebook, Apple, Microsoft, Amazon and Alphabet/Google (MAMAA). To the Forbes list of the biggest 100 pub-licly traded companies, Britain contributes just three – fewer than Switzerland, Germany, France, Canada, Japan, China or, of course, the US, which can claim 39 of the top 100.[15] And, tellingly, all three UK entrants – GSK, HSBC and Unilever – have their origins not in the dot-com boom, or even in the post-war period, but in the nineteenth century.[16]

For all the hype, it is notable that the FTSE 100 had more domestic tech firms in the year of its founding, 1984, than it has today.[17] The story of one of them, Standard Telephones and Cables (STC), is revealing.

In 1984, STC employed 51,000 people, mostly in the UK, pro-viding telephony services that included deep-sea Atlantic cabling and, through a subsidiary, mainframe computing across UK gov-ernment departments.[18] In the decades before, STC invented and patented technology to allow fibre-optic cables to transfer data at the speed of light over any distance. And these innovations, developed in STC's optics lab in Harlow in the 1960s, made the cost of global communication negligible and, decades later, helped enable the World Wide Web.

Yet, like 68 of the original FTSE 100 companies, STC is no longer British-owned. In 1991, it was sold to the Canadian telecoms giant Nortel. And, in the same year in which former STC lab manager Charles Kao received the Nobel Prize in recognition of his fibre-optic work for STC, Nortel filed for bankruptcy. The end came in 2011, when a consortium led by Apple and Microsoft outbid Google to pay $4.5 billion for Nortel's patents and the residual IP.

Over the decades, other tech firms have fallen in and out of the FTSE 100 index. While some offered innovations that really could have reshaped modern communication, they did not make it. They could not grow. They did not scale.

Consider the UK computing firm Psion. It evolved the first effective pocket computers several years before Apple developed the Newton and Microsoft developed Windows for handheld devices. Today, the Psion Organiser is seen as a forerunner to the smartphone, and its technology certainly foreshadowed it. For example, the low-power operating system developed by the firm was the core of 250 million mobile devices by 2009 before ultimately losing market share to Google's superior Android platform and Apple's IOS. Psion entered the FTSE 100 in March 2000 before dropping out after just two months. In 2012, it was purchased by Motorola Solutions of Chicago, Illinois. By 2023 the FTSE 100 contained just three tech firms: Sage, Rightmove and Auto Trader, although arguably only the first of these is really a tech company.

If the UK government is embracing entrepreneurial tech investment, is anything changing? Not really. Even Tech Nation has noticed that one pound in three offered to UK tech firms by institutional investors is American. As for the 'unicorns' and the 'futurecorns', US investors also dominate larger investment rounds. All of which is a little awkward for Tech Nation itself, which has received some £29 million in sponsorship from the UK government to help boost a start-up culture.[19] As a result, its 2021 report seemed distinctly hedged about the consequence of all this US investment, observing: 'On the one hand, this could be seen as a sign of strength and burgeoning international reputation for investment returns in UK tech, but on the other, this may be seen as potentially problematic if UK tech firms with significant profit and influence are owned by non-UK actors.'[20]

It seems unthinkable that any of the UK firms backed by US institutional investors will grow to a size that could challenge already dominant US businesses. Sometimes, they are simply bought out by the US giants to take the innovation out of the hands of competitors. In recent years, Google has snapped up the UK companies Dataform and Redux and, perhaps most controversially, the AI innovator DeepMind, bought in 2014.

As UK investor and SongKick co-founder Ian Hogarth has written, the talent pool for serious AI development is small. In 2018 he estimated that there are perhaps 700 people who can contribute to the leading edge of research. 'I find it hard to believe,' he wrote, 'that the UK would not be better off were DeepMind still an independent company. How much would Google sell DeepMind for today? $5 billion? $10 billion? $50 billion? It's hard to imagine Google selling DeepMind to Amazon, or Tencent or Facebook at almost any price.'[21]

Google paid just £400 million, with no questions asked by the UK government.

Britain's groundbreaking semiconductor innovations have also drifted away from our shores over the years. Hermann Hauser of

Amadeus Capital is an Austrian-born tech investor who is used to making money from selling UK tech firms. Some of Amadeus Capital's biggest deals have been with US firms such as Microsoft. And, in 2011, Hauser sold UK semiconductor innovator Icera to the US chip-maker Nvidia for $367 million. The sale was designed to help Nvidia engage with the smartphone revolution, but four years later it closed the UK firm with the loss of 300 jobs in Bristol.

Today, Hauser's view is that Britain's tech firms suffer not from a lack of ideas, talent or research capacity but because they cannot scale up effectively: 'Europe actually doesn't have a startup problem. We produce more startups than the US. It's not a startup problem, but we have a scale-up problem.'[22]

Arm

There is, however, one exception: Arm Holdings. Growing out of the innovative but unsuccessful Acorn Computers in the 1980s, Arm developed chips and software that allowed computer processors to run far faster and with less power than many rivals.

Starting in a barn in Cambridge and backed by an investment of £1.5 million from Apple, Arm has grown into one of the most important tech companies in the world. With technology in more than 200 billion devices, the firm has successfully pioneered a business model in which it licenses cutting-edge computer architecture to developers across the globe. The UK company has been so successful for so long that its profits even kept Apple afloat when the US titan sold its modest investment in Arm for $800 million back in the early 1990s.[23]

Hauser saw it all because as well as running Amadeus Capital, he also helped to found Acorn Computers and Arm itself. And it is notable that, in 2020, he led a campaign to persuade UK and EU authorities to intervene to stop Arm being sold to Nvidia in the US by its Japanese owners SoftBank. In a letter to the *Financial Times* he warned that the sale to a US firm would allow that nation to decide who gets to keep Arm's innovations or, as he said, it would mean 'that the American President can decide which companies Arm is allowed to sell to worldwide'.[24]

This raises the vital issue of the loss of tech sovereignty where the UK and EU authorities have been overwhelmed and effectively neutered. The dominance of Silicon Valley companies in search (Google), social media (Facebook), entertainment (Netflix) and e-commerce (Amazon) has become a pressing issue, fostering a belated debate on how we could have allowed it to happen.[25]

As for Arm, in 2023 SoftBank decided that it should relist the business on the stock market but anchored to a US exchange. The British prime minister, Rishi Sunak, joined numerous discussions to bring Arm back to Britain, and begged SoftBank to offer a secondary listing of Arm shares in the UK. This too was denied. Victoria Scholar, the head of investment at Interactive Investor, told *The Guardian*: 'Arm's abandonment of London is another kick in the teeth for the Square Mile's attractiveness among international investors as a go-to destination for technology giants.'[26]

Size matters

The headline figures speak for themselves. The UK economy grew sluggishly in the years following the great recession of 2008 but, in the same period, the UK earnings of America's biggest tech firms skyrocketed, as shown in Table 2.

Table 2. UK turnover of the US tech giants in £ million[27]

COMPANY	2008	2022	GROWTH
Meta/Facebook	4	3,000	750×
Apple	42	1,500	35×
Microsoft	591	4,860	8×
Amazon	94	23,500	250×
Alphabet/Google	150	3,391	22×
Netflix	0	1,400	–
Oracle	400	1,800	4.5×

Today, Amazon collects more than 30 per cent of all UK online spending, and is growing steadily. That is profit-producing income that could have remained in the UK but that will now ultimately return to, and be controlled from, Amazon's headquarters in Seattle.

Meta and Google receive two-thirds of all the UK's expenditure on search and display advertising. The profit from that could have travelled to UK broadcasters and local newspapers, but it now ends up in California.

The profits made by US firms in the UK may help deliver value to consumers. But they have also built up market power that small domestic businesses do not have, forcing them to become US business rule-takers in their own economy. And the position of UK domestic business is weakening.

For example, of the biggest US tech companies operating in the UK, most reap the benefits of 'network effects' in which as more users join a platform, the more useful the platform becomes, and the harder it is for customers to switch to a rival. Microsoft's

LinkedIn site and its Office products are all more useful because others also use them. In the aftermath of the Cambridge Analytica scandal, in which Facebook user data ended up in the hands of an unscrupulous political consultancy, one reporter put it like this: 'Facebook knows that as long as your 2 billion friends are online, you're probably not going anywhere.'[28] Similar network effects explain why Threads found it impossible to displace Twitter/X in mid-2023. Users build up a platform's power because innovations and revenue streams can be rolled out internationally to billions of people at once.

In media streaming, scale is critical. For example, Netflix boasted that it invested $17 billion in content in 2023 and was instantly able to distribute that content to 238 million subscribers in more than 150 countries. In contrast, when the production companies that feed UK broadcasters seek international deals for their shows, each one must be individually negotiated.

Scaled businesses using the network effect are well placed to diversify, too. In addition to its own distribution business, Amazon has expanded into streaming services, home entertainment and, of course, broader tech services. As if to demonstrate the power of scale, Amazon has created a platform through which many UK-based suppliers can sell. It has become so large that 60 per cent of Amazon sales are now made through its 'Amazon Marketplace'. Amazon takes a margin on all these sales, builds its brand, dictates service quality and refers all problems back to the suppliers. The major advantage to Amazon is that for these Marketplace sales it does not need to hold any stock: it has become for many UK businesses the toll bridge which they must cross. Jeff Bezos's vision that his platform should become the 'everything store' offering limitless selection and seductive convenience at disruptively low prices is now entrenched as the dominant force in UK retail commerce.

Amazon Web Services (AWS) began as an attempt by Amazon to control its own web hosting, creating a system that could handle the growing data storage and traffic to its site. By 2002, Jeff Bezos had dispatched a team of data scientists to South Africa to develop a product for others to use, now known as 'the cloud'. It took just two years to launch but it grew fast without dramatically increasing overheads. 'This has to scale to infinity,' Mr Bezos instructed staff, 'with no planned downtime. Infinity!'[29] Today, AWS is worth at least $500 billion to its parent company.[30] Most of the UK government's websites and data are on AWS, which hosts everything from websites to streamed video. Even Britain's most popular porn site, Pornhub, of Canada, with 2 billion UK visits annually (yes, billion), is hosted on AWS. Although Amazon does not have the UK market to itself, it does have about 40 per cent, and its competitors are all American: the other big players being Google Cloud Storage and Microsoft's Azure.

Even for the smaller US tech firms, diversification and innovation are at the heart of their plans. Despite lack of profitability, Uber and Lyft have poured billions of dollars into research-and-development projects such as driverless cars.

Larger firms, meanwhile, push to buy up potential competitors and out-innovate their rivals to create unassailable market positions. In the past decade, Facebook decided to out-compete social media rival Snapchat by buying and rebuilding Instagram. Tesla, while selling electric vehicles more successfully than other car manufacturers, is also developing driverless systems. It is diversifying further, pledging to parlay its driverless-car research into developing a humanoid robot – called 'Optimus' or the 'Tesla Bot'. Ultimately, these businesses hope to build what investor Warren Buffett calls 'moats' around themselves: a set of unique characteristics that ensure consumers are hooked and their behaviour is predictable and predictably advantageous for the company. Following Buffett's investment in Apple, one of his colleagues described Apple's moat: 'Once you are fully invested in the Apple ecosystem and you've got your thousands of photographs up and in the cloud and you are used to the keystrokes and functionality and know where everything is, you become a sticky consumer.'[31]

One of Amazon's moats is its compelling sales offering, with an intuitive website and speedy delivery. Another is the 'Kindle ecosystem' for digital book sales, which is unrivalled. Uber offers special value and convenience through its app and dense network of vehicles on the road. Airbnb has an unmatched roster of landlords prepared to offer rooms, huts and homes on short leases. The sheer scale of Facebook's popularity is a moat – which includes 73 per cent of all regular internet users in the UK – and the platforms owned by Facebook/Meta combine to reinforce it: Instagram, Messenger, WhatsApp and Facebook.

Each of these businesses builds momentum: surplus revenue is poured into R & D, and into diversification. The new products and services are themselves also scalable, and they bind customers more closely to the original brand, creating new customers for it. Quickly, this process repeats until the business's position becomes entrenched, creating a de facto monopoly. At that point it can churn out profits. A virtuous cycle – but if your firm is on the outside, failing to scale and at the mercy of impatient investors, you might sell out instead. The quick return has mostly been the British way.

In 2010, the Bank of England's chief economist warned of short-termism in the UK markets, and since then academic studies have provided more evidence that 'systematic pressures exist in the UK context for the over-payment of dividends, leading to potential underinvestment'.[32]

Consider the position of one of Britain's biggest public technology companies: Aviva. At the start of 2024, the proportion of earnings paid out as dividends to shareholders was 280 per cent. In August 2023, Aviva's half-yearly report boasted: 'The consistency and strength of our performance supports the delivery of attractive outcomes for our shareholders.'[33]

Compare the tone with that of Netflix in their 2017 annual report: 'We are in no rush to push margins up too quickly,' it told shareholders, 'as we want to ensure we are investing aggressively enough to continue to lead internet TV around the world.'[34] Amazon has a similar vision for a strategy of domination: in his report for the first quarter of 2020, Bezos said: 'If you are a share-owner in Amazon, you may want to take a seat, because we're not thinking small.'[35] Amazon may have paid for its founder's trip to space, but it has never paid a dividend and is not thinking of doing so any time soon.

In Britain it is said that dividends keep managers 'honest'. But in the tech economy, the demand for dividends helps keep UK businesses small – and potential US competitors want them to stay that way. And if British businesses are small, they are discovering that they feel it when dealing with scaled, diversified and 'moated' US corporations as they have little power and little choice about what they pay, how they pay it or what information they must disclose to do business.

For Hermann Hauser, all this comes down to three questions, as paraphrased in an article for Forbes: 'Do we control the critical technology in our own country? Do we have access to the technology from multiple independent countries? Do we have long-term, guaranteed, unfettered and secure access to the technology from a monopoly or oligopoly supplier from a single country?' Hauser elaborated as follows: 'If the answer to the above three questions is no, you have to make changes. There is a danger of becoming a new vassal state to these tech giants. It's the danger of a new kind of colonialism, which is not enforced by military might but by economic dependence.'[36]

As we shall see, Britain's consumers, workers and businesses are learning exactly what it means to be a twenty-first-century vassal and to be plundered by a more powerful nation. They are learning the advantages of scale in technology, but also how the tech giants and the US platforms have become deeply embedded in the UK. And how US companies take a slice out of almost every transaction.

4

A SLICE OF EVERYTHING
PAYMENTS, PUBLICITY AND PLATFORMS

The best business is a royalty on the growth of others, requiring little capital itself.

– Warren Buffett, 1997[1]

The death of cash and building the payments toll bridge

In 2010, half of the purchases on the high street were made with cash, but now more than 90 per cent are cashless, according to the British Retail Consortium.[2] At incredible speed cashless convenience has drawn consumers away from a system of exchange used for millennia. But this is not just a story of innovation winning out; it is also about a policy of 'war' pursued by two major US corporations.

Ajay Banga, CEO of Mastercard, announced in 2010: 'I have declared war on cash.'[3] His 'accomplice', Al Kelly, CEO of Visa, later admitted to being part of what some would call a conspiracy, saying, 'We're focused on putting cash out of business.'[4] British authorities also joined the battle, on the side of these American firms, wishing to achieve their own ends: to reduce tax evasion, cut the number of robberies and make money traceable.

The big US card companies approached their targets using all available tactics to quell their opponents. They successfully prevented shopkeepers from charging extra for the use of cards, and at one stage Visa was even paying lump sums to selected businesses as a reward for refusing to accept cash.

Mastercard went on to acquire the company which controls the UK's LINK cash machines in 2016. In the aftermath, the cash-dispensing network has shrunk.[5] They slashed the payments that had made it worthwhile for petrol stations and retailers to host the LINK machines. One of the cash machine hosts said he had been forced to charge a fee for cash or take out the machine. Site owners started ripping out cash machines at a rate of 300 a month. Between 2018 and 2023, more than a quarter of ATM machines were decommissioned (16,000).[6] For many of those ATMs that remained there was a new customer charge of £3 for every £100 withdrawn.

Now, electronic payments have infiltrated places which were once bastions of cash: at festivals and craft fairs, stall-holders wave mobile card readers and often don't accept anything else. Even buskers on the London Underground are accepting credit card payments. The demise of cash has contributed to the waves of branch closures on the high street: since 2015 more than half of bank branches have been closed.[7]

In parallel with the demise of cash, plastic has rapidly gained wallet space. As a nation the British hold 160 million credit and debit cards, so a typical adult has at least three cards.[8] The American card issuers must have thought they had invented money – with credit card fees of between 1.5 per cent and 3.5 per cent they take a royalty on most of the retail spending in the UK economy.[9] Although British banks get some of this commission it is the US payments companies who are in control.

A decade on from Banga's statement, Covid-19 further cut supplies of cash to users, many of whom feared that touching coins or notes could lead to viral infection. It has gone so far that tens of thousands of shops and cafés now display the sign 'card only'.

It need not have been like this. Germany and France still use cash everywhere: in both those countries notes and coins account for around half of all retail transactions, something that gives significant benefits: cash makes people more aware of their spending and so helps millions to manage their finances. The well-off in society often ignore the usefulness of cash, but a survey by Which? showed that half the British population use cash to help with budgeting.[10] The loss of cash may well have made life meaningfully harder for ordinary people.

Responding late in the day to the disappearance of cash, the British establishment woke up in 2022. In that year the Access to Cash Action Group was set up by eight major banks, Age UK and the Post Office to try to stop the tide going out.[11] As Jenny Ross, money editor of Which? says: 'Cash remains vital for many on a tight budget.'[12]

Despite this, it seems unlikely that cashpoints will be reopened and probable that much more debt counselling will be needed.

Shopkeepers always knew that they could save money by taking cash because the handling fee is only about a tenth of the cost of plastic, but most customers wanted to use their cards and retailers just had to accept the change – and the charges. It has now grown to a point where, according to the British Retail Consortium, retailers pay fees of more than £1.3 billion every year.[13] Credit cards have become indispensable, and because it is illegal for shopkeepers to charge less to customers offering cash, the card companies can demand high fees – they hold the pricing power and can squeeze up the percentage they take. Following a hike in charges in 2022, economist Callum Godwin pointed out that card fees can be a business's second-largest cost after staff, and he said: 'UK retailers are now shouldering more than half a billion in estimated fee increases.'[14]

The big card companies and banks do not just take a cut of sales: they make as much from interest charges as they do from transaction fees. With interest rates on some cards at 24.9 per cent a year, the borrower's debt of £1,000 increases to £4,741 in just seven years. Millions of Brits drift into borrowing on credit cards because it is so convenient. Apart from profiting through cardholder inertia, the card companies are perfectly positioned to take advantage of two other very human conditions: self-deception and desire. Credit card users have, on average, twice as much debt as they report in surveys.

Confirming this observation, researcher Joshua Frank showed that cardholders also underestimate the interest they are paying by about a third.[15] A typical UK household has credit card debt of £2,500, and often much more, creating a treadmill that is difficult to step off. With this level of debt they rack up interest costs of about £600 a year – much of which is profit going directly to Visa and Mastercard. Reflecting this bonanza, in the period since 2010 Mastercard's share price has gone up by a factor of 17, from about $23 a share to more than $400.

But card fees are only part of the model. As Ajay Banga has said: 'The mistake that most people make is of assuming that Mastercard is a card company. We see ourselves as a payments company and have a presence in every form of cashless transaction.'[16] The US card companies have expanded across the whole payments ecosystem: they are deeply embedded in the money-transfer mechanisms, and the other banks' debit cards are usually linked to Visa or Mastercard. Their reach now means they can offer prepaid cards as well as business payroll and supplier

payments in addition to tap-to-pay systems. Widespread accept-
ance of Visa cards for 'tapping in' on buses or trains is very convenient and helps Visa achieve its CEO's goal of keeping a presence, and a slice of commission, in every form of transaction.

Looking at the other tap-to-pay options offered by Transport
for London, commuters can also use phones from US tech giants
Apple or Google, or devices on the wrist such as those produced
by Fitbit (based in San Francisco) or Garmin (headquartered in
Kansas). This exposes a common feature of technical change: as
new consumer behaviour emerges, the best-placed companies
are the incumbents with technical expertise – in this case US
payments companies and the US tech giants. That also applies
to payments beyond tap-and-pay, where shoppers do not even
have to take their cards or phones out of their pockets. Amazon's
bricks-and-mortar stores do not need checkouts: cameras and
smart software know what has been taken off the shelf and auto-
matically charge the Amazon card as the customer walks out.
Depending on which of their cards is used, the interest rate could
be 19 per cent or 29.9 per cent.[17] It is the same with verbal orders
through Alexa: there is no mention of money but the cost is added
to your Amazon card.

Behind the scenes in the payments world, every day vast sums
move between card companies and banks. Until 2010 these payments were processed by the Royal Bank of Scotland. However,
when that bank had to be bailed out following the financial
crisis it was forced to sell that division. The buyers were the US
private equity groups Bain Capital and Advent. According to
Peter Morris, a private equity expert at the University of Oxford,
when they resold the business just five years later these groups
multiplied their capital by a factor of five.[18] The next buyer was
Vantiv, an American payments processor that renamed the business Worldpay, and, like a growing snowball, it was subsequently

absorbed by another giant US financial corporation, Fidelity National Information Services (FIS), based in Florida. In July 2023, Worldpay was once again taken over, with the new owner GTCR saying it expected 'sustained, long-term growth' from the company.[19] At each stage Worldpay increased the number of UK transactions from which it was taking a cut. As Luca Bassi, a director of Bain Capital, put it: 'Everything where cash isn't there, is good.'[20]

Cashless payments represent a tariff on ordinary trade that transfers money out of the domestic economy and into the pockets of US corporations. Far from watching carefully and acting to protect consumers and producers alike, the UK government does not seem concerned.

In 2022, Al Kelly, the chair of Visa, had a reported personal fortune of $177 million while, at Mastercard, former chairman Ajay Banga, who remains a shareholder, had assets said to be worth $162 million.[21] And, each time a cashless transaction is made using their corporations' services their personal wealth will rise again.

Visa and Mastercard, Worldpay and the other payment companies represent only a few of the many toll bridges assembled to suck money out of Britain's domestic economy and blow it over the Atlantic. But tolls are due not just at the point of the transaction but also almost every time British businesses advertise to find customers.

The new world of advertising and publicity – with stars and stripes

For 50 years the UK's newspapers flourished with 'the twin rivers of gold': recruitment and classified advertisements. Building up their reader numbers and advertiser base allowed them to take a royalty on business activity, and they had enough pricing power to protect against both inflation and occasional downturns. Back in 2005, 13 million national newspapers were printed each day, which was wonderful business for their owners, needing little working capital and riding the waves of economic expansion. By September 2023, the number of papers printed each day had plummeted to about 4 million – only a third as many.[22]

Readers moved online and, released from their narrow silos, became promiscuous in their search for a good story. Even though they jumped around the internet, people mostly had three interests: talking, searching and shopping. So, to cater for these interests, three new rivers of advertising income emerged: through their social lives (Meta/Facebook), from what they searched for (Google) and from what they might buy online (Amazon). For all these activities, adverts could be precisely targeted, with no purchase necessary. The days of advertisers carpet-bombing readers with random adverts were numbered. In pursuit of eyeballs, as the industry puts it, more than two-thirds of ads had moved online by 2022, with UK advertisers spending about £28 billion every year.[23] The US giants had eaten the newspapers for breakfast, and today an equivalent of £1,000 for every British household is spent annually on digital advertising, with most of it going to the US.

And the three online advertising whales (Meta/Facebook, Alphabet/Google and Amazon) really do want to know you intimately. More than just where you live, what music you listen to and what you usually buy, they want to know your plans. They know your friends, too. Never forgetting anything about you, they also have the superpower of knowing what people like you typically choose to buy. Whether you suffer from haemorrhoids or are trying to conceive, they know stuff that even your family does not. And they can target their advertising with products and services that match your desires, often before you even realise what you want.

We apparently give them permission to build this treasure trove of information about us, technically at least. We sign terms and conditions, don't we? To check whether anyone reads these, the computer games seller Gamestation once inserted a clause in their terms and conditions which stated: 'By placing an order via this website on the first day of the fourth month of the year 2010 Anno Domini, you agree to grant us a non-transferable option to claim, for now and for ever more, your immortal soul.' Out of the 7,500 customers who agreed to those terms and conditions that day, not a single one raised any issue about their immortal soul – nor, presumably, did anyone read them.[24]

More positively, PC Pitstop buried a clause in their terms and conditions offering $1,000 to anyone who emailed them. It took four months and 3,000 downloads before someone noticed it and collected the money, demonstrating starkly how meaningless these conditions are for giving informed consent.[25] What really matters is how much the advertising groups can get away with, and despite some limits, mostly set by the EU, they continue to learn more and more about us, click by click.

The online giants are not just experts at targeting ads; they are scientific about what they charge for the ads. Their pricing ensures they take the biggest slices from the biggest businesses. So, when you search for a term such as 'tissues' on Amazon, 11 of the first 12 results are for Kleenex, owned by Kimberly-Clark in Texas, with the twelfth for Amazon's own brand, Presto! To get to that position Kleenex will have had to outbid everyone else. Except Amazon, obviously, who are playing both gamekeeper and poacher.

Along with online shops run by eBay, Google and Facebook, Amazon takes a significant portion of the leading brands' margins.

Vendors expect to pay a fee to be the first sponsored answer provided to users, and this captures as much of the margin as possible in an automated auction process that runs day and night. To rank number one with Google for the term 'locksmith', for example, vendors will have to pay 9p per click, but for the more valuable term 'gambling' they will be charged 58p per click: the US giants are not just asking for a slice of your advertising budget; they have engineered a way to get a slice of your profits, and the more profitable the industry sector the more they take.

Platforms – most roads lead to the West Coast

If toll roads exist for finding customers, others have been constructed for businesses attempting to seal the deal with them, through digital platforms which cut a recurring slice out of the British economy. One promise of internet retail was the prospect of 'cutting out the middleman' – the sales intermediary who makes a profit for stocking goods from suppliers and selling them on to consumers. But it has worked out very differently. Middlemen are back in force, but they have switched nationality.

Virtually everything is available online through a digital platform. To get a ticket for an event you might look at Ticketmaster (California), or to travel you might visit Expedia (Washington State). If you want a taxi you will summon Uber or Lyft (both California), and when you want a date you will hook up through Tinder or Grindr (both California). For a new computer game you will take on the bots at Steam (Washington State); to sell your house you will list with Zoopla (California), and for stuff you need at home you will source it from eBay (California) or Amazon (Washington State). Using social media you might use Twitter/X, Facebook or Instagram (all based in California).

If you want to watch a streamed film it is probably going to come through Netflix (California), Disney (California), Amazon Prime (Washington State) or Apple TV (California). Or maybe you want to share ideas through Reddit (California) or pictures through Pinterest (California), with its 450 million users, or maybe just connect with your neighbours using the remote-community platform paradoxically called Nextdoor (California). Or you could make a real-life visit using a bike or scooter from Lime (California).

Platforms reach into every part of life to match your needs with an array of suppliers. And it is not just for consumers: businesses depend on platforms such as Slack (California), GitHub (California), LinkedIn (Washington State) or Yahoo (California) for their interactions, but they also use platforms such as Oracle (California), Google Cloud (California) or Getty Images (Washington State) for storing or processing their data. Quite likely your company will take some of its payments through PayPal (California) after they have been processed by Stripe (California).

The geographical pattern could not be clearer: all these companies are based on the West Coast of the US. And every day tens of millions of interactions between British people go through California and Washington State, 5,000 miles from London. The hub of this region, Silicon Valley in Northern California, has become a uniquely productive area for growing and incubating tech businesses like these. Home to thousands of successful tech entrepreneurs, it has a large population of programmers and marketers who are experts in promoting platforms, and they host a myriad of events where new ideas are spawned and nurtured. A unique culture of enterprise and collaboration has evolved here. The region has also grown wealthy from the spillover benefits of hosting dozens of leading tech companies. San Jose, the city at the heart of Silicon Valley, has the world's third-highest income per person, after Zurich and Oslo.[26] Crucially, it is also home to some of the most sophisticated tech investors in the world.

One of these investors, Katherine Boyle, believes that the successful techniques of 'the Valley' can be applied in other US cities. She says: 'What I'm now seeing and what we're seeing in our own portfolio is that those people [founders] can build from anywhere... It is an extraordinary thing that Silicon Valley could be exported to the rest of the country.'[27]

There are already many platform companies with world-wide reach beyond the West Coast, in cities such as New York (Etsy and Peloton), Atlanta (Mailchimp) and Austin (Bumble). Technology has enabled these platforms to grow exponentially: in just ten years Etsy increased the number of sellers on its platform from 600,000 to more than 7 million, with a million of these in the UK.[28] Such growth could not have happened in the 1990s, even when the cost of digital copies dropped to just a few pence: it was still expensive to send out CDs by post and the programs were always out of date by the time they arrived. The internet eliminated these costs and meant platforms could be freely accessed from anywhere and updated instantaneously. This gave enterprises the potential to grow at lightning speed, as shown by the spread of ChatGPT: within just six weeks of its launch in late 2022, the AI chatbot already had more than 100 million users.[29]

The advocates for the platform companies paint a picture of organisations that promote sharing and creativity. From the outside it all looks frictionless, but under the surface is another story. Surveys of users show that three-quarters of them think it is too hard to make complaints, and 80 per cent think that more needs to be done to protect people's safety and privacy. Some suppliers also complain that the platforms make them jump through too many hoops and that they can still find themselves arbitrarily banned.

Despite appearing to be competitive, many platforms have established monopolies in their sector, becoming virtually impossible to displace with their massive quantities of high-quality content. As well as this monopoly power, some of these platforms rely on deceptive design patterns that are carefully crafted to trick users into buying expensive add-ons or giving away more information than they intended. Critics have attached colourful names to some of these techniques, such as 'privacy zuckering' for tricks that obscure ways to opt out of sharing private information. Another is the 'roach motel', whereby a webpage makes it easy to start paying a subscription but fiendishly hard to cancel it. For Trump's 2020 presidential election campaign the WinRed fundraising platform used a technique whereby intended one-off gifts committed the donor to recurring monthly donations. And 'confirmshaming' pressurises users into becoming subscribed to an email list.[30]

Ironically, the market strength of most platforms is underpinned by their consumers producing so-called 'user-generated content'. In the case of Airbnb, its hosts do all the legwork of listing and guests give free feedback, allowing the automated platform to take an eye-watering commission from Brits who are mostly just renting property from each other. Together the 'host' and 'guest' send 17 per cent (a sixth) of the income back to California, and that comes out of UK rentals of about £1 billion a year.[31] Each of these platforms takes whatever slice they can get: Eventbrite clips 7 per cent off ticket receipts; Deliveroo gobbles up 30 per cent of what is paid for a meal; and the really big platforms like the Apple App Store or Google Play demand 30 per cent of revenue from app sales.[32]

These businesses gained first-mover advantages and have often become highly lucrative monopolies. The prospect of such profitability leads US venture capitalists to pour money in to help establish platforms in new sectors. A whole cohort of West Coast investors has helped evolve a highly effective funding system from seed capital to public listing (initial public offering, or IPO) while also supporting and mentoring the founders.

The founders of digital enterprises have also worked out smart strategies to expand quickly and keep out competition. Many of them offer the 'freemium' model, allowing some free use but charging for full access, and they all design seductive and intuitive interfaces. Their marketing trades on the many weaknesses of human nature, and they also generate 'breadcrumbs' to lead customers along the path to signing up. Most of all, they tell stories and create myths that make customers want to spend time on their platforms.

As Simon Sinek, motivational speaker and author, says: 'People don't buy what you do – they buy why you do it.'[33] To convey why they run their businesses, each company promotes an origin story, the most powerful element of which is often the 'founder's story'. It is bizarre to see how many of these tales contain a version of 'the Silicon Valley garage myth', but there are good reasons for spinning the yarn.

A small garage in Palo Alto was the 1938 birthplace of Hewlett-Packard (HP). Here, William Hewlett and David Packard started building the pioneering audio oscillator that revolutionised sound engineering. Today, that garage appears in the US National Register of Historic Places with a plaque which reads: 'Birthplace of Silicon Valley'.[34] Microsoft also claims to have been started in a garage in 1975 by college dropout Bill Gates, and Apple fans insist that Steve Jobs and Steve Wozniak built their computers in a garage, though 'Woz' has since explained that it was little more than a drop-off point. Google also relates that it was started in a garage by Sergey Brin and Larry Page, although online footage of this location reveals it to be a comfortable office that happens to have double doors at the front.[35] The myth of the 'garage as birthplace' is also claimed by Californian companies Disney, Mattel and Wham-O, as well as by Xerox and Dell.

A garage origin story helps ordinary people identify with the founders and builds their hero status, as it shows them fighting against the odds, bringing disruption and defeating the giants of the past. It is also an aspect of the American dream: these fairy tales inspire workers to believe that one day they too might make it big, and that they are working for just an ordinary Joe. Or perhaps just an ordinary Jeff, if they are one of the 1.5 million Amazon associates (staff). He, too, claims to have started the 'everything store' in a garage, which feels a bit of a stretch as he spent the previous ten years as a well-paid executive on Wall Street and received $300,000 of start-up funding from his parents. Bezos's origin story includes the claim that to save money in the early days, rather than buying desks, he used cheap wooden doors supported on legs made from four-by-four timber.[36]

These founders' stories add to the celebrity status given to the men who still lead their companies, such as Mark Zuckerberg, Marc Benioff and Elon Musk. But the star-struck reporting on business celebrities can easily overlook the essential part of the story, as happened with Musk's purchase of Twitter/X late in 2022. The BBC reported extensively on whether Musk paid too much, on the will-he-won't-he takeover process and on whether he was employing enough content moderators.[37] The real story, at least in the UK, should be why the 'town square', which sits at the heart of British political life, is owned and controlled – and reportedly manipulated – from California.

Peter Thiel, founder of both PayPal and Palantir, has set up the Founders Network, where entrepreneurs offer each other support.[38] Thiel says: 'If you're a founder starting a company you always want to aim for monopoly and you always want to avoid competition.' He adds: 'You want to be a one-of-a-kind company, where it's the only one in a small ecosystem.'[39] Founders in Silicon Valley have created hundreds of such companies, and the British are usually only invited into their ecosystems as paying guests.

Perhaps one consequence of the deeply embellished 'founders' myths' is to make the success of the platforms more digestible to consumers. It seems to work too – even if numerous traditional British businesses such as travel agents, estate agents and department stores have closed their doors across UK high streets and US main streets. Even local accountants feel under pressure to team up with companies offering back-end number crunching, such as fast-growing QuickBooks of Mountain View, California. In the short term this offers a reliable platform on which accountants can store and process client data, but in the longer term their clients are locked into paying an annual or monthly toll charge.

One of the most successful investors in Silicon Valley, Marc Andreessen, famously wrote that 'software is eating the world', predicting, back in 2011, that West Coast companies would disrupt most traditional industries.[40] Silicon Valley is still eating the UK byte by byte, one transaction at a time.

Labour as a commodity, brokered from California

While digital platforms now dominate the markets in goods and services, they are also transforming the labour market. One in seven of the UK workforce (4.4 million people) now gets work through a platform.[41] These so-called 'gig economy workers' may often seem invisible, even if they do bring us our pizzas from Just Eat or Deliveroo and they deliver 'your stuff' from Amazon. These platforms have grown really fast: in the four years before 2020 the number of such workers doubled. They are working in what is often labelled the 'gig economy', a term implying that it is cool, flexible, individual, but the reality is that it is often tough, impersonal and insecure. Whatever the conditions, jobs are found through an app, which is often a US-owned platform taking a fee for matching workers with work.

Giant automated agencies like Taskrabbit naturally demand their pound of flesh, extracting a royalty from British labour. And firms such as Uber and Deliveroo are built almost exclusively on zero-hours 'gig workers'. A typical such worker, Anton Barker, told me his experience: 'The training course to become a Deliveroo cycle courier took much less than a day – all they did was show me how the app works and gave me my branded kit. After that I just did what the app told me – I never met colleagues. It was totally impersonal. I liked working in a hilly part of London because I got really fit, but in the winter I also got really cold. I was paid £7 an hour plus £1 for each meal delivered and it went OK for three months until I got an injury. Then I was out of work and on my own.'

The government has done little to stop the growth of insecure working conditions and some of its contractors even use gig workers for cleaning and catering at government buildings. Instead of challenging the working conditions and considering whether this is debasing the labour market, government ministers focus on making sure such workers are properly taxed.[42] The gig economy has created a workforce toiling long hours for the minimum wage – and many claim they earn even less than that. This contrasts with the much better position of most European workers and, even more sharply, with those who are managing these companies, especially those holding equity stakes. If this is a new feudal order there is a nobility now – mostly algorithmic and American – which provides work to the majority, who are subject to the authority of the ruling elite, a reality the UK government seems uninterested in reversing.

But whether the UK government is paying attention or not, US multinational innovation has reshaped the way the country is run: building toll bridges to draw revenue from every innocuous transaction, making consumers dependent, and turning suppliers into supplicants and workers into a cheap and disposable resource.

For the UK, the consequences of all this extend beyond money: our payments systems, social media and the personal data of almost every citizen are controlled from across the Atlantic. While the British have been watching passively, these companies have been creating a new world. They think in systems, concentrating not on products but on processes used by British businesses as well as consumers. But what about the big US brands themselves? They are already streets ahead, having learned how to make recurring sales, how to increase prices effortlessly and how to present this as customer service. After the transaction toll bridges come the payment treadmills.

5

LIFE-AS-A-SERVICE
THE TWIN TREADMILLS OF SUBSCRIPTIONS AND DEBT

We realized the best way to monetize content was through a subscription model.

> – John 'Trip' Adler, founder of Scribd,
> a platform with 80 million users[1]

In February 2000, a protest appeared outside a technology conference in San Francisco, signalling the start of a transformation which is still reshaping economies across the developed world.

Inside, the venue was packed with businesses which used Siebel software for running customer databases and marketing. Outside, there were chants and placards proclaiming 'No More Software'. But this was not a Luddite protest, or even an anti-globalisation rally. On the contrary, the whole scene was fake. Even the TV news crew that turned up had been coordinated, along with the protestors, by a man called Marc Benioff.[2]

Benioff was an unknown businessman who would, in two decades, grow his company, Salesforce, into one of the biggest in America. He did it by smashing the business model of firms like

Siebel. At that firm's annual conference in Cannes, Benioff hired every cab in the city, and placed salesmen in them who subjected each Siebel delegate to the full force of Salesforce's pitch.

The pitch was not complicated: instead of buying expensive software outright, businesses could rent what they needed when they needed it online. Benioff was aggressively persuading buyers that 'Software-as-a-Service' (SaaS) was a better proposition than purchasing single-user licences.

By 2003, Salesforce had grown its annual sales to $100 million, and since then it has multiplied them by 300, making it one of America's largest tech firms. It has the objective 'of making enterprise software as easy to use as a website like Amazon'.[3]

But the idea of transforming software from a product you buy and install into one you rent did not just build one business: it revolutionised first the entire tech sector and then the rest of the economy, in Britain and across the business world.

The change is easy to track: from 2011, Microsoft encouraged its customers to rent Office 365 rather than buy its software outright. In March 2015, Microsoft's CEO Satya Nadella told a conference that every kind of business would soon become an SaaS business.[4]

The SaaS revolution spread to include Adobe, Intuit and HubSpot. Salesforce is now ranked as the number-one customer relationship manager in the UK, and its UK sales alone exceed £160 million every month. What drives IT chiefs to sign up for SaaS is having a powerful off-site resource in exchange for predictable monthly payments.

The monthly fee is the key to the success of SaaS. And by charging in this way the company reserves the right to raise the fee at any time. It goes up when the customer needs extra software or storage space, or perhaps because the company thinks it can get away with raising the prices.

Erik Bullard, from the market experts UpperEdge, has observed that much of the software business happens in the dark: 'The lack of transparency that Salesforce provides to the market is astounding when you consider the millions of dollars that are simply taken as "the cost of doing business with Salesforce" by many organizations.'[5] Once they have signed up, customers are extremely sticky: inertia kicks in and the costs of switching suppliers can be crippling.

According to entrepreneur Mario Grunitz: 'The subscription-based model is revolutionising every major industry on the planet and reshaping consumer behaviour in real-time.'[6] 'Finance-as-a-Service' offers accounting, invoicing and payroll services in return for monthly payments. 'Agriculture-as-a-Service' helps farmers with crop management and analytics. Caterpillar Inc. now offers 'Diggers-as-a-Service', connecting its machines to the cloud, with customers paying a monthly fee. These services tell drivers when they need fuel, a new tyre or engine tuning. Tom Barker, a Caterpillar dealer says: 'The Cat Productivity platform gives customers the information they need to improve site productivity… and track individual assets to ensure they are optimally positioned to reduce cycle time.'[7]

Even jet engine makers offer an 'Engines-as-a-Service' business model, nicknamed 'power-by-the-hour'.[8] The manufacturer leases the engine to the airline, providing services for maintenance, repair and overhaul, in exchange for a monthly fee adjusted for the number of hours the engine runs. This helps the airlines by cutting their upfront capital costs and transferring to others the management of 'their' engines. Airlines, like most businesses, always want to cut down on their use of capital, that scarcest of resources, to stop it from becoming a brake on their growth. And the same drive to eliminate capital spending has opened opportunities for 'Furniture-as-a-Service' for office chairs and desks, and 'Art-as-a-Service', with a monthly subscription for paintings which can be regularly swapped out. Other, larger 'as-a-Service' sectors are human resources, disaster recovery and marketing (HRaaS, DRaaS and MaaS), each running on a subscription basis. Corporate life is now all about predictable, recurring revenues and spending.

The leasing life has spread beyond business to personal spending too – including in high fashion: for the Earthshot Prize ceremony in 2022, Catherine, Princess of Wales, wore a spectacular green dress rented for just £74 from HURR in London. Alexandria Ocasio-Cortez also hired a designer outfit for the 2021 Met Gala. These examples nudge others to become renters rather than owners.[9]

For consumers, paying for a service is an alternative to buying a product outright and can have useful advantages. A rented dress doesn't need storage or mothproofing, and this same pay-as-you-use model also drives car rentals. In London, Zipcar has 200,000 customers (oddly called 'members'), who pay for the use of cars and vans by the hour, or minute. Based in Boston, Massachusetts, the company's website announces: 'we're on a mission to enable simple and responsible urban living – a future filled with more car-sharing members than car owners… from the Big Apple to Big Ben.'[10]

Owned by the Avis Budget Group of New Jersey, Zipcar also satisfies drivers' desire for less polluting solutions with the positive message of a 'sharing economy'. Theirs is a very top-down version of 'sharing': the company owns the asset and many people rent it. It works even better for other car-sharing organisations, such as Uber and Lyft, whose chauffeurs themselves provide the cars while the platform collects a payment every time the vehicle is used.

Although companies that rent out equipment earn a high return on their capital, it is the next level that gets them excited, the stage beyond one-off rentals. What finance directors crave is a regular, repeating rental: the subscription model. This is nectar for suppliers. Their bankers and investors love it too: a recurring rental contract where the cash arrives every month, come rain or shine. And that is exactly what many businesses have established in the UK, often in sectors where no one thought it would be possible.

European businesses have also followed where the Americans have led. BMW of Munich ran a short-lived scheme in which drivers of some new cars were forced to pay monthly to access heated seats (£15 per month) and a system that alerted the driver to nearby speed cameras (£25 per year).

Why has renting become so popular? The answer, in part, is a matter of behavioural science.

Nudge, nudge

As a 26-year-old marketer at Oracle Corporation, Marc Benioff was an admirer of leading behavioural economist Richard Thaler, a professor at the University of Chicago. Thaler, who would later explain his life's work in an influential book called *Nudge*, studied why people choose one option over another.[11] Again and again, he found they seek to avoid hard choices.

Thinking about his own customers' choices, Benioff noticed their preference for renting on a monthly basis rather than making large, one-off capital investments. It struck him that instead of selling software licences he could just rent software to customers from a central hub where he could also store their data, and that insight set off the 'Life-as-a-Service' revolution.

Ordinary consumers, too, have been encouraged to buy services on a subscription model, and the option of purchasing outright is taken off the table. The shift to monthly payments was no accident: it has been the result of systematic changes decided by the big US multinationals harnessing the research of psychologists.

Daniel Kahneman's 2011 book *Thinking, Fast and Slow* became particularly influential within US companies.[12] And in the years that followed, consumer-facing tech giants hired behavioural scientists. Adjusting the wording of a message or altering the placement of a button encourages users to take a particular action. This was not just about marketing a fixed product: it was also about redesigning the offer to make it easier to say yes. Central to this was helping buyers to avoid making a big decision and to agree, initially at least, to pay a month's subscription.

Take the case of video streaming, where the main offerings are from the five US giants Netflix, Apple, Disney, Amazon and Sky (bought by Comcast of Philadelphia in the autumn of 2018). At the beginning of 2024, each of them required a monthly payment of, respectively, £10.99, £8.99, £7.99, £8.99 and £19.00. These are all-you-can-eat offerings and, as with other 'Sales-as-a-Service' models, there are many tricks behavioural scientists use to increase sign-ups. For instance, Apple includes three months' free subscription with the purchase of any of its devices. This is part of CEO Tim Cook's plan to boost recurring income. In 2017 he said: 'We have a goal to double the size of the services business over the next four years.'[13] That was achieved in only three years, and in November 2023 Cook said: 'We have well over 1 billion paid subscriptions across the services on our platform, nearly double the number we had only three years ago.'[14]

All the video-streaming companies offer free trial periods, and discounts when the whole family signs up – making it very hard, socially, for them ever to unsubscribe. And each channel offers exclusive content to recruit subscribers, knowing that inertia will make most of them stay subscribed even when they only signed up for one particular film.

The combined effect of these techniques, coupled with improved technology, has been an explosion in UK subscriptions. According to Ofcom, the number of UK households paying for streaming video services ballooned from 1.6 million in 2012 to more than 28 million by 2022.[15] This represents a 16-fold increase in a decade.

Taking this a step further, George Loewenstein, a professor of Economics and Psychology at Carnegie Mellon University, Pennsylvania, looked at what stops people from buying. He found that regular smaller payments made online by direct debit or by credit card feel much less painful than parting with a lump of hard cash, and he concludes: 'Credit cards effectively anesthetize the pain of paying.'[16]

US psychologists have studied in depth how to nudge someone just browsing into becoming a purchaser. One critical question is how much choice to offer a potential buyer or subscriber. Researchers from Columbia University set up an experiment with a stall selling 24 kinds of jam. Shoppers showed plenty of interest but made very few purchases. On another day at the same stall, they offered only six types of jam and discovered that shoppers were much more likely to make a purchase from the smaller selection.[17] When it comes to this sort of choice, less is more. And one sees this when facing options for buying extra storage space on Dropbox, Google or Apple: they give a very small number of choices and nudge people into signing up for the one that works best for them.

Marketing departments have taken careful note of studies exploring how people make decisions. Monthly payments are easier to choose than bigger one-off purchases, and most buyers prefer having more granular control over services received. In his book *The Paradox of Choice*, American psychologist Barry Schwartz shows that people have different decision-making styles: some are 'maximisers' and want to consider all available options, while others are what he calls 'satisficers' and make 'good enough' decisions from limited information.[18] US marketers are careful to cater for both groups.

Bundling services together for a single charge means that larger operators can keep out competition and this appeals to customers' desire for simplicity and the perception that they are getting a bargain. 'Bundling bias' means that people prefer to buy services together even though ultimately they will often not consume enough of the bundle to justify paying the combined cost. Single purchases would often have been cheaper, as shown by the ski-pass experiments done by psychologists Soman and Gourville.[19] They found that when people buy weekly ski passes rather than daily ones they are more likely to miss a day's skiing and, more generally, that buying in a bundle makes consumers more willing to pay for a service but not use it. Selling services in a combined package means that the bigger players can keep out smaller, often local, competition. Smaller suppliers do not have enough offerings to create a bundle. No British online seller can plausibly collect £95 each year in the way that Amazon does with Prime. This is a single subscription which includes free delivery, access to streamed videos, special offers, a music collection, a library and much more.[20] While the UK's Competition and Markets Authority (CMA) recognises the anti-competitive effects of bundling in financial services, they have not dared to challenge US bundlers such as Amazon or Microsoft.[21]

A unique position in the market has advantages, allowing Amazon to push up the price of Prime by 75 per cent since its introduction, and Prime subscriptions alone garner $25 billion each year from across the world. The US Federal Trade

Commission (FTC) has said that some of the methods the company has used to create this deluge of cash have been 'manipulative' and 'coercive'. The US regulator accused Amazon of using deceptive user-interface designs, known as 'dark patterns', to trick consumers into automatic renewal of their subscriptions.[22] According to a complaint filed by the FTC in 2023, Prime consumers have had to 'navigate a four-page, six-click, 15-option cancellation process'.[23] This contrasts with the signing-up process which only needs one or two clicks.

The genius of the US-led SaaS subscription model is that, at any point, customers can simply opt out – it is inertia and psychology that bind them in. This is in contrast to Britain's own troubled history with rented goods and services, which has led to a series of scandals around companies exploiting consumers through unfair contract terms. BrightHouse and PerfectHome were each chastised and fined by the Financial Conduct Authority (FCA), in 2017 and 2018, respectively, for using unfair contracts and for not checking customers' ability to pay.[24]

US corporations have developed the art of moving people from being free users to being subscribers, which is exactly what the 'freemium model' does. Originally, freemium was evolved to sell software, and it is now widely used in gaming, music and news media. The basic idea is to offer a free version to attract a large user base, and then monetise that base by offering premium features or extra paid-for services. It originated in the 1990s US software world as part of the open-source movement. Open-source software is freely available code which anyone can modify and distribute and is at the core of initiatives such as Linux, Apache and MySQL. As these projects grew, several software companies began developing commercial products, offering a free basic version and then selling add-on services. AVG's antivirus software was the first of these: it was free but had paid-for upgrades for real-time scanning and updates. By 2008, AVG had 80 million users, many of whom chose to pay for the add-ons – and freemium was born. It has been crushingly successful in the world of apps: Dropbox, Hootsuite and Candy Crush Saga each make millions of dollars a year through the freemium model. Candy Crush Saga has more than 300,000 daily users in the UK and worldwide 2.7 billion people have downloaded it – that is one in three people globally.[25] In most years its owner, Activision of California, makes more than a billion dollars of revenue from the game.

So the suck-it-and-see freemium model lures users onto the payments treadmill, and they often find it hard to get off. According to a 2023 study by Stanford economists, this inertia can boost subscription firms' revenues by up to 200 per cent: many customers were continuing to pay simply because they had not taken the time to cancel the service or did not know how to step off the treadmill.[26] Escape routes can be well hidden according to Citizens Advice, who have shown that 2 million Brits struggle to cancel unwanted subscriptions. They estimate that at least £300 million worth of payments are taken each year for unused services.[27]

Once it has become fully embedded, a platform such as WhatsApp becomes a latent treadmill whose owner – Meta of California in the case of WhatsApp – can at any point decide to charge users a subscription for access. And the UK's reliance on services such as WhatsApp is demonstrated by the fact that when there is an outage, as happened for just two hours on 24 October 2022, it becomes national news.

While it is reasonable for suppliers of services to charge for them, the British authorities have allowed many online monopolies to develop that have the effect of excluding local suppliers. Indeed, the big US platforms have already started turning dependence on them into a new payments treadmill. In 2023, three social media platforms started charging for extra services, such as the 'blue tick' to prove status, for which Twitter/X charged £84 each year. Instagram subscribers can pay for exclusive content highlighted by a purple ring, and Facebook is introducing 'Meta Verified', where a 'verified badge' (also a blue tick) will cost over £140 a year, charged monthly through the app. Even Snapchat has adopted a similar scheme, claiming that 'subscription will allow us to deliver new Snapchat features... and allow us to provide prioritised support.'[28]

Any services we currently use for free are potential treadmills and there are plenty of emerging ones: the AI tool ChatGPT was free to use in the three months after it was launched, but very soon a $20-a-month subscription was introduced for the premium version.

Debt

Being on the subscription treadmill leads many towards the second great treadmill: debt. And with debt you cannot simply unsubscribe.

Fraser Sutherland of Citizens Advice in Scotland described the situation in his region: 'Around 1 million Scots last year had reason to cancel a recurring payment... we know from the number of clients we help on the subject that many thousands are being duped into subscriptions they didn't want.'[29] One person receiving debt counselling told me: 'I didn't realise how much of my pay was going towards subscription services until I started budgeting and tracking my expenses. It was eye-opening.' Over 50 per cent of the UK population report being in financial difficulty, and the FCA says subscriptions are significantly to blame, with consumers feeling social pressure to maintain multiple subscriptions.

A typical consumer spends £46 each month on subscriptions, with one in six paying more than £100.[30] According to researchers at Compare the Market, half of them have at least one subscription which they no longer use.[31]

The average credit card debt per household in the UK was £2,409 in 2023, according to the Money Charity, and the Bank of England shows that consumer lending in 2022 and 2023 reached its highest levels for a decade.[32] But it is worse for lower-income homes and minorities: 27 per cent of black people describe their debts as 'a heavy burden', compared with 15 per cent of UK adults generally.[33]

The debt charity Christians Against Poverty (CAP) has worked hard to publicise the terrible human cost of debt. One of their clients explained:

> I thought about doing away with my life; I thought about it many times. I was so depressed I didn't want to see anybody. I was incapable of repaying the debts I had built up while I was not working; so I turned off the heating, stopped eating and was unable to afford essential things like toiletries.[34]

For those readers who do not carry any debt, much of this may seem to be 'someone else's problem', but financial stress is a much wider issue. Justin Welby, Archbishop of Canterbury, says that the scale of problem debt is at 'epidemic levels'. He is a patron of CAP, whose chief executive Matt Barlow says: 'Debt isn't just a maths problem, it touches every area of life: relationships, health, housing and children's welfare.'[35]

High interest rates make it especially hard to escape the debt treadmill. Typically, those in financial difficulty struggle with any unexpected outgoings, illness or simply the lack of funds. A third of those under financial stress live in homes with less than £15,000 of annual income; two-thirds are receiving benefits – and yet, despite this, two-thirds are also working. That household debt hits unequally is shown by the fact that 42 per cent of those who are financially stressed have a physical or mental health issue.[36]

Problem debt is only made worse by monthly subscriptions. Martyn James of *The Times* says: 'Cancelling unwanted, unused or poor value subscription services can save you big money. Our consumer champion did just that and clawed back £1,207.'[37]

While subscriptions are not the only cause of the UK's collective household debt, they must be a substantial contributor when the average UK household pays £1,100 a year on them, creating what has been described as a 'subscription society'.[38] The link between paying monthly subscriptions to US corporations and high-interest borrowing is inescapable.

Britain is in a worse position than others. The most expensive mainstream borrowing is by credit card (typically charging 22 per cent annual interest), and the British have much more credit card debt than the Europeans: the French have half as much, the Germans two-thirds and the Italians only a quarter.[39] These debts are mostly via American corporations such as Visa or Mastercard, and the British have been uniquely tempted to climb aboard the treadmill of high-interest debt. Maybe it is because of the unusually British desire to 'keep up appearances' or because of their reticence to talk about money and financial pain. One survey by the Money and Pensions Service shows that although half the UK population regularly worries about money, 29 million adults (over half) do not feel comfortable talking about it because of a combination of shame, their upbringing and a desire not to burden others.[40]

The depth of personal borrowing in Britain is shown in comparison with the US and Europe using OECD numbers for

2022.[41] Average debt as a percentage of disposable income may seem high in the US at 101 per cent; for Italy it is 110 per cent; and in Germany it is 111 per cent. But the UK takes the prize for personal indebtedness, with average debt of 148 per cent of disposable income. The British consumer is quick to latch on to new forms of borrowing, of which the latest is 'BNPL' – 'buy now, pay later' – dominated by market leader Klarna. The company is owned by US investors, led by Sequoia Capital of Menlo Park, California.[42]

Life-as-a-Service, with its unavoidable and potentially crippling outgoings, has become a way of life not just for millions of consumers but for UK companies and the government. Organisations have signed up en masse to pay monthly for software and other services. There has been exponential growth in 'cloud computing' such as Software-as-a-Service (programs), Platform-as-a-Service (hardware and software for running apps), Infrastructure-as-a-Service (hosting of websites) and Communications-as-a-Service (communications systems).

So the Brits and their companies are being rapidly moved from being owners of their assets to being renters and then borrowers, and much of what they consume and pay for is done through the monthly treadmill.

The switch to the monthly pulse of money transfers has been coming for a long time: in 1973 about 80 per cent of British workers were paid weekly, usually on a Friday, whereas today the vast majority are paid monthly. And the US multinationals have jumped onto that monthly cycle for collecting almost all payments: reducing credit card balances, collecting direct debits for streaming channels and taking payments for apps.

Some of the biggest winners from Life-as-a-Service revenue models have been the US private equity titans, who since 2008/9 have been reshaping the British economy. Much of the £700 billion the UK pays annually to US companies goes out in this monthly cycle and frequently to businesses owned by US private equity. For their acquisitions they usually borrow heavily, and private equity buyers often need these reliable, growing cash flows to pay their interest costs.

6

PRIVATE EQUITY
THE EXTRACTION MACHINES

Basically any predominantly British-listed company, with one or two exceptions… is vulnerable to a takeover offer in a way that doesn't apply elsewhere in the world.

– Lord Paul Myners[1]

Acrobats, live camels and a spectacular firework display entertained 600 guests at Stephen Schwarzman's seventieth birthday party in 2017.[2] It was held at his Palm Beach house in Florida, just a mile and a half from Mar-a-Lago, and the Trumps were among the guests – as they had been for his sixtieth birthday bash in New York.[3] At that earlier Manhattan event there was a giant replica of the Schwarzmans' apartment, with outsized copies of their art treasures. Rod Stewart and Patti LaBelle performed, and the actor and comedian Martin Short was the compere.[4] It took three days to assemble the towering birthday cake, and the cocktails were served in ice sculptures. Each of these parties was reported to have cost at least $5 million, but for a man worth $37 billion such amounts barely register. Looked at another way, even without earning any further return on his assets, he can afford to throw one of these parties every week for the next 140 years.

Beyond extravagant birthday bashes, Schwarzman, the most prominent of the private equity chiefs, is a philanthropist – and does not mind if people know it. He has made $100 million-plus donations to the New York Public Library and the Yale School of Management, and has funded the construction of a new humanities centre at Oxford University.[5] Naturally, the new facilities he funds or builds will all carry his name. Explaining why he gives these vast amounts, he says: 'I find myself giving to large projects that I think can make a large-scale impact.'[6]

Schwarzman's project making the largest impact is his private equity group, Blackstone, with a trillion dollars of assets under management. But critics claim its practices seem to be far from charitable.[7]

Blackstone leads the pack of businesses working to acquire great chunks of Britain. Using a combination of private capital and heavy borrowing, it buys large businesses, and slices and dices them to crank out profits. Blackstone – and private equity in general – has been devastatingly effective, typically purchasing undervalued companies and restructuring them. Usually they buy cheaply and cut costs, as well as often raising prices to earn fabulous returns.[8] The process often increases efficiency and allows companies to grow, though critics say this is sometimes at the expense of service quality and workers' interests.

Right from the outset, Schwarzman wanted Blackstone to do more than just execute a few profitable deals. His ambition was far greater: to build a financial juggernaut that would buy and sell whole businesses and, when profitable, keep hold of them for the longer term. The machine he envisaged would be opportunistic, constantly sifting through the economies of the world to find hidden value that he could capture. He says: 'To be successful you have to put yourself in situations and places you have no right being in… through sheer will, you wear the world down, and it gives you what you want.'[9]

Including the staff at acquired companies, Blackstone employed around half a million people around the world by 2024.[10] It controls more than 200 large enterprises, and within that collection the UK offered a rich seam of bargains: listed companies, government assets and family firms. Blackstone has had a hand in the purchase and sale of scores of UK enterprises, including Legoland, the NEC in Birmingham (the UK's largest event space), Madame Tussauds and Blackpool Tower. As Schwarzman says: 'Some of the people in finance touch enormous parts of the economy.'[11]

Blackstone is only one of dozens of such buyout companies, and they are all constantly scanning the UK economy, and others, for attractive assets. Private equity interests already own hundreds of UK and US businesses, and in the process their founders have become influential and immensely wealthy. At the start of 2024, Apollo's Leon Black and KKR's Henry Kravis, both based in New York, had reported net worth of $12 and $10 billion, respectively.[12] In Washington, David Rubenstein's Carlyle Group had earned him more than $3 billion personally, and in Chicago Orlando Bravo had amassed a fortune of $8 billion through the Thoma Bravo company.

Thoma Bravo is an unusual private equity investor because it is a specialist. Rather than looking for bargains across the whole economy, it specialises in software companies. One of its typical purchases was Sophos, a British cybersecurity business purchased in 2020 for $4 billion. Formerly controlled from Abingdon, Oxfordshire, the sale allowed co-founder Peter Lammer to pocket more than £250 million. I know Peter Lammer a little and wonder if the company is less humane without him – he has certainly been generous in sharing the proceeds of his sale. The Sophos deal helped to power Bravo's meteoric rise, and the group now runs 200 different software companies. Perhaps even Orlando Bravo, the CEO, has been surprised by the speed of its growth, since he boasted: 'We're doing nothing different now than we used to. It's just add another zero, and then another zero.'[13]

However, private equity never makes everyone rich. Sometimes the very deals which enrich private equity's leaders can harm staff. Almost as soon as Sophos was bought the job cuts began. Thoma Bravo reduced the overall headcount by 16 per cent, with claims that more jobs disappeared in the UK than elsewhere.[14] Management axed non-critical administrative costs and reduced spending on legacy and non-core products. Just like many other private equity purchases, a premium had been paid and that was best justified by making the company leaner, and maybe a little meaner.

As with big tech in Britain, which is utterly dominated by American enterprises, so with private equity: of the top 20 private equity companies, 17 are from the US.[15] Virtually all of these are active in the UK. Following these larger companies there are a host of 'boutique' private equity players often owned by the big US banks, such as the subsidiaries of Morgan Stanley, Citigroup and Bank of America. Even within this wider group of a couple of hundred players, three-quarters are American. And, in the last 20 years, the UK economy has welcomed them to a feeding frenzy that has transformed the UK's commercial landscape – not just changing who owns the UK but how we work and live. Increasingly, Britain's most successful businesses are private equity-owned, which means they are more cut-throat, less accountable and usually highly tax efficient.

One study by the universities of Harvard and Chicago showed that, on average, during the first two years of owning a company private equity managers cut one in seven staff, reduced wages and raised prices in a process financiers call 'margin expansion'.[16] Back in 2005 a senior German politician famously described such buyers as a 'swarm of locusts', and the private equity industry is still struggling to persuade politicians that it contributes to economic well-being.[17] In the US, senator Elizabeth Warren was so incensed by what it does to communities and workers that she introduced a 'Stop Wall Street Looting' Act in 2021.[18] Senator Warren says: 'Washington has looked the other way while private equity firms take over companies, load them with debt, strip them of their wealth, and walk away scot-free – leaving workers, consumers, and whole communities to pick up the pieces.'[19]

For Blackstone's critics in the UK, its role in the management of a doomed care home business called Southern Cross showed Warren's warning in action. Blackstone helped to build Southern Cross into England's largest care home provider, with 31,000 residents, through aggressive acquisition.[20] It was five years after Blackstone's interest in associated companies had ended that the business was declared insolvent.

By the time it failed, one in three of Southern Cross's 581 centres in England had been served with improvement orders by inspectors from the Care Quality Commission (CQC). After Blackstone's time, in one London centre there were 19 unexplained deaths. A coroner's report described one care home as 'mismanaged and understaffed', but it was not the poor standard of care that led to collapse.[21] Southern Cross failed because the number of elderly residents using the homes fell after the 2008 financial crisis and the business was no longer profitable. After its collapse there was considerable speculation that Southern Cross could have survived if it hadn't been for its business plan, introduced by Blackstone managers, which made the company particularly vulnerable to a downturn.[22]

Blackstone's plan had been ingenious: it bought the business in 2004, and expanded rapidly through 'sale and leaseback': buying smaller companies, splitting off the property assets and signing long rental agreements with ever-rising 30-year rents to be paid by the care homes to the landlords of the buildings. Southern Cross as the trading company subsequently floated on the stock market, and the much safer property rental business was later sold to Qatari investors.

There was a flaw: margins were slim, and the moment Southern Cross's revenue fell, it could not pay the rent even after cutting staffing to the bone. Jamie Buchan, who became chief executive of Southern Cross in 2009, stated that the 'model doesn't work through hard times', but by the time these came, and the care homes could not make the rent payments, Blackstone was long gone.[23] It denies any responsibility for Southern Cross failures and during its tenure the company experienced growth and was profitable at the time of its flotation.

Self-evidently, the interests of business owners, customers and workers are often in competition. Private equity concentrates the power of ownership to create good outcomes for owners like Blackstone. Sometimes the companies are traded quickly, and they are usually run for maximum short-term profit, which makes them vulnerable during downturns. This can mean slicing off many of the elements that make a business robust for workers and customers: a solid pension fund, a host of buildings owned debt-free, generous terms for employees and enough staff to ensure good customer experience.

'I've learned,' says Stephen Schwarzman in one Blackstone marketing video, 'that it's really helpful to be with nice people and that's an essential part of building a great business: you have to build a great culture.'[24] However, his critics claim the culture is not always so 'great' for the nice people who do not work with

Schwarzman in the boardroom but rather beneath him, thousands of miles away, on the ground floors of the businesses Blackstone controls and trades.

Hidden stars behind the household brands

Despite the surge in takeovers and restructurings, the bulk of the British public still have no idea what 'private equity' really means, or how much of the UK economy it controls. That's partly because British politicians rarely discuss it, but also because acquired companies invariably continue with the same trading names and offices. Behind closed doors the businesses are radically reorganised. Veterans of private equity mostly keep a low profile so that their straw-to-gold machines can carry on expanding. Few consumers realise how many household names are owned by North American private equity: in 2024 they controlled Morrisons, Travelodge, the AA, Alton Towers, Gatwick Airport, Biffa, Center Parcs and Burger King. And there are far more within the business-to-business sector. In 2021 the former City minister, Lord Paul Myners, said: 'Britain is open for business in the same way that a car boot sale is open for business.'[25]

This eating up of UK enterprises has removed hundreds of listings from the London Stock Exchange (LSE), undermining its reasons for existing. In the 15 years following 2008, the number of firms trading on the LSE has plummeted by more than 40 per cent, which means that many more purchasing decisions are made outside the UK.[26] This is partly because firms prefer to have their listing in New York, and partly because they have been swallowed up by private equity buyers. Martin Sorrell, the leading UK marketeer of this generation, is quite clear: 'Private equity is rampant… they are the dominant force now'.[27]

Profiting from the pandemic

As the pandemic swept across Britain in 2020–22, people feared for the most vulnerable in their families and communities, and so homes and workplaces were locked down. But for private equity it was quite different: precisely because the consequences of Covid weakened many listed companies they created frequent buying opportunities. In the early months of the crisis private equity firms announced approaches to more than twice as many listed companies as they had ever done previously.[28]

Private equity had learned the lesson of the 2009/10 financial turmoil: downturns bring opportunity. Bain Capital's managing partner John Connaughton commented: 'One of the most productive periods for us was after the global financial crisis... Investors wish they had deployed more capital in 2010, 2011 and 2012.'[29]

Schwarzman's Blackstone went on a UK buying spree during the pandemic, picking up housebuilder St Modwen, aviation supplier Signature and Bourne Leisure. Bourne owns Butlin's, Haven and Warner Leisure Hotels and its takeover was a typical private equity deal: some of the founders wanted to retire; the business was suffering from the effects of the pandemic, and it was packed with property assets which the buyer was able to borrow against. As a domestic holiday operator, it also stood ready to profit from the staycation boom.

KKR, Apollo, Carlyle, Advent and Bain also bought businesses in the hospitality, retail and travel sectors. Low valuations prompted the takeovers of infrastructure group John Laing (KKR), defence contractor Ultra (Advent), waste company Viridor (KKR) and housing developer Beechcroft (Carlyle). Large companies were equally vulnerable: a bidding war broke out for Morrisons, and each of the two American private equity buyers understood what a bargain it was even at £7 billion, selling for less than the value of its freehold property. By August 2021, Reuters was reporting 'UK for sale'.[30]

While these takeovers were going on during the Covid crisis, some of the private equity-owned companies did find themselves without customers, such as restaurant chains Prezzo and Bella Italia, but the British government jumped in to pay their staff, and their business rates. The financiers still wanted more, and lobbied hard for further government support: some pundits argued that large emergency loans at low interest rates, 80 per cent guaranteed by the government, should not be offered to the private equity firms. Despite this, the industry's lobbying prevailed and they were fully included in the bailouts. The strength of their structure became apparent: each subsidiary was in its own silo, so it could, where necessary, plead poverty. The central private equity houses were insulated from the damage and were actively acquiring other businesses.

When a public company is bought by private equity, it is information as well as capital that becomes private. Each of these takeovers has led to a loss of transparency and accountability: published accounts become nearly impossible to interpret and company boards become less responsive to wider stakeholders. This is compounded by the flight since the pandemic of many publicly listed companies from London to New York, which has made London less attractive as a place to list: in March 2023 the large construction group CRH announced it would move to the US, following in the footsteps of plumbing merchant Ferguson. Even the oil giant Shell has considered relocating its headquarters to the US.[31]

How has such aggressive capitalism emerged?

Today, private equity has a reputation for producing dramatic increases in values, and the re-engineering for profit is well understood by anyone who has seen the 1987 film *Wall Street* or read the papers. In short, private equity gains are achieved by offering lifestyle-changing incentives to managers, using debt, focusing single-mindedly on cash flows and margins, and where possible stepping away from regulation. The standard model for private equity firms has been to buy companies with strong cash flows and the potential to make higher returns on capital, then steer them through a rapid increase in profit, before selling them. While many of the individuals are well intentioned, private equity firms have found systemic ways to insulate themselves from any negative consequences of their management style.

So far, so simple, but, in recent years, there have been two significant evolutions: first, more investors have been willing to put up 'permanent capital', removing the pressure to resell the business, and in total far more investment money has flooded in. Second, the scale of capital available has grown, and by the start of 2024 it was estimated that private equity groups had more than \$2.5 trillion of cash available for acquisitions, or 'dry powder', as the industry calls it, taking a term from the lexicon of pirates.[32]

Blackstone and the pack did not just stumble upon their business model: they built on the leveraged buyouts in 1980s New York, led by Jerome Kohlberg, Henry Kravis and George Roberts (now KKR). These were takeovers where the buyer effectively borrowed heavily against the assets of the company being acquired; they often found they could make an offer for a huge company that required very little of their own capital. If they had done their sums carefully and picked the right target, they could multiply the value of their capital within just two or three years, sometimes even more speedily.

Profits like this sucked in new players, and Blackstone, Apollo and Carlyle saw that the model could work on a larger scale and on both sides of the Atlantic. They have since trained their banks to lend, their investors to support them, and lawyers to battle the competition authorities. In order to expand, private equity managers outsource almost everything they can: accountants for tax planning and due diligence, surveyors to organise sales of surplus property, and lawyers for the purchases.

Schwarzman has said: 'Blackstone is not really a business per se. It's a mission to be the best.'[33] There are different ways for a group like Blackstone to generate profits. A company can be bought, restructured and sold on. Sometimes this is a sale to the public market (an IPO), or it can be to a US multinational, crystallising a large capital gain. But private equity can now buy up 'cash cows', load them with debt and collect long-term, and growing, cash flows. The great new strength of private equity is to have what insiders call optionality: if an industry buyer comes knocking, they can sell at a premium; if a public listing looks profitable, they float the company, but if these windows don't open up, they can just collect the profits each year.

When Blackstone purchased the UK's 5,000 railway arches from the government in 2018, it got hold of reliable cash flows with no restraints on raising rents.[34] Best of all, it was bought cheaply: paying only £1.46 billion to have the right to collect annual rents which were expected to grow shortly to more than £150 million, implying a yield of over 10 per cent. The rents are a steady and rising income stream, which means that, after interest payments, the buyer will get all their capital back in just a few years. Since the takeover, rents have been doubled for many tenants using the railway arches as work premises – often mechanics and skilled craftspeople unused to negotiating with a professional landlord of this sort. George Grant, who runs an MOT business in Clapham, says he spent a lot on legal fees and 'fought tooth and nail' against a steep rent increase, but: 'After all that our rent has doubled.'[35] Many others have been forced to leave their premises completely, such as Peckham tattoo artist Moby Kenyon, who was employing 12 people.[36] For chief engineer Schwarzman, this purchase was just another morsel fed into his machine to be processed and optimised for profit.

After that sale, the UK Parliament's National Audit Office (NAO) lamented the almost total failure to consider the interests of the tenants. While the hoped-for cash was raised for the public purse, the disposal failed to offer any 'business support, tenant protection or community cohesion'.[37]

I interviewed Philip Hammond, who had personally initiated the railway arches sale as minister of transport and completed the deal once he became chancellor. He was pleased to have found a mechanism to separate out the commercial property management from Network Rail's business of running a railway, and he was brutally frank about the government's inability to manage its own assets effectively: 'Network Rail is the worst of all animals… bureaucratically unable to ever get anything done… They are hopeless people.'[38]

If the price of an acquisition is too high, a private equity buyer can team up with others, as with the UK's only satellite supplier, Inmarsat, in 2019. In order to pay the $3.4 billion required, Warburg Pincus of New York joined forces with Apax of London. Within three years they had agreed to resell the company to California's Viasat, for almost twice their purchase price. Apax did a similarly lucrative deal when it bought Auto Trader from Guardian Media Group and sold it on to Cox Enterprises, a conglomerate from Atlanta, Georgia.

Private equity groups cooperate easily because they have a shared culture, which also allows individuals to move freely between the companies. The culture is mostly American and sparky, and uses a lot of shared jargon, such as 'unlocking value', 'sweating the assets', 'value-add' and 'levering up'. One of the cognoscenti told me how the new owners always improve and streamline management – and, critically, avoid paying tax. They split up companies so that most of the profits end up in tax havens. Using the best tax advisers, they stop the UK government getting much out of them, and are helped by the revolving door between HMRC and the big accountancy firms. Their advisers don't just know how the tax inspectors operate; they often know the individuals themselves. Tax is always minimised, significantly boosting returns. For some purchases, reducing tax is a big element in making a target attractive: companies are worth much more to owners after a restructuring has virtually eliminated the tax bills. It is quite different from public company operations: as one accountant pointed out to me: 'Most listed companies pay more tax than they need to.'

Cheap borrowing – the secret sauce

The magic ingredient of private equity is borrowing, so good relations with banks are vital. Schwarzman's insight is that while he needs banks, they also need him. They have lending targets to meet and they want to get a return from their deposits. As he says: 'Blackstone is a major client of many of the largest banks around the world.'[39]

In borrowing, what really matters are the promises, or covenants, that private equity firms have to make, and it is critical for them that they do not guarantee the loans of their subsidiaries.

This avoids a house of cards: if one enterprise goes bust the banks cannot come to Schwarzman and ask him to take on those debts. Often, by the time anything like that does happen, he has already recouped his capital through special dividends and capital distributions.

Big private equity firms are notorious for driving hard bargains with the banks. They start by making the lenders compete against each other. Each time they borrow they try to negotiate a better deal than the last time: lower interest rates, more flexibility on repayment terms and less onerous covenants. Whether the high-borrowing model can withstand higher interest rates is uncertain, but higher borrowing costs might work to the advantage of private equity: they will find more opportunities as companies get into difficulties and they will still be borrowing more cheaply than almost anyone else.

The magnifying power of this debt can be seen in Blackstone's purchase of Thomson Reuters's financial-data business in 2018 for $17 billion, financed by $14 billion of debt.[40] Blackstone changed the name to Refinitiv, reorganised the business and sold it on for a handsome profit – after only three years – receiving $27 billion from a sale to the LSE. In round numbers the borrowing turned the return on the investment from 60 per cent into 330 per cent.

Private equity riding the waves

An economy is always in flux, especially when technology changes everything so rapidly, and private equity can profit from this constant reorganisation of businesses: whenever there is a crisis, private equity investors show up. The financial crash in 2008/9 threw up opportunities for the next several years, but Brexit and Covid have also given private equity the chance to swoop in and buy 'distressed assets': in reality, it is buying hard assets with distressed owners. It is said in hospitals that a bad day for the patient is a good day for the medical student. Similarly, a bad year for the economy is often a good year for private equity.

Apart from facing lighter regulation, there are many ways for the private equity buyer to cut costs in the acquired company. One lump of cost is often the obligation to pay into the pension scheme, and if the company is a long-established one the pension scheme liabilities may be huge. So much so that, to a financial analyst or corporate raider, a company like BT or British Airways is really a pension scheme with a company attached: BT has a market value of £11 billion with pension liabilities of £65 billion, while British Airways has a market value of £7 billion with pension liabilities of £31 billion. This demonstrates the potential attraction for acquirers of escaping pension commitments. Telling me not to use his name, one pensions expert at PricewaterhouseCoopers (PwC) told me that the bulk of his work is from private equity firms trying to find legal ways to minimise their pension obligations.

And there are mechanisms to get the government to take on these pension liabilities, as happened with bed manufacturer Silentnight. This was a family-run business, founded in 1946 by Tom Clarke, who used the money he got from the Royal Navy when he was demobbed after the war. It became the UK's largest bed manufacturer and flourished in part because of its reassuring name, which was suggested by Clarke's wife, Joan. Based in Pendle in Lancashire, the company eventually got itself into financial difficulty. According to the UK's watchdog, the Financial Reporting Council (FRC), in 2011 Miami-based private equity fund HIG Capital spotted an opportunity and bought bonds in Silentnight, creating a credit line which they later withdrew, throwing the company into distress. They then demanded repayment, which couldn't be made. Along with the auditor KPMG, they then arranged a pre-planned bankruptcy so that HIG ended up owning the bed company outright. The effect of the transaction was to divorce the company's operations from its heavily underfunded defined-benefit pension scheme, and so, as if by magic, they owned the company without the pension obligations. The result of this bankruptcy was that these liabilities were taken on by the government's pensions lifeboat, the Pension Protection Fund (PPF), and many staff had their pension claims reduced.[41]

Taxpayers had suddenly found themselves on the hook to pay these pension promises. Private equity has contributed to the growth in the obligations of the government's back-up fund: in 2009 it had total commitments of less than £9 billion, but by 2023 these had grown to more than £32 billion.[42] And it is not just the government that takes a hit: if a pension scheme is rescued by the PPF, many of the pensioners get reduced payments.

Private equity groups use other people's capital and charge heavily for their efforts. The traditional model was dubbed '2 and 20', meaning that they took an annual fee of 2 per cent of the funds under management and on top of that they got 20 per cent of any profits. In recent years that means that their total fee has worked out annually at 6 per cent of the funds they control. Although the level of those fees has come under pressure, private equity is still phenomenally profitable – but largely for the owners of the private equity companies themselves. While bosses such as Schwarzman have amassed huge personal fortunes, their investors – who are mostly pension savers – have done much less well. According to Oxford professor Ludovic Phalippou, rewards for outside investors in private equity funds are often the same as, or lower than, returns from owning traditional listed shares, mainly because of the high fees.[43]

'Wealth-extracting geniuses'

Financial journalist Nicholas Shaxson argues that 'collectively, private equity firms add little of value, extract a great deal and have persuaded everyone that because they're so rich they must be wealth-creating geniuses. They aren't; they are wealth-extracting geniuses.'[44]

Other critics too, such as Phalippou, accuse the private equity companies of extracting wealth rather than creating it, and of avoiding tax on an industrial scale. Their defenders, such as former chancellor Philip Hammond, who is now involved in private equity, says that, in his experience, 'Many businesses struggle to prosper in public markets with their focus on quarterly earnings. They can operate a lot better in private markets: when you are owned by private equity your owners are all over you in trying to help you grow, and are typically not interested in dividends.'[45]

Certainly, managers of listed companies can feel isolated, over-regulated and vulnerable to opportunistic takeovers. There is also a genuine clash of cultures between Europe and America: should companies be out-and-out profit maximisers or should they contribute to society and balance the interests of their different stakeholders?

Some US law firms actively promote these takeovers. Squire Patton Boggs has a big presence in London, and at one point its website explicitly appealed to US firms to buy up UK companies. It stated: 'The process for effecting a UK takeover is swift, relatively cheap and rarely subject to legal challenge or third-party legal claims.' It went on: 'The quality of assets potentially available to purchase through a public company takeover is often high, with UK public companies being subject to stringent disclosure and transparency regulations.'[46] The law firm concluded its pitch by pointing out that other buyers are nervous because of Britain's uncertain relationship with Europe, so there was less competition for quality UK companies and their assets.

At the dawn of the private equity era, quick money could be made from restructurings, but the sector has matured and is investing for the longer term. Private equity firms have built up hoards of 'permanent capital' and created 'continuation funds'. These take the pressure off a private equity fund to sell a company if it thinks it can squeeze out further increases in earnings. Blackstone's long-term portfolio shows how US ownership is deeply embedded: private capital is no passing phase, but nor is it static. As the UK economy ebbs and flows, Blackstone tightens its grip. In a 2015 promotional video about their famous Monday meetings, at which they review their purchases, Tony James, the chief operating officer, said: 'We're not in this for a quick hit: we want to build lasting value.'[47]

Technology, thinking in systems, and transforming markets

Private equity is eager to take advantage of technology, especially where it disrupts markets and creates new royalty streams. On 1 January 2008, Zoopla! – with an exclamation mark in those days – was launched, offering 'free, instant value estimates on over 26 million UK homes'.[48] The company had scraped the data from the databases of the Royal Mail and Land Registry to generate its valuations, and it even offered a service called 'TemptMe', where visitors could make offers on homes even if they were 'not on the market', and another called 'AskMe', which was designed to start online discussions. The market was overturned: suddenly everyone could look up the value of their home online instead of asking an estate agent. Before long a million people were using the website every day. Conventional agents flocked to list their properties on Zoopla. Ten years later in 2018, California's Silver Lake private equity group spotted the business and made an offer, even though Zoopla was 'not on the market'. The business, including Primelocation, was bought for £2.2 billion and a high proportion of UK property owners now look up the value of their home, and maybe sell it, through Menlo Park in California.[49]

Private equity buyers such as Silver Lake seek out and digest their targets systematically. While a British predator might look for a single juicy takeover target, each US private equity company is itself a machine for takeovers. They are pursuing the highest returns possible – whether that means disposing of parts, selling the whole business or holding on and investing in it – and for this they have built teams of experts rather than relying on just one or two senior executives. Private equity giants Blackstone, KKR, Carlyle and Apollo have each developed an entrepreneurial culture: rather than make a single profitable deal, they create an environment in which profitable deals become almost inevitable. In parallel with the honing of these takeover machines, the public have stopped regarding takeovers as newsworthy, as shown by the response to Apollo's purchase of 400 UK restaurants in October 2023.[50] There was barely a grumble as a business with £900 million of turnover was handed to new American owners.

A few holdouts and residuals

After this banquet of takeovers, many of the remaining British-owned companies look either indigestible or unappetising, and they often have poor economic prospects. Even though there are still some very desirable family-owned companies, such as J.C. Bamford Excavators Limited (better known as JCB), many remaining companies have large legacy liabilities and poor growth prospects, such as BT, Shell or BP. A group of smart, well-financed, highly motivated buyers, mostly American, has thoroughly picked over anything that offered good returns and what remains is unattractive or unavailable. Some UK sectors, such as utilities, have a degree of protection through their regulators, but private equity is already circling the UK banks and insurance companies, as well as pharma and engineering. Whenever management falters or the market fails to recognise value, private equity will move in. And more often than not the buyer is from the US.

The private equity endgame

Ultimately, private equity has changed the way business works in Britain. Having transferred numerous UK companies wholesale into American ownership, private equity has transformed the climate for those that remain. They are forced to rein back nonfinancial objectives. Companies can no longer spend resources on staff and communities without making themselves more vulnerable to buyouts from private equity. Unilever's Port Sunlight model village and Cadbury's housing for workers at Bournville are distant dreams, and public companies must now think carefully about any spending which is not directed towards maximising returns.

While private equity machines efficiently extract wealth through takeovers, incentivising managers with a laser-like focus on profit, a central part of their strategy is to limit tax payments to HMRC. Along with the US tech giants and other US multinationals they have realised that minimising tax, or avoiding corporation tax altogether, is one of the surest ways to increase returns to owners.

7

WHY YOU CANNOT MILK AN EAGLE

In a rational system, a corporation's tax department would be there to make sure a company complied with tax law, but in our system there are corporations that view their tax department as a profit center.

— Len Burman, former US Treasury official[1]

Visiting an industrial estate in Switzerland on a chilly Monday morning I expected to see machines being repaired and fork-lift trucks buzzing around. But the unit I visited turned out to be a quiet, almost deserted, office. 'Oh, that's quite normal here,' explained a receptionist. 'These buildings are mostly headquarters of big companies used for board meetings and some strategic planning. Lots of the offices here in the Zug canton only have one or two staff – they just need to look like headquarters because this canton has the lowest tax rate in Switzerland, so hundreds of companies are based here.'

I was in Zug to visit Jan Marck Vrijlandt, the man responsible for his company's 145,000 vending machines across Europe. Selecta, his company, feels very Swiss. Its vending machines are emblazoned with red and white to reflect the colours of the national flag; it prides itself on precision engineering, and it has machines throughout Switzerland's 26 cantons. Yet there are also strong American connections. It was founded by Joseph Jeger, a factory worker from Basel who made a life-changing business trip to the US in 1950. On that visit he spotted automatic machines selling snacks and was so inspired that he set up his own vending business, Selecta, in Murten, in the canton of Fribourg. The company has since migrated to low-tax Zug. Its strongest American link came in 2015, when it was taken over by KKR, the New York-based private equity giant. KKR has since gone on to use the company to buy Selecta's UK competitor, Express Vending, and Pelican Rouge, a coffee-roasting company in the Netherlands. In the UK the company operates 36,000 vending machines from its base in Hemel Hempstead, Hertfordshire.

Google Maps showed me that almost next door was the European headquarters of Bristol Myers Squibb, a pillar of the American pharmaceutical industry, and on the other side of the road was the headquarters of Coca-Cola Hellenic Bottling Company, one of the biggest partners of Coca-Cola from Atlanta, Georgia. Probably they, too, were here for the low tax rates.

Switzerland has been a favourite place for the headquarters of US corporations' 'EMEA' operations, an acronym which stands for their businesses in Europe, the Middle East and Africa. Dozens of examples include the Dow Chemical Company in Horgen by Lake Zurich, where there is a symbiotic relationship between the town and the company: the company supports the town's events, offers jobs to local people and, of course, has for many years sheltered under Zurich's low-tax umbrella. Similarly, General Motors of Detroit has its European headquarters in Zurich.

The effect of a myriad of multinationals basing themselves in Switzerland has even distorted the country's GDP figures. Subtracting the sales of US multinationals reduces the size of the

Swiss economy (GDP) by about 27 per cent, and its ranking in the table of the world economies drops significantly – from about twentieth to twenty-third. That effect is even greater for other tax havens: Singapore drops from about thirty-second to about fifty-eighth position when US multinational revenues are taken out, and Ireland plummets from twenty-sixth to about fifty-seventh. In Ireland the effect is so big that removing US multinational sales cuts the size of the economy by about two-thirds.[2] The tax tail has also been wagging the GDP dog in the economies of Luxembourg and the Netherlands, which are similarly bloated by US corporations' tax manoeuvres. Until 2021, the 14 million UK residents who subscribed to Netflix were invoiced from the Netherlands, and the billions of pounds of Apple's UK sales continue to be routed through Ireland.

For any sales it puts through Ireland, Apple has for some years apparently paid the astonishingly low tax rate of 0.05 per cent on its profits.[3] Seeing the unfairness of this, the European Commission blew its whistle, complaining that this amounted to 'an illegal tax benefit'.[4] The EU demanded that the Irish charge Apple at least €13 billion of back taxes, plus interest. That would have been the biggest tax fine in history, but, to the surprise of many, the Irish refused to play ball. Instead of welcoming the windfall, the Irish parliament declared they wouldn't take Apple's money and that this was 'an intrusion into Irish sovereignty'.[5] Their reasons were enlightening – US multinationals represent 25 of Ireland's 50 top companies and even at low tax rates they contribute 80 per cent of Irish corporation taxes. More important still, they employ a big chunk of the population: about 172,000 workers, or one person in 14.[6] So the Irish economy has become highly dependent on US corporations. The Dublin government declined to bite the hand that was feeding it. This case is still to be concluded after an appeal to the European Court of Justice.[7]

Ireland maintains that Apple received no selective advantage and paid the correct amount of tax. Apple says that the initial finding did not take into account that $20 billion of tax had already been paid to the US on the same profits in the decade to 2014. The final judgment is expected by the end of 2024.

As well as selling into the UK from Ireland, Apple has directed a chunk of its financing through Ireland and other tax havens, something that works out very tax-efficiently because of an obscure financial loophole nicknamed the 'Bermuda Black Hole'.[8] Essentially, profits are routed to Bermuda, where they are untaxed and can stay in a subsidiary that *lends* the money back to the parent company in the US. Following Ireland's refusal to accept money from the EU's fine, Apple's CEO Tim Cook appealed the judgment, and he won on the basis that Ireland could decide its own tax rates.

This case helps explain why such modest amounts of tax have been collected by HMRC from the 1,000-plus multinationals operating in the UK. They make up about 30 per cent of the UK's trading economy but the tax they pay on their profits makes up little more than 1 per cent of the government's total tax take. This is even more striking considering that US companies tend to be the most profitable ones. The problem has been steadily growing. According to Gabriel Zucman, a leading tax researcher at the University of California, in recent years at least 55 per cent of foreign profits of US multinationals were redirected to tax havens, whereas in 1970 the figure was only 8 per cent. Zucman has shown that a typical US company was shifting over half of its true profit into a tax haven where the tax rate averaged only 7 per cent.[9] A study using HMRC data over a 15-year period showed that foreign multinational subsidiaries were paying half the rate paid by comparable purely domestic companies in the UK.[10] A large proportion of these subsidiaries claimed in their HMRC returns that they made little or no taxable profits, even though their financial accounts showed they were profitable.

This effect has hit Britain hard: of the world's top 50 countries, the UK has been losing more tax from the offshoring of profits than anyone else. One way to quantify the loss would be to say that, typically, US multinationals make 10 per cent profit on their turnover, so that their combined UK turnover should be generating declared profits of about $70 billion.[11] With the UK's 25 per cent corporation tax rate they should be paying $17.5 billion in UK tax, but typically in recent years they have been paying less than $10 billion. But this does not take account of the sales to the UK made direct from tax havens such as Ireland, Luxembourg and the Netherlands, which may well be more than double that number. If those estimates are right, the annual tax loss is likely to have been more than £12 billion, enough to build an extra 150,000 new homes each year, or twice the current rate of construction.[12]

When British politicians say they cannot afford to reduce hospital waiting lists or that they are compelled to increase personal tax rates, some of this is a direct result of their failure to collect tax from the multinationals.

The British government has followed a dysfunctional approach to international tax: the so-called 'arm's length' principle. This means that affiliates of a multinational group are taxed as if they were independent entities, and allows them to siphon off royalties or fees for services to other subsidiaries, often offshore.

The attitude of Starbucks, of Seattle, is typical. It is said to contribute almost no UK corporation tax, but declared in 2012: 'We don't write this tax code; we are obligated to comply with it. And we do.'[13] For a powerful brand selling millions of hot drinks in the UK every year it has some very neat, but legal, ways to slash its declared profits. According to a 2012 article by Tom

Bergin, an investigative journalist at Reuters, Starbucks held its IP offshore, and its UK business made a payment for the right to use the trademarks, which shifted profits from the UK to the Netherlands – where a very low tax rate had been negotiated.[14] This kind of behaviour is widespread among US multinationals and contributes significantly to the prosperity of cities such as Amsterdam and Luxembourg. Starbucks is also said to route its purchases of coffee through its Swiss subsidiary, where profits will probably be taxed at only 5 per cent, without the beans physically needing to travel to the country.

In addition, Starbucks UK has loans from other group companies, and the interest on these effectively moves profits away from the UK. These strategies have meant that, for its first 26 years of operating in the UK, Starbucks made very small tax payments.[15] By 2014 there was such a public outcry that the company 'voluntarily' agreed to pay £20 million of tax over the next two years. This pressure arose because Starbucks is such a well-known brand, but there are hundreds of other, lower-profile US corporations following very similar policies. And the leopard had apparently not changed its spots seven years later: for the three years up to 2022, Reuters reported that Starbucks declared no profit and paid no tax on its £1.2 billion of sales.[16] In spite of this, the UK operation is described to investors as profitable. The company's annual report said that it paid 31 per cent tax to the US government but only 13 per cent to overseas authorities.[17] The UK's TaxWatch research body says that, in 2020, Apple paid an overseas tax rate of 8.3 per cent.[18] The rise of a culture of tax avoidance over the last 25 years has been rapid: academics Alex Cobham and Petr Jansky found that, in the 1990s, US corporations under-declared profit by about 7 per cent, but by the first decade of the new millennium that had risen to more than 25 per cent.[19]

While the problem has been growing for many years, it became widespread around the turn of the millennium, when PepsiCo decided to restructure its supply chain. According to *The Guardian*'s Felicity Lawrence, this outwardly innocent process was largely tax-driven. Lawrence describes how Walkers, a UK brand established in 1948, was reorganised by its owner PepsiCo so that a big part of its business was routed through tax havens. Even though the company uses British potatoes, processes them in the UK and sells to UK customers, the tax bill for Walkers Snack Foods reportedly dropped from £28 million in 1998 to just £8 million in 2002. Other multinationals paid attention and followed PepsiCo's lead.[20]

Big US tech is particularly unlikely to pay significant UK tax: Google and Microsoft at points have housed their IP units in tax havens and then charged their subsidiaries significant royalties for using the company's IP – such as software, branding and patents. A popular place for the big companies to put their IP rights is the Cayman Islands, a territory with no corporation tax, or Switzerland, where earnings from royalties can be taxed at rates as low as 2 per cent.

Over the last few years this shift to tax havens intensified, and the US profits in Europe of $1.2 trillion each year have been typically taxed at 5 per cent or below, according to the IRS figures. Much of this has been channelled through Europe's own tax havens: in the four years up to 2020, total sales recorded through Luxembourg and Ireland more than doubled, and through Switzerland they increased by two-thirds.

Tax havens represent a particularly embarrassing problem for the UK because the majority of them are located in British territory, placing the UK right at the centre of the infrastructure of international tax avoidance. Researchers from the UK's Tax Justice Network say that eight out of the ten major tax havens are

British.[21] These are Guernsey, Jersey, the Isle of Man, Bermuda, the Cayman Islands, the Turks and Caicos Islands, Anguilla, and the British Virgin Islands. For many decades the UK has profited nicely from these arrangements, which makes it exceptionally hard for Westminster policy-makers to challenge their use by US companies. To be effective, the British would first have to dismantle their own ancient structures, but would then come up against the strong vested interests in those territories. Naturally, those outlying dependencies always fight tooth and nail to preserve their status and income.

Tax-driven employment is moving jobs away from the UK

Tax avoidance does not only slash the UK tax take, it also moves employment abroad.

While US multinationals employ 4.5 million people across Europe, many of them are strategically located to help minimise their tax payments. The stand-out country is Ireland, with 7.5 per cent, meaning that one Irish worker in every 14 is a US employee, while Luxembourg has almost one in 20 working directly for a US corporation, along with thousands of accountants and lawyers who are working for them as professional advisers.

The speed of the US's move into Europe has been dramatic: in just the last four years for which figures have been published, American companies have taken on more than a million extra employees across the continent. Most of these new workers are in manufacturing, distribution or financial services, and plenty have become US employees through takeovers. One measure of the profitability of the American companies is their much higher return on capital: corporate Europe's return on equity (7 per cent) lags well behind America's (10 per cent).[22] Another demonstration of US success is the country's trade surplus with Europe: annually the US exports more than it imports.

US corporations' love affair with the tax havens has moulded Europe to suit their needs: without the US giants, Luxembourg's economy would be less than half the size it is, and in Ireland about 200,000 workers would be unemployed or working in different jobs. It has boosted those economies, as shown by their infrastructure spending: Ireland has massively expanded both its road network and its Luas light rail system, while Luxembourg has been able to introduce free public transport.[23]

The Luxembourgers offer multinationals the three key ingredients of a tax haven: stability, secrecy and low tax rates. This has been very helpful to many companies such as General Electric (GE), of Boston, Massachusetts, whose former tax department head, John Samuel, said in 2013: 'The government puts incentives out there, and we take advantage of them. That's the obligation we have to shareholders.'[24] GE is a large industrial and leasing business with total assets of $200 billion, and its tax team has been nicknamed the 'Harvard of tax departments' because of its skill in minimising tax liabilities by legally arbitraging tax rules in different countries.[25] In a rare public challenge by HMRC, it was revealed how GE arranged its affairs without the duty of candour that HMRC claimed was required. Tax officials said that the company moved $4.9 billion between subsidiaries in the UK, Luxembourg, Australia and the US to avoid about $1 billion of tax. The barrister Philip Jones, acting for HMRC, claimed in court that the whole thing was set up to gain a tax advantage.[26] Part of the case went on for so long – it began in 2005 – that eventually it was struck out by the Court of Appeal in 2018. Despite much criticism from Parliament and tax lobbying groups, HMRC eventually settled for less than $100 million – less than a tenth of its original assessment of the liability.[27]

As well as offshoring profits, big US corporations are experts at exploiting any legal loopholes or allowances they can find, and have the resources to do it – in contrast to the cash-strapped HMRC and its civil servants. In the UK, spending on R & D generates generous tax credits. Naturally, tech firms tend to make large R & D tax credit claims, and it is clear that these are worth £1–2 billion a year to US corporations, although this has to be an estimate: HMRC breaks down small and medium-sized enterprises (SMEs) by region, but oddly they do not break down large company claims by nationality of ownership.[28] And the Americans are big spenders on R & D, out-spending both the Europeans and the Brits. According to the European Commission's 'EU Industrial R & D Investment Scoreboard' for 2022, of the 2,500 biggest spenders, 822 are in the US, only 361 are in continental Europe and 95 are in the UK.[29]

The US tech companies have been so effective at avoiding paying tax that in 2018 the chancellor, Philip Hammond, declared: 'It's clearly not sustainable, or fair, that digital platform businesses can generate substantial value in the UK without paying tax here.'[30] So, in his 2018 budget, Hammond promised to introduce a 'Digital Services Tax' (DST) targeting the turnover of the US tech giants. The idea was to secure at least some tax revenue by taxing sales rather than profits, as sales are harder to transfer into tax havens. The DST was set at the low rate of 2 per cent of turnover and only applied to the 30 largest US tech companies, and was projected to bring in just £400 million a year. Other European countries, such as France, legislated for a similar tax, but US corporations co-opted their government to stop this in its tracks. Democratic senator Ron Wyden said in July 2019 that a trade agreement between the US and the UK 'will not happen with your digital services tax, period'.[31] He was backed up by US treasury secretary Steven Mnuchin, who added:

'If countries choose to collect or adopt such taxes, the United States will respond with appropriate commensurate measures.'[32] In January 2020, even the French were forced to climb down on their DST, after the US threatened to put 100 per cent tariffs on imports of French food and wine.[33]

Private equity – slicing and dicing

It is not just big US tech and the multinationals who refuse to contribute: US private equity companies have always taken advantage of any tax sheltering they can find – and for this reason they usually split an acquired business into different parts, often setting up an 'OpCo' (operating company) separately from a 'PropCo' (the property-owning part) and labelling the holding company as 'Topco' or 'Hubco'. These are commonly based in different countries. Private equity companies usually register their assets in Luxembourg, which allows them to avoid most taxes – such as stamp duty and corporation tax – altogether. It also adds a layer of secrecy, preventing the UK tax authorities even getting access to information. In this splitting of companies they have occasionally forgotten to change the name of the actual enterprise. That seems to be why the acquirers of Heathrow Airport left the holding company's name as 'FGP Topco', and in turn the largest shareholder in that company is 'Hubco Netherlands BV'. According to TaxWatch, Hubco Netherlands BV (known to most of us as 'Heathrow Airport') pays very low corporation tax, despite being the country's most profitable car park.[34]

Private equity groups and multinationals take advantage of another large tax loophole for those with heavy borrowing, which helps them cut tax systematically. Their borrowing costs are treated like any other costs, so that their interest payments reduce taxable profits, which incentivises heavy borrowings: when eventually they do crystallise their gains, they navigate the legal chicanes to take these to low-tax jurisdictions. This incentive to borrow, along with low interest rates, has fuelled the private equity boom over the years since the financial crash of 2008/9. The direct result has been the takeover of countless UK companies, and the sending of UK tax and profits across the Atlantic, often via tax havens. Even though most of the horses had already bolted, the UK tried to limit this tax advantage through the 2017 'restriction on corporate interest tax relief'. But it is fiendishly difficult to do this effectively, and, as Eloise Walker, head of corporate tax at law firm Pinsent Masons, says: 'The rules are detailed and complex.'[35] It is another tax game that is routinely won by the smartest accountants and lawyers, who, inevitably, do not always work for HMRC.

You can get a good sense of how the Americans feel about making payments to their British 'hosts' from London's Congestion Charge Zone (CCZ). Drivers are supposed to pay to drive into the zone, but the US embassy simply refuses to pay its CCZ fines, of which it has accumulated more than 102,000, which means that it owes Transport for London in excess of £12.6 million.[36] This obviously defeats the purpose of a measure intended to reduce pollution and encourage use of public transport, but it shows how much the eagle hates being milked.

In contrast, the IRS has a worldwide reach and often bears its powerful claws. In 2015, Boris Johnson was caught out: because of his dual UK–US citizenship he was handed a US tax bill for around £100,000, on the profits from selling his North London home. He decried this as 'absolutely outrageous', saying: 'I haven't lived in the US... since I was five years old.'[37] The IRS website clearly states: 'If you are a US citizen or a resident alien living outside the United States, your worldwide income is subject to US income tax, regardless of where you live.'[38] Even Mr Johnson was forced to pay up, but at the first opportunity, in 2016, he renounced his US citizenship. Such an approach contrasts with that of the British authorities, who are not resourced like the IRS and have less success in collecting tax from those who have emigrated or even those who work abroad.

US tax receipts under threat – so 'all change'

Perhaps because of their efficiency in collecting taxes, in 2009 even the Americans got fed up with how little tax their multinationals were sending to Washington, and President Obama complained that they were practising illegal overseas tax evasion and only paying 2.3 per cent on $700 billion in foreign earnings.[39] This was taken up by Donald Trump, who was troubled by the $4 trillion of cash US companies were holding offshore when he came to power in 2017. So he cut the tax rate for repatriating profits in order to create an incentive for their return to the US: it worked, and the tax authority, the IRS, raised billions of dollars in new revenue. Bundled into the new tax laws was 'Global Intangible Low-Taxed Income' (GILTI) – a US tax on foreign income. This ensures that the IRS collects at least 12.5 per cent on any foreign income that is repatriated. Here there is a large element of poacher turned gamekeeper: having used all available tricks to avoid taxes around the world, the US authorities and their presidents know very well how to prevent others from doing the same. They have stopped companies from dodging taxes on profits as they come ashore – and they ensure that the IRS gets its cut. But there is one further twist, and it is important for understanding how useful Britain is to the US.

While it is clear that tax-avoidance strategies are rampant in US corporate finance departments, we are all missing a trick if we think the effect of them is simply to deny revenue to the UK exchequer in favour of shareholders. On the contrary. As soon as the barely taxed revenue of US corporations leaves UK shores, often via tax havens, and enters the US, the IRS intercepts the cash and demands its share. The result is that the profits which were not taxed by the British are then taxed by the Americans – effectively creating an ongoing transfer of wealth from the UK government to its US counterpart. An HMRC official might reasonably shout: 'Hey, those are our taxes you guys are collecting over there!'

A similar loss is being suffered by all other national tax collectors around the world, and much of it is happening through the eight British-controlled tax havens. So Britain is not just losing tax revenue: it is acting as the Americans' handmaiden in moving multinationals' tax money from around the world into US government coffers.

Lost tax is only one part of the outward flow

Inevitably, many people get a little frustrated when they understand the epic scale of US tax avoidance, but they often miss the bigger picture: it is not just about avoidance. Even if US corporations were to pay the official rate of 25 per cent tax on all their UK earnings instead of a small fraction of that, they would still be taking the other 75 per cent of UK profits and sending the cash back to their American owners. This extracts increasing amounts of wealth from the UK and leaves the country poorer.

It is also highly convenient for the multinationals that the bulk of the UK's tax load is borne by workers through payroll taxes and by consumers via VAT.[40] As the footprint of the US multinationals expands, the burden on UK workers and savers increases.

There is a further associated tax effect: the ability of US corporations to eliminate tax has also encouraged the swallowing up of local companies: the first cost that a US corporate raider cuts when acquiring a British company is the payment of tax. And, like a ratchet, this progressively erodes the UK's tax base of those who can be relied on to contribute towards the nation's hospitals, essential services and state pension.

Global tax deal means multinationals will pay 15 per cent – or less

For decades there has been a desire to stop multinationals shifting profits to tax havens and to prevent countries from competing by setting ever lower rates of company tax. In the 1990s, Europeans were looking for a minimum global rate of 30 per cent, and many still argue for 25 per cent. Americans typically charge their own 'homeland' companies 25 per cent and, in some states, such as New Jersey, it is more than 30 per cent, while the UK's company tax rate is 25 per cent.[41]

But to get the global deal agreed in October 2021, the 136 countries that have signed up have been forced to agree to the US demand for a 15 per cent tax rate for most multinationals. Although it is presented as a minimum rate, it is likely to end up as a maximum rate and provide US companies with a cap on their overseas taxation. Many multinationals' tax departments will be able to push their tax rates below 15 per cent using legal techniques and special allowances.

The deal is structured so that, if one country charges less than 15 per cent, the difference goes to the home country of the corporation. For example, if Ireland charges Apple a tax rate of, say, 12.5 per cent – its current official tax rate – then the extra 2.5 per cent goes to the US Treasury. According to Reuters: 'Economists expect that the deal will encourage multinationals to repatriate capital to their country of headquarters, giving a boost to those economies.'[42] This is ideal for America, where the majority of multinationals are headquartered.

As the 136 signatories have to get it incorporated into their national laws, the transitional process is complex and potentially contentious. It should eventually reduce the significance of tax havens, but it will still leave a two-tier system in the UK, where local firms pay 25 per cent tax and the multinationals will pay 15 per cent or less.[43] US companies with turnovers of less than $750 million may be able to pay far less.

Another element, or 'pillar', of the global deal applies only to the largest multinationals: those with more than $20 billion of annual turnover. It addresses the problem of companies who have little physical presence in a country but have large user bases, such as the US digital giants (MAMAA). It will redistribute some of the excess profits of the multinationals to countries where the customers are based.

The other great triumph for the Americans in the new global tax deal is that it will probably kill the 2 per cent Digital Services Tax (DST) that former chancellor Philip Hammond sought to impose, alongside similar schemes introduced by finance ministers in other countries. That would have taxed turnover from big tech and platform companies, but the US flatly insisted that each country would have to abandon these or there would be no deal. Other countries had much higher DST rates, of up to 9 per cent of turnover, but all these will be swept away by the new deal. George Turner of TaxWatch worked out that the US tech giants will almost certainly end up paying less tax in the UK than they would have been liable for under a modest DST.[44]

Free rider problem

The trouble with tax is that when someone does not pay their fair share, everyone else has to pick up more of the bill. It follows that the very low tax payments by US multinationals mean there is less money to pay for infrastructure upgrades, and local people have to shoulder a correspondingly heavier burden. Worse, there are specific parts of UK infrastructure where US corporations are really heavy users, making the running costs higher and raising the amount required from everyone else.

Just think about Amazon's core business. It is completely dependent on the UK road network, where that corporation is, effectively, the largest private courier, covering 15 per cent of deliveries. Yet its road tax payments fail to cover the costs of its road usage, partly because lorries are significantly more damaging to the environment than other vehicles, and because Amazon's vehicles do above-average mileage – typically 100,000 miles a year. This is an incidental tax bonus for Amazon because road taxes do not pay for the full costs of maintaining the network. The extra is paid for from general taxation. Now consider Amazon's packaging – along with that of other online retailers. Amazon generates thousands of tons of cardboard and plastic, which are fed into the UK waste network and dealt with by local authorities across the country.[45] These are also subsidised through general taxation. That is the context when a multinational pays little or no corporation tax: the rest of us pay commensurately more to clean up after it.

Next, consider telecoms systems, which, across Europe and the UK, are at breaking point largely because of the high volume of US traffic. More than half of the data going through their cables is accounted for by just six US companies: the five biggest customer-facing tech companies (MAMAA) plus Netflix.

Except that it is not 'accounted for', because these companies pay negligible European tax, so upgrades have to be funded by the telecoms companies or by national governments. The European Commission's competition chief, Margrethe Vestager, wants to force the US tech companies to contribute to the roll-out of connectivity, and the expensive shift from copper to fibre. France, Italy and Spain are particularly incensed because in those countries it is the governments themselves who must pay for the upgrades. Struggling phone companies (telcos) are also unhappy because they have made huge investments in networks over the last ten years. BT, for example, planned to spend £12 billion to get broadband to 20 million homes and premises by 2028. The UK government promised to chip in £5 billion towards broadband connectivity.[46]

The problem is so widespread that even the US's Federal Communications Commission (FCC) has said that big tech should pay more in Europe as well as in the US. Its chief, Brendan Carr, said: 'It's a ripe issue and it's at a pivot point... The time where big tech was untouchable has passed.'[47]

There is an additional and critical cost to which US multinationals are not contributing their share. That is the cost of running the British state. Their businesses rely on a stable government, law and order, the protection of their property and IP rights, sound money, viable national defence and a social security system – to all of which they are making only a small contribution.

Bit by bit, you can trace a pattern of policy decisions by the UK government and ingenious choices by the US government and US corporations that work against ordinary taxpayers in the UK. Large companies can revel in the fact that about 80 per cent of UK tax is collected from taxes on individuals: payroll taxes (income tax and National Insurance), property taxes (council tax and stamp duty) and sales taxes (VAT and excise duty). Less than

8 per cent of UK government revenue comes from corporation tax, of which multinationals pay only a small fraction.[48] The new global tax deal won't change that significantly, so the multinationals will continue their free ride while the UK government demands that its citizens pick up the tab. It is fair to ask whose interests are served by this and whether it allows for adequate funding of the things that matter most to British people – chief among them the NHS.

8

THE NHS CASH COW

The reason we have the vaccine success is because of capitalism, because of greed, my friends.

— Boris Johnson, March 2021[1]

The Covid-19 pandemic of 2020–22 was an era of risk and fear, of human losses and business profits. Speaking with MPs one spring evening in 2021, UK prime minister Boris Johnson credited the profit motive with helping to deliver Britain safely through the crisis by prompting the effective development and distribution of vaccines. His comment in defence of 'greed', Downing Street later clarified, was just a joke.

Nonetheless, Covid-19 made the rich richer. The wealth of the world's billionaires increased more in the first 24 months of Covid-19 than in any two-year period over the previous 23 years. In the food and energy sectors, profits boomed, but the titans of 'Big Pharma' were some of the most high-profile winners.

The pandemic created at least 40 new pharma billionaires, with two major US vaccine providers – Moderna of Cambridge, Massachusetts, and Pfizer of New York City – reportedly making

$1,000 profit every second from their Covid-19 vaccines in 2021.[2]

In Oxford, British scientists were the first to announce a Covid-19 vaccine.[3] British companies and innovators offered much to governments in the crisis, but they did not win the lion's share of pandemic revenues – not even in their home country. Perhaps that would matter less if the UK government's response to the pandemic had delivered 'success' across the board, but the solutions chosen were mostly inadequate, as well as costly.

An analysis of Britain's government spending after six months showed that American companies were picking up over half of all the Covid-19 contracting. In business terms, the country did not pull together to solve the crisis. On the contrary, the government often looked for help anywhere but at home.

In May 2020, Honeywell of Charlotte, North Carolina, won a deal to supply 70 million face masks. Hologic of Marlborough, Massachusetts, won a £150 million contract for testing kits, and another £68 million was given to Thermo Fisher of Waltham, Massachusetts. When the 'Test and Trace' scheme required call centres, these were operated by Sitel of Miami, Florida. Testing kits were largely delivered by Amazon and ID checks were made by the consumer credit company TransUnion, of Chicago, Illinois. Brake Bros, owned by Sysco of Texas, shared a £205 million untendered contract to deliver food boxes to vulnerable people who were isolating during the pandemic.[4] The company also received a £600 million government loan at 0.5 per cent annual interest under the Covid Corporate Financing Facility (CCFF) – a particularly valuable benefit in light of the inflation that followed the crisis in Britain.[5]

The fact that call centres, deliveries and credit checks were deemed beyond the cost-effective capacity of UK-owned companies says much about the British government's attitude to domestic businesses, but all these deals are dwarfed by the cash paid by Her Majesty's Government for vaccines. By the end of 2022, the UK had ordered 654 million jabs, of which more than two-thirds were bought from Pfizer and Moderna, despite those costing more than the Oxford vaccine (AstraZeneca). The exact cost of buying vaccines has not been published but, based on what we know about dose charges, this probably cost more than £7 billion, or about £120 for each UK adult.

Pfizer's pricing shows the power of market pre-eminence: in spite of the obvious economies of scale from producing such huge volumes and the very high returns on investment, in late 2021 they ramped up the price for each jab by 26 per cent, from €15.50 to €19.50.[6]

Moderna, too, made the most of its strong market position by holding prices at $16.50 for US customers but raising them to between $22 and $37 for each jab sold outside the US – a cost, some might say, of vassalage. Britain, however, could do little to argue, since the majority of its vaccine programme was contingent on US companies delivering US products. So dependent did the UK choose to become on US vaccines that the government even announced it would stop purchasing the Oxford vaccine completely in the summer of 2022. Should Covid reappear in the next decade, our response will be reliant, as usual, on American businesses. And we will pay dearly. The British firm AstraZeneca had committed to supplying the Oxford vaccine at cost, but it lost out badly and has since vowed never again to supply a vaccine at cost.[7]

If many of the rewards for fighting Covid-19 flowed to Big Pharma, health workers were the troops on the front line and they suffered for it. In 2020, 150 nurses died from Covid-19, and by the end of the following year 50 doctors had lost their lives – nearly half of these were consultants.[8] Coroners started registering their cause of death as 'industrial disease'.[9]

In gratitude, householders across Britain emerged onto their doorsteps to 'clap for carers' each Thursday during the early months of the crisis but most healthcare staff knew they lacked the kit to keep themselves safe. '[It was] like going over the top in WW1 with a bow and arrow,' one GP told the British Medical Association (BMA). Without the correct safety equipment, another doctor said, 'many of my colleagues and I became ill.'[10]

Across social media, medical staff would post pictures of expired, damaged and even mouldy personal protective equipment (PPE), which they were expected to wear to face patients. In hospitals and care settings, particularly big risks occurred during 'aerosol-generating procedures': tasks in which infected patients expelled very high doses of the virus at the staff treating them. One of these, intubation, when a tube is inserted into the airways of very sick patients, helping them to keep breathing, was routine. And to keep the medical staff safe, normal masks were not enough. Instead, thicker, technically complex face coverings called respirators were needed.

It is an accident of history that the epicentre of the global pandemic, the city of Wuhan in Hubei Province, China, was also the global centre for the manufacture of the non-woven fabrics used to make respirators. In 2020, this coincidence caused mayhem – and nowhere more so than in the UK.

To start with, at least, the UK government insisted that it had remedies in hand. One of these was the pandemic stockpile established ten years earlier, which held 26 million single-use respirators in a warehouse near Liverpool. In the early months of the pandemic, government ministers boasted of it regularly.[11] Another of their solutions was careful and determined purchasing of extra supplies throughout 2020. Both responses were deeply flawed – with PPE held in the pandemic stockpile being old or unusable, and government appearing to avoid domestic manufacturers such as JSP Safety in Oxford.[12]

At the start of 2020, JSP had three UK factories, which combined employed 320 people, others in Germany and the UEA, and two in China. Like so many other factories in the Hubei region, these produced respirators, but, at the very moment when JSP might have hoped to call on them to supply customers in the UK and Europe, much of China was locked down.

In February 2020, JSP announced that its two Chinese factories had been formally reserved, with all output remaining in China. The company stated that it had shipped all excess pandemic inventories from the UK and 'were no longer taking enquiries', so, at this early stage, China had dealt a body blow to Europe's leading independent supplier of life-saving equipment. By April, JSP was ramping up production in Europe. In Germany, respirator manufacturers were even able to take advantage of millions of euros of government grants to rapidly increase production.

And in the UK? Well, here the story is not as you would hope. Despite every effort from established domestic PPE suppliers, the government's buyers were slow to engage. Instead, in the whirling scramble for equipment, the UK government chose to award contracts to a string of businesses with little or no expertise in PPE but who claimed to source products from China more effectively, such as PestFix, a pest-control firm with 17 staff, which received £342 million in contracts.[13] Priority was given to firms with contacts in Parliament and government, so that, according to the National Audit Office (NAO), proposals from such sources were fast-tracked and were 14 times as likely to be awarded contracts.[14]

A significant proportion of the PPE supplied in this way did not work. And JSP, far from leading the fast lane of ministerially sanctioned PPE suppliers, tried to supply hospitals and NHS trusts directly.

The rot started early. NHS Supply Chain Coordination Ltd, a hybrid private business under the ultimate control of the Secretary of State for Health, was responsible for the pandemic stockpile. But the stockpile was maintained in poor order, there was too little of it, and it was poorly distributed.[15] The stockpile storage contract tender had been won in 2018 by a subsidiary of US firm Owens & Minor of Mechanicsville, Virginia.[16] It was Supply Chain Coordination that allowed much of the equipment held in the £500 million stockpile to expire. Owens & Minor sold the subsidiary managing the stockpile in April 2020 – at the peak of the crisis. By September of that year, Supply Chain Coordination's chief executive had departed after criticism for not being able to get supplies to the required destinations.[17]

Again and again, the pandemic crisis exposed how Britain's health service was let down by poor procurement practices that left genuine British innovators and businesses out of the main fight, often provided poor outcomes, and relied heavily on large and expensive US private providers that totally out-negotiated UK public sector buyers. Greed did not deliver success for Britain. It cost us greatly, 'my friends'.

It is a little more than a footnote, perhaps, that JSP's respirators were overlooked by the UK government when it bought its pandemic stockpile in 2010. With metronomic predictability, the 26 million held in the UK's emergency store had all been bought from three American companies: 3M of Two Harbours, Minnesota, Cardinal Health of Dublin, Ohio, and Kimberly-Clark of Irving, Texas. Even in a period of peace and plenty, money that could have funded domestic businesses and thereby increased what would become critical infrastructure was paid, instead, to America.

Before and after the pandemic

The era of English exceptionalism in healthcare is over.

– Simon Stevens
(NHS chief executive 2014–21), New York, 2004[18]

The UK's reliance on private – and therefore usually foreign – sources for its healthcare provision is often discussed in terms of the employment of foreign health workers, but the most costly dependency is on private companies. In the five years before the pandemic began, NHS procurement costs rose from £60 billion to £75 billion, and rose higher still in the years following the crisis. It has been a creeping shift, said to provide value and innovation in service provision, but the swelling procurement budget has achieved something further: it has allowed Britain's single biggest public sector entity to mesh neatly into the business plans of major, and mostly American, multinational companies.

The growing US involvement in private provision in the UK was kick-started by Tony Blair's Labour government in 2002, when many elective procedures were outsourced. As outlined by Blair in 2006, the aim was to increase private provision up to 40 per cent of operations, and this has been actively supported by successive governments, mostly Conservative, since then.[19]

A man who understood the trend better than most was Simon Stevens, now Lord Stevens, who steered the NHS through the pandemic and perhaps more than anyone was responsible for maintaining high public spending on health and securing improved outcomes for patients in the seven years in which he served as the chief executive. From an early point Stevens argued for greater private sector involvement in the health service. In 2004, while the NHS was going through one of its regular

'modernisations', he was at the forefront, advocating for the adop-
tion of some aspects of the US healthcare model. Addressing the
question of choice, Stevens said the NHS needed 'constructive
discomfort' and he argued for setting up free-standing surgical centres run by international private operators as a first step.
He added that 'private diagnostics and primary out-of-hours
services are next'.[20] In a panel with UK health secretary John
Reid in New York, he welcomed the parallel between the new
UK Health Trusts, which 'buy' health from doctors and hospitals, and the US 'managed care' supplied by companies such as
UnitedHealth Group of Minnesota.[21] Stevens went on to become
UnitedHealth's European president, during which time he guided
its controversial takeover of two UK GP practices.

Unfairly, some people used Stevens's background to imply his
involvement in a conspiracy against the NHS. The fact is that
advocates of further private sector intervention have a powerful
case: it often results in cutting fixed costs, ensuring just-in-time
style efficiencies, outsourcing risk as well as profit and offering
increased choice for patients. The 'vassal state' analysis would
suggest, however, that unless the NHS bucks a national trend and
acquires ruthless, world-beating negotiators to make its private
sector contracts, there will inevitably be two very negative and
costly effects of greater private sector involvement. The first is
that domestic, tax-paying businesses will not provide as much
of the NHS's services as most people would wish or expect. And
the second is that large numbers of services will be provided by
US-owned businesses, and that the profits too will flow out of
the country.

So, how much of the NHS's public sector contracting already
goes to the US? In an attempt to discover the answer, I submitted
a Freedom of Information request to the NHS. In reply it said:
'We are not able to separate the cost of US goods and services

procured by NHS England from goods and services procured elsewhere… We hope this information is helpful.' It was not. Although it did indicate the lack of any analysis or interest in the issue.

Fortunately, the answer can be cobbled together from data that is out there. Let us start with NHS spending on drugs, which costs over £20 million annually – equivalent to more than £700 for each UK household every year.[22] Although the UK has two large pharma companies of its own (GSK and AstraZeneca), they are seriously outgunned by the top US drug companies, such as Pfizer, Eli Lilly, Merck, Amgen, Bristol Myers Squibb, Gilead, AbbVie and Johnson & Johnson. These are just some of a much larger herd of US pharma companies (most of Big Pharma) that together have annual worldwide sales of half a trillion dollars, and they are generating recurring revenue that rises rapidly in countries with ageing populations, such as the UK. Even though the NHS does not break down its purchases by country, the US is home to five of the top seven pharma companies, and each of these is a big supplier to the UK. They have been effective at growing their share through development pipelines and networks of sales reps and lobbyists.[23]

Hospitals also spend copiously on equipment and medical devices. Of the world's top ten medical device companies, seven are from the US, and all are highly profitable suppliers to the NHS. The biggest is Medtronic of Minneapolis, which makes cardiovascular kit and a wide range of surgical supplies. It also has a joint venture with DaVita of Colorado to supply kidney care equipment and services: dialysis is a treatment typically given three times a week, which also generates a long-term income stream.

Another big need for NHS equipment is in diagnostics, where the NHS spends around £10 billion each year.[24] The healthcare industry loves diagnostics, which leads almost seamlessly to treatment solutions: even just telling someone that they have nothing to worry about is still a useful and profitable business. One result of the increasingly litigious approach to health is that doctors with any doubts usually order extra tests. As one medical friend told me: 'In the back of my head I hear a tribunal judge asking me, "But why didn't you do that test?"' The NHS buys diagnostics in volume from Abbott Laboratories of Abbott Park, Illinois, and from Becton, Dickinson (BD) of Franklin Lakes, New Jersey.[25] BD is also the NHS's main supplier of blood collection tubes and needles. This is a sizeable business because, on average, a British citizen has 14 diagnostic tests a year, of which two are blood tests.[26]

Then there is medical ultrasound, an extraordinary technology that allows doctors to look inside the body without using a scalpel, and that has enabled many innovations for heart and lung interventions, orthopaedics, keyhole surgery and foetal medicine. Its lead inventor was British obstetrician Ian Donald. While working in London in 1952 he built the first respirator for newborn babies; he then moved to the University of Glasgow as its new professor of obstetrics, and here his inventiveness continued. On a factory tour of nearby engineering firm Babcock & Wilcox in 1955, he was shown a sound-wave device used for finding flaws in steel welds, and he noticed that the operative tested it by bouncing sound waves off the bone in his thumb. Donald immediately started work on adapting the technology for medical use, and by June 1958 his team had built their own imaging machine and published pictures of a 14-week-old foetus.[27] Although in its infancy, ultrasound scanning had been born. Today, GE Healthcare, of Chicago, is the market leader supplying the NHS.[28]

Orthopaedics departments largely buy American and often go to Stryker of Kalamazoo, Michigan, for hip and knee joints, each costing a few thousand dollars. And in ophthalmics, Johnson & Johnson are the biggest suppliers of contact lenses as well as many consumables for eye departments: in total they make 4.5 billion contact lenses each year. Another healthcare giant, Cardinal Health of Dublin, Ohio, is the NHS's major supplier of those little-discussed but important products to help with bowel and bladder management.

There are now 25 private hospitals in the UK, and dozens of private clinics clearing waiting lists for elective operations for hernias, weight loss and tonsil removal. Three of the biggest operators are Aspen Healthcare of Texas, HCA Healthcare of Tennessee and BHI Healthcare, whose parent company is in Missouri. For staffing, these hospitals often use part-time NHS consultants, and, because they pay generously, they have the advantage of being able to pick and choose which consultants to work with. Almost half of NHS consultants work only part-time in the health service and supplement their earnings with private work like this, which makes up a third of their income – but the system is set up to ensure they still get full NHS pensions. Far from being an independent and parallel provider, these private hospitals have big contracts for government-financed work: every year they carry out 500,000 elective procedures for the NHS, meaning that the NHS pays the private rate but is at least able to contain its waiting lists.[29] The NHS commissions £18 billion of services like this from non-NHS organisations annually. As well as taking the strain off the health service, they perhaps give an impression of 'consumer choice'.

And the list goes on: one in seven in-patient beds in UK mental health services is now provided by American suppliers: while the NHS cut its own mental health beds by 6,000, the private sector has increased its beds by 9,000. This outsourcing costs the NHS about £2 billion a year, with profit margins that are typically 15–20 per cent.[30]

General practice, dentistry, opticians and pharmacies, which have been provided by private contractors since the NHS's formation in 1948, are now also squarely in the crosshairs of the American corporations.

In 2021, health insurance group Centene, of Missouri, quietly took over 58 GP surgeries. When patients discovered that their GP practices were now American-owned, some of them took the local NHS to the High Court. They complained that the process had been secretive, with no public meetings. One local councillor asked: 'Without my knowledge, my surgery has been sold to a giant American healthcare company, one with a very poor reputation. How can that be right?'[31] The case, however, was dismissed.

In dentistry, private equity advisers Lincoln International of Chicago published a guide for would-be acquirers of UK dental practices in January 2020, stating: 'The elderly population is typically in need of more dental care and is more willing to pay for it privately.'[32]

That guide cites the significant takeovers in the dental sector that have already happened, such as that of Integrated Dental Holdings (branded as 'Mydentist') by private equity company Palamon, funded by US capital.[33] The biggest chain is Portman Dental Care, with 350 clinics and 1.5 million patients, all backed by the private equity group Core Equity Holdings, a spin-off from Bain Capital of Boston.[34]

And then there are the bureaucratic functions. In 2022, the NHS was offering a new £1.7 billion contract for a 'workforce management solution' with the condition that solutions would have to be built on working with the existing database.[35] That is to say, it must be built on the software from Oracle of Santa Clara, California, and be hosted on the six production servers running on the AIX operating system of IBM, of Armonk, New

York. As often happens in government work, US firms become too entrenched for other options to be viable.

Consider Palantir of Denver, Colorado, which has a five-year, £360 million contract to manage vaccines, waiting lists, population health and the supply chain in the NHS. This follows the work that the company did during the Covid-19 pandemic to coordinate the delivery of PPE and vaccines as well as manage waiting lists, which had grown to 6 million patients – almost one in ten Brits. But the deal is more than it seems. It will very likely run longer because, as one insider explained: 'Once Palantir is in, how are you going to remove them?'[36] In November 2023, the NHS doubled down, awarding it a £480 million contract to run a data platform that allows the medical histories of patients to be shared across the health service. A competing bid from the UK start-up Quantexa was discarded, with that company's CEO warning that opting for a single US contractor risked 'having people over a barrel'.[37]

As for patient data held in the regions, each trust chooses its own software supplier, but the NHS has produced a shortlist of recommended and trusted companies they should pick from. There are just eight suppliers that it considers have adequate software to 'help clinicians access and share data effectively', and five of them are from the US.

The challenge of acquiring and analysing medical data operates on many levels: genetics, medical data, patient data and NHS-wide data. In all of these, it is corporations from across the Atlantic that dominate. In the case of genetics, gene sequencing has been developing very rapidly, and the cost of sequencing an individual's genome has plummeted, creating great opportunities for personalised medicine. According to the National Human Genome Research Institute (NHGRI) in Maryland, over the last 20 years the price has dropped from $100 million to under

$1,000.[38] In this field the top three firms supplying laboratories around the world, including in the UK, are Illumina, Agilent Technologies and Thermo Fisher, the first two from California and the last from Massachusetts.

One of the leading companies offering computerised medicine is Babylon Health, now owned by eMed of Miami, Florida, which provides an app called 'GP at Hand', and with funding from the NHS it already has more than 100,000 patients. Technically, the app does not offer diagnosis, but it acts as a clinic so that clinicians can prescribe medication, issue sick notes and make referrals to specialists.

Very roughly, then, about 40 per cent of UK health spending, apart from staff costs, is already with private suppliers, and around half of that is with North American companies. The services offered are so competitive, diverse and embedded that it is now difficult to see private domestic entrants 'taking back control'.

That is today, but we can already see the shape of tomorrow. A future of medicine involving big data, AI and genetics will, very likely, be dominated by US companies. And big tech brands are likely to get in on the act. Today, Apple tracks well-being through its iPhone, and Alphabet/Google sells wearable devices while pumping money into biotech research. We might predict that these functions will feed and then subsume more formal health services. Amazon has already got there. In November 2022, the 'Amazon Clinic' was launched, a service linking users with third-party health providers that will probably soon be rolled out to the UK. According to Amazon's 'chief medical officer', Dr Nworah Ayogu, the clinic will address 'more than 20 common health conditions, such as allergies, acne, and hair loss'. He makes clear that users of the service are not just patients but buyers, who can get 'treatment within hours, instead of days – helping customers achieve better health'.[39]

It will be easy for these and other companies to click into the NHS network because it has already been reshaped to fit more neatly with American business models.

In his 2018 book *Too Many Pills*, the British doctor James Le Fanu diagnosed Britain with a crisis of polypharmacy in which the proportion of adults given more than five drugs doubled in less than 20 years.[40] Some pills are given to cancel out the side effects of the others, leading to a cascade of additional prescriptions – and of profits for Big Pharma.

It is impossible to detach the influence of the US medical industry from the mindset criticised by Le Fanu. Back in the 1970s, Henry Gadsden, chairman of Merck, told *Fortune* magazine that he wanted to extend the market for the corporation's drugs beyond just the sick.[41] He wanted to sell to the healthy as well, and that is what his company now does. Merck, Pfizer and others have persuaded the NHS that a whole-population approach is needed, in which drugs are taken on a preventative basis. Le Fanu reports that 90 per cent of doctors believe they are over-prescribing pills. This was never the plan for the NHS. The vision was for Britain to work together to make sure everyone was looked after.

Ultimately, how we fund and organise our healthcare must serve domestic and not foreign interests first. Those interests are undermined if we have to pay more for the same products than patients and customers in countries from which products originate. If we grow ever more dependent on foreign healthcare, we will only further engorge their profits and undermine our own tax base, domestic expertise and resilience.

After the pandemic, Dr Clive Dix, who chaired the UK's vaccine taskforce, was eager to apply the lessons of the crisis to ensure that Britain would come through the next one more easily. He ended his tenure emphasising the need to capitalise on Oxford's breakthrough and ensure that the UK was not dependent on others to fix its problems by building an infrastructure for diagnosis, testing, developing and manufacturing vaccines.[42] Instead, however, the proposed infrastructure would be wholly dependent on US-designed and -owned mRNA vaccines, which may not work, and would include mechanisms for developing traditional viral vector vaccines like Oxford's Covid-19 breakthrough.

By the start of 2022, the UK government had poured around £205 million into a new Vaccine Manufacturing and Innovation Centre (VMIC) in Harwell, outside Oxford. The plan was to build a resilient, forward-looking and independent body that would secure Britain against future pandemics. By the spring, the facility had already been sold to US medical giant Catalent, of Somerset, New Jersey, which pledged £105 million to finish the building.[43] By the autumn of 2022 Catalent had cancelled the investment, leaving the UK government to pick up the pieces.[44]

Vaccine developer Moderna, meanwhile, signed a partnership with the UK government that binds the country to the use of their mRNA vaccines in the next decade and announced its own manufacturing facility in Harwell.[45]

In a subsequent interview with the *Observer*, Dix could barely contain his indignation:

> We had the vaccine manufacturing initiative. We worked with a lot of pharmaceutical companies to show them how good the UK was with our clinical trials network. Most of that has gone… The government has basically put all their money on mRNA vaccines. They've gambled recklessly… 'Let's forget about all these other vaccine technologies. Let's forget about manufacturing. Let's just encourage the likes of Pfizer and Moderna to come to the UK, then we're covered.' That's our

pandemic preparedness. Quite frankly, it's not just reckless. It's fraught with danger.[46]

Who knows what Simon Stevens really meant when he said that the era of English medical exceptionalism was 'over'. That exceptionalism involved not just the inclusive and monolithic NHS of the twentieth century but also the manner in which our scientists pursued unique and highly successful solutions to pressing public health concerns through observation, inventiveness and cooperation. They invented vaccines in the eighteenth century and produced vital new ones in the twenty-first. They made British healthcare effective as well as resilient and the rest of the country flourished for it. Perhaps that era really did end in 2004, as Lord Stevens said. Perhaps Harwell represented a last stand. Or perhaps the UK should change course and put its trust and resources in the hands of its own exceptional people once again – in healthcare and, as we shall see, across the rest of government procurement. After all, it is what the Americans would do.

9

SUPPLIERS OF CHOICE
TO HM GOVERNMENT

The Advocacy Center works... to ensure that exporters of US products and services have the best possible chance of winning government contracts. Advocacy assistance... often involves the US Embassy or other US Government agency officials expressing support for the US exporters directly to the foreign government.

– US International Trade Administration
webpage on selling to the UK public sector[1]

Beyond the NHS, other parts of the UK government are huge customers for US companies, and these buyers are ideal: susceptible to marketing pressure from across the Atlantic, blind to the totality of their own interests and often showing little concern about prices. For salespeople, government buyers are the holy grail because they are spending big dollops of 'OPM' (other people's money), their orders are by nature recurring and there is no risk of the customer going bust. Even better, these customers have a preference for dealing with large corporations, and their buying decisions often cascade into more purchases from the same supplier by other departments, agencies and local authorities.

It was these government buyers that Mike Kelly was targeting when, in 2013, he started up DataCentred, which offered cloud computing services. The plan was to create 200 skilled jobs in his home town of Manchester, and the venture had backing from the Greater Manchester Investment Fund, the North West Fund for Venture Capital and veteran investor Jon Moulton.[2] Mike Kelly expected off-site computing to become important to government and was soon supplying part of HMRC's critical infrastructure along with two other UK companies offering cloud services.[3] I met him at an internet conference, where he told me he hoped to win more government contracts because of official support for small and medium-sized enterprises (SMEs). Suddenly – without consultation or concern for the wider consequences – HMRC changed its policy and decided to switch exclusively to using Amazon Web Services (AWS). Officials were following the same centralised guidelines as the Department for Work and Pensions, who admitted they had adopted a policy of procuring public cloud services only from Amazon, Google or Microsoft. Soon after the DataCentred contract was terminated in 2017, an HMRC official explained: 'Hyperscale cloud technology is newly available in the UK and the larger cloud capability offers more resilient services at a significantly lower cost to the taxpayer.'[4] The UK start-up went into administration just a few weeks later. It was therefore no help to him that, by 2023, the UK government was spending almost £3 billion annually on cloud services, mostly with AWS.[5] Nor was it any comfort that in October 2023 the UK's Competition and Markets Authority (CMA) launched an investigation into the 70–80 per cent market share held by Amazon and Microsoft.[6]

West Coast software is wall-to-wall

The UK government has very few significant domestic suppliers for its IT and computer systems, and instead buys from Oracle, IBM, Microsoft and other US companies. All its cloud storage is bought from US companies, and citizens depend on AWS when they deal online with the DVLA, the Post Office, Companies House, the Met Office or the Ministry of Justice.[7] That applies to almost all the state's public-facing websites. Beyond that, the government's social media is published on Meta/Facebook's platforms or Microsoft's LinkedIn.

The extent of the UK's dependence is often masked by the way US software is supplied through local contractors. This happened when Whitehall decided to digitise the Passport Office (in 2017) and the Land Registry (in 2020).[8] In the past these had undertaken cumbersome tasks: every year 7 million new passports are issued, and 26 million property titles across Britain have to be kept up to date. Contracts to shift these functions online were awarded to the British software company Kainos, based in Northern Ireland.[9] For passports, the project would end the use of tedious paper forms collected from the Post Office, on which tiny boxes were filled in by hand so that a computer could read them. With the old paper system half the forms had to be rejected: the most common mistakes were incorrect postcodes and dates of birth (applicants often fill in the current date when writing by hand). The new online system would prevent these errors and be quicker and cheaper. For the digitisation of the Land Registry, Kainos used clever software to match plans and complete the land transfer process, with help from artificial intelligence.[10] But, in both cases, Kainos needed software from US firms whose computer code does the heavy lifting: in this case AWS hosts both the passport and Land Registry services. Kainos did smart work developing the online system, but the ultimate beneficiary was not just a Northern Irish software company but AWS, which is paid handsomely to host the service.

Other British businesses begin to seem like 'front companies' since their principal work is supplying US technology products. BT resells routers and cloud storage from Cisco, Amazon and Microsoft. The London-listed Bytes Technology Group won a bid to supply Microsoft's Windows operating system across government departments and also markets the whole suite of Microsoft products to the government, including Azure, Microsoft's cloud platform.[11] Bytes specialises in the public sector, selling cyber-security and IT services to government departments. Virtually everything it sells is US-made, coming from VMware, Dell, Microsoft, Adobe and Sophos.

This pattern of working through local agents suits the big West Coast tech companies as it saves them the costs of regional offices. Another of the largest agents is Buckinghamshire-based Softcat, with annual sales of more than £1 billion. Its 2022 report lists 33 companies whose software it sells to the UK government. All but four of these are American.[12]

For larger software contracts, the US tech firms prefer to sell direct without having to hand over a slice to the locals. Hewlett Packard Enterprise (of Texas and California) took £1.7 billion from the UK government in a two-year period, mostly supplying the Department of Work and Pensions (DWP) with computing power, and contracts have been placed directly with DXC Technology (of Ashburn, Virginia) by the Crown Prosecution Service (CPS) for IT infrastructure. In late 2023, AWS (of Washington State and Virginia) won three-year contracts worth £450 million to supply hosting services to the Home Office and DWP.[13]

Reliance on US tech is broadscale

These bigger contracts often hide the thousands of smaller purchasing decisions, especially around software, where government buyers lean heavily towards American suppliers: government offices pay millions in licence fees for the use of Excel, Word, PowerPoint and a host of other day-to-day programs.

The problem was recognised in 2011, with a House of Commons report entitled 'Government and IT – "a recipe for rip-offs"', which stated that the UK government was 'over-reliant on a small "oligopoly" of large suppliers, which some witnesses referred to as a "cartel"'. It went on to say: 'The government needs to break out of this relationship.'[14] However, the Covid-19 crisis demonstrated that, nine years on, the relationship had only intensified. When desk workers were forced to move online, their video conferencing was all-American, from Google Meet, Microsoft Teams, Skype (owned by Microsoft) and Zoom (based in San Jose, California).

According to Tussell, a private company which closely monitored UK government spending during the Covid-19 crisis, for every three pounds that was spent by the government, one pound went to a US business. Much of this was for non-medical supplies.[15] It was as if the UK simply lacked the infrastructure to respond on its own. The problem with too much foreign procurement is that this lack of resilience becomes self-perpetuating: if you have not given contracts to domestic companies, they will not be there when you most need them.

Tussell also produced an analysis of government spending that showed that between 2017 and 2020 the UK spent more than £19 billion on foreign suppliers, and more with US suppliers than with any other nation. The true number will be even higher because, in addition to these direct contracts, there will also have been a lot of indirect purchasing from US companies. Tussell's analysis of spending over the ten years up to 2021 shows one government department spent three times as much as any other private provider: the Ministry of Defence (MOD), and it paid £26 billion to US suppliers in the period.[16]

Locking in defence spending

While the British military have always worked closely with the US, the relationship has moved steadily from one of partnership to one of loyal, paid-up dependence. The UK has committed to buying much of its military equipment through the US's Foreign Military Sales (FMS) programme, which allows the US significant influence over UK defence. In 2023, the MOD spent £733 million on FMS agreements – the actual supplier will end up being either the US government itself or a favoured US company, and the system seems designed to strengthen the US arms industry.[17] The costs of this FMS programme are funded by a levy on foreign governments, and it is one of a number of such schemes that put much of the UK government spending into foreign hands. The purchaser does not deal directly with the defence contractor: instead, the US Department of Defense (DoD) serves as an intermediary, handling logistics, delivery and even the building of infrastructure such as hangars and runways. FMS programmes often have two-word code names beginning with the word 'PEACE' to indicate the oversight of the US Air Force headquarters. The DoD website states: 'FMS is a fundamental tool of US foreign policy and national security and strengthens the United States' unmatched network of allies and partners.'[18]

When successive US governments press NATO allies to spend more on defence they are, on one level, trying to make the

Europeans share more of the burden, but they are also urging more spending with their favoured defence contractors. The US spends more than 3 per cent of GDP on defence, while the UK spends 2 per cent. Boris Johnson signalled in 2020 that he wanted to see that raised to 3 per cent; the war in Ukraine also pushed the UK to spend more. Such increases will boost buying from the US and its influence on the UK.

Increasing dependence for the army's front line and back end

Over the last 30 years, all branches of the UK military have cut their personnel by around 40 per cent, and, in 2023, the British Army had only 77,000 regular full-time staff. The move away from a standing army towards modern warfare systems increasingly means replacing soldiers with US hardware. One middle-ranking officer told me that, with these numbers, in an emergency the army might only be able to raise one or two divisions: around 10,000 soldiers each. This was confirmed in 2022 by the admission by an MOD official that at most it could only muster two divisions.[19] The military is far more dependent on the US and NATO than the public realises. In one year, the Royal Navy relied on NATO to protect British waters on 20 occasions.[20] The UK also needs the key member of NATO to provide and maintain its nuclear weapons. At every level, from weaponry to joint exercises, British defence is ever more tightly folded into American arms contracts.[21]

US companies have dug in solidly and now supply much of the MOD's 'back end', with very large contracts going to little-known companies like KBR (of Houston, Texas). In May 2020, the government's buying department awarded this company a contract for £2 billion to manage the military's catering, building works, logistics, housing and training for the next four years.[22]

The US government even produces analysis to help its companies to identify British takeover targets: its International Trade Administration recognises the UK's aerospace industry as 'the crown jewel for UK exports and… 90% of domestic aerospace production is exported'.[23] In the 2019–22 period, American companies have taken over three of the largest six UK companies in the sector: Cobham (£4 billion), Meggitt (£6 billion) and Ultra (£2.6 billion). These UK companies were leaders in the emerging technologies of drones, 3D printing and space technology, which demonstrates how US executives think: they concentrate systematically on sectors that will see the greatest growth in coming years. An old adage states that 'when California sneezes America catches a cold, and when America sneezes the world catches a cold', but it could also be said that world consumer and industrial demand is led by the US, and within the US it is led by California. As well as being the hub of US software, California is the centre of the US weapons industry. The state gains over $180 billion in revenue annually from defence spending, which supports 800,000 jobs.[24]

Looking westwards for fighter jets and choppers

The turning point in weapons supply came back in the 1960s when Britain had streamlined its aircraft-manufacturing industry down to three major groups: the British Aircraft Corporation (BAC), Hawker Siddeley and Westland Helicopters. BAC was successfully developing the TSR-2, a high-speed, low-level strike and reconnaissance aircraft. It was an expensive project, but would have allowed Britain to maintain its position as a world-class aircraft manufacturer. At the same time, the Americans were developing a similar aircraft, the F-111. The UK Treasury was wary of the costs of such projects and the more limited markets available to the British company. It was also in economic trouble, with a threatened devaluation of sterling and the need for an IMF loan. Harold Wilson took the agonising and seminal decision to scrap the TSR-2 project and instead buy F-111s from the Americans.[25] Similar decisions were made with other aircraft types, and since then Britain's aircraft industry has never recovered. Julian Amery, who had been a Conservative aviation minister, believed that the Americans made the IMF loan dependent on dropping prestige projects such as the TSR-2 and Concorde. As he put it, the American sentiment was 'Why don't you cancel the TSR-2 and we'll let you have the F-111 fairly cheap?'[26]

Within a few years, Britain's world-class home-grown aeronautical industry had withered to almost nothing, and, in 1985, the helicopter business followed. Westland Helicopters, of Yeovil in Somerset, was in a poor financial state and could only be saved with a takeover by another helicopter maker. The American defence contractor Sikorsky offered to buy out Westland but the UK's defence secretary, Michael Heseltine, believed a European solution should be found. He hastily organised a French–Italian–British consortium to buy the company. Unfortunately, the Westland board and Margaret Thatcher supported the Americans, and Sikorsky of Connecticut became the new owner.

The contrast with France's aeronautical industry is acute, where Dassault remains a world-class exporter of military planes whose independence is strongly supported by the French government. Even beyond its manufacturing of submarines and armoured vehicles, it has three other companies focused on military aircraft: Thales, Safran and MBDA.

American school dinners and high-street prescriptions

Lorries belonging to Brake Bros are a familiar sight to British drivers. They are often delivering food to schools, where they are the UK's leading supplier of school dinners. The company's story follows a familiar pattern: set up in 1958 in Ashford, Kent, it had long been a profitable wholesale food supplier when, in 2007, it was bought up by Bain Capital of Massachusetts, who then, in 2016, sold it on to Sysco, a Texan corporation.[27] A similar ownership path was followed by another large supplier to the UK government, Boots UK Limited, which sells more than £2 billion of prescriptions each year. Established in Nottingham in 1849, Boots was bought by private equity group KKR in 2007 and sold on seven years later to Walgreens, a large US drugs supplier in Illinois.[28] In each case, the rewards for restructuring and reorganising the company went to the various US owners, with, one might assume, negligible UK taxes paid along the way. US ownership has now been established for the long term, with both these companies being indispensable government suppliers.

In the case of Sysco, with its Brakes lorries mostly delivering highly processed school dinners, the outsourcing has made life easier for government officials and maybe cheaper in cash terms. It has, however, had many unintended downsides: because so much is pre-processed, children do not see the activity of cooking and food preparation in school life, more packaging is needed, the link between food and seasons is lost, and, of course, the profits flow to Texas, where the company's strategic decisions are also made.

Prisons, office management and events

The British and London-based company G4S came to public prominence with the 2012 Olympics, for which the company won a contract for £284 million to provide 13,700 security guards. However, just 14 days before the opening they only had 4,000 lined up. One of the trainees, an ex-policeman, described the recruitment process as 'an utter farce', and another former policeman pulled out because, he said, it was 'totally chaotic'.[29] In another controversy, G4S were discovered to be overcharging for the tagging of criminals; it was also found that they had been collecting fees for tagging prisoners who were already back in prison and even for some who had died.[30] G4S executives admitted their wrongdoing and paid back £109 million to the government. Within a year it was cleared to bid again for new contracts.

It was not just the government who were unhappy with the company: some inmates protested too. In December 2016, Birmingham Prison, which was being operated for profit by G4S, experienced its fourth riot in six weeks.[31] Prisoners phoned the BBC to say that they were rioting because of inadequate staffing, poor food and lack of medical care.[32] After the incident, the chief inspector of prisons, Peter Clarke, identified ineffectual management and declared that it was the worst prison he had ever visited. Some people asked how prison privatisation could continue. G4S said it 'welcomed' the development as an opportunity to 'urgently address' the various problems.[33] It retained the contract to run Birmingham Prison and has since been awarded dozens of other significant government contracts. In 2021, the company (which had been listed in London and Copenhagen) was taken over by Allied Universal.[34] It is now part of a US private prisons empire with 750,000 employees, headquartered in both Pennsylvania and California.

You might hope that the US owners will improve G4S's services – the British government certainly does: in May 2023 G4S won a significant five-year contract to provide security services to the Foreign Office, where it took over the employment of 300 staff members. According to Bidstats, which monitors procurement, over the previous 12 months G4S had won 50 UK government contracts running into billions of pounds in value. It is paid variously by the Ministry of Justice, NHS, Department for Work and Pensions, and MOD, and has been awarded a series of contracts to collect cash. Some work is jointly awarded with others, such as the facilities management contract for the NHS, where G4S partnered with US multinationals such as CBRE (property) and commercial window-cleaning company OCS, now owned by New York private equity firm Clayton, Dubilier & Rice (CD&R).

Management failure in government has led to widespread outsourcing that plays straight into the hands of the US multinationals. The UK has contracted with G4S to run four private prisons, several detention centres (two of which I have visited, but not as a detainee). As a result, 15 per cent of the UK's prison population is held in privately run prisons, which are mostly larger and newer.[35] Time will tell if the US model of incarceration is adopted even more enthusiastically in the UK.

Big projects mostly run by Uncle Sam

One might assume that the British are capable of organising their own infrastructure building as the French do. Such projects include the HS1 railway for the Channel Tunnel, HS2, connecting London to the Midlands, Crossrail, the Gatwick Airport extension and the new terminal at Heathrow Airport.[36] In fact, a principal contractor for each of these was Bechtel, which is based in Reston, Virginia. While the Virginians are clearly effective project managers, the profit goes west, and their research teams are mostly in that state, as well as Texas.

GPS is positioning the UK as a customer of both US companies and the federal government: GPS-based systems such as Trimble combine with US satellite networks to supply the British government's expanding demand for mapping and surveying services. Indeed, GPS is itself a commercial service owned by the US government and operated by the US Space Force. Almost 90 per cent of all commercial satellites are manufactured by US firms and – of those in orbit – they are mostly controlled by the US, which has 3,433 of the 5,465 total.[37] China, its next largest competitor, has 541. SpaceX is on target to increase its rate of launching fourfold over the next 20 years. In 2018, it was planned that the UK Space Agency would operate an independent satellite system, but within two years the idea was scrapped as being too expensive and unnecessary.[38] Space has therefore become a place of Stars and Stripes where Britain, like other countries, must pay economic tribute.

There have been some in government who have realised the problem of awarding mega-contracts to just a few suppliers. Lord Young's review in 2013 was intended to give small and medium-sized enterprises (SMEs) more access to government contracts, and the Federation of Small Businesses (FSB) showed that endlessly throwing money at large corporations was not delivering value for money or helping SMEs.[39] Such is the ideological commitment to open markets that none of the reforms explicitly addressed why so many billions flow out of the UK exchequer and into the bottom lines of foreign businesses.

Buy American, but no buy-British policy

Many sales from US companies are made through the government's buying agency, the Crown Commercial Service (CCS), whose existence must be one of the country's best-kept secrets, considering its £27 billion annual spend (which would be equivalent on a per-household basis to almost £1,000 each year). It is part of the Cabinet Office and acts for the state in buying almost everything, from vehicles to laptops. Its 2022 annual report lists all its objectives, but none of those includes a preference for buying from the UK or even from Europe, and it chooses not to record the nationality of the companies from which it buys.[40] This is quite different from the policies of other countries' buying agencies. The US tracks government contracts awarded to foreign-owned companies through its Federal Procurement Data System (FPDS), which shows where the supplier is based. And Europe similarly requires member states to publish the details of contracts including the supplier.

The British belief in nationality-blind buying contrasts with the 'buy national' policies of other such agencies around the world, including those in the US. In 1933, President Hoover used his last day in office to sign into law the Buy American Act, which gave preference to the buying of home-made goods, and 50 years later the very similarly named Buy America Act (no *n* this time) gave preference to US supplies in mass-transit buying, where the requirement to buy American can only be overruled if the domestic supplier is 25 per cent more expensive than the foreign tenderer. More recently, in 2021, the Build America Buy American Act established that for all infrastructure projects there must be a strong national preference: all iron, steel, manufactured goods and construction materials must be produced in the US.[41] Compliance is enforced with help from the 'Made in America Office', which states that it aims to 'reduce the need to spend taxpayer dollars on foreign-made goods.'[42] There are no such policies and there is no such office in the UK.

The US has gone much further in boosting its economy at the expense of others. The misleadingly named 'Inflation Reduction Act' (IRA) of 2022 has given an enormous injection of $369 billion of state aid to US companies to subsidise certain industries and create a playing field sloping in its favour. The IRA requires high percentages of electric vehicle components to be made in the US for any cars sold there, and acts like a magnet in dragging businesses onto US soil. As a result, Tesla has decided to switch its battery cells factory from Germany to Texas.[43]

Waste and local authorities

Local government represents a big government buyer, spending more than £100 billion a year, and as with central government they have become very dependent on US-owned suppliers. Responsible for waste and recycling, they outsource much of their waste management to private companies who are reliably profitable: as they say in Yorkshire, 'Where there's muck, there's brass.' During the Covid-19 lockdown US private equity groups emerged as the most active dealmakers. In March 2020, KKR, one of the biggest and oldest of the pack of private equity companies, spent £4.2 billion buying Viridor, based in Taunton, Somerset.[44] This waste disposal company 'covers the entire waste value chain' and has contracts with 150 local authorities and 3,000 employees. If the private equity playbook is followed, the company may find itself with extra debt, and may increase margins through cost-cutting and price increases. KKR's co-president, Joe Bae, put the firm's purchase in context: 'Our active investment pace since the beginning of Covid has been quite intentional… [we are] capitalising on the unprecedented level of volatility and dislocation in the markets to buy high-quality businesses at attractive prices.'[45]

Similarly, Biffa was bought by private equity group Energy Capital Partners (ECP), of New Jersey, in September 2022 for £2.1 billion.[46] ECP said it was attracted by the strong brand and 'powerful barriers to entry'.[47] In other words, Biffa is a supplier to the government in a sector where new competitors are rare and will not be nurtured by the state, so its margins will stay high. Now there are no large UK-owned listed waste companies.

Total numbers and the lack of measurement

While two large departments (the NHS and MOD) have a particularly large dependence on US suppliers, contracts throughout government are routinely won by US companies or their UK distributors. In total the UK government spends more than £1,100 billion every year, of which the bulk is used to pay its 5.8 million employees. The rest is heavily skewed towards American suppliers. Taken together, the true cost of US supplies to the UK government each year must be around £30 billion, but of course no government department bothers to measure. This spending dwarfs the £10 billion or so that the large US companies typically pay in UK corporation tax each year on their profits.[48] In addition, companies selling to the government have learned much from those who are selling to consumers and have persuaded government departments to step onto the treadmill of regular payments – with open-ended contracts and annuity-style deals where the default is that the purchase of services just carries on.

Often US products are the best in their field, and this tour through some of their conquered markets should in no way detract from that. But in many cases dominant companies can shape the tender documents to match what they already supply, and they lobby hard to get contracts awarded. The US government works hand in hand with its companies to get regulations changed to promote US industry at a high level. In one example from 2019, the US ambassador to London, Robert 'Woody' Johnson, wrote a *Daily Telegraph* article encouraging more imports of US food, saying that chlorinated chicken was 'a public safety no-brainer' and that the perceived dangers of hormone-fed beef were 'myths'.[49] In response, the National Farmers' Union (NFU) president, Minette Batters, made the point that changing the regulations and accepting US agricultural products would 'put British producers out of business'.[50]

The question for policy-makers is not merely about America, however. It is whether they should be doing more to build up domestic capabilities so that buying the best also means buying British.

Targeting foreign workers rather than foreign ownership

The UK has a long history of 'British jobs for British workers' sloganeering – for instance, the memorable aspiration of Gordon Brown at the 2007 Labour Party Conference.[51] A similar theme was adopted by Amber Rudd at the Conservative Party Conference in 2016, where she also suggested that businesses should declare how many foreign workers they employ.[52] Since then, public attitudes to foreign workers have softened, and the political emphasis has moved to migrants and asylum seekers crossing the channel on dangerous small boats. Absent from these debates, however, is the government's attitude not to foreign workers but to foreign owners. Public procurement policies expose the confusion of the UK state about economic forces originating from outside its shores. The emphasis on the dangers of foreign workers was folly at best and misdirection at worst. They are much less of a threat to people's jobs than the UK government's handing out of tens of billions in gold-plated contracts to US companies.

If strong American corporations are behaving like lions in the zoo we should not be surprised. It is in the nature of such beasts to be forceful, dominant and carnivorous. The behaviour that we should be concerned with is that of the zookeepers.

Consequences: jobs, skills, security and taxes

The sum of all these contracts is not just the money flowing abroad but the loss of jobs, opportunity, skills and taxes. And the bigger picture is of a UK government which is, directly and indirectly, beholden to the US. The power of these corporations and the UK's dependence on them means that the UK has ceded control of much of its economy, and is cooperating in the continuing loss of wealth and income.

10

CONSEQUENCES
WHY DOES US DOMINANCE MATTER?

If you don't build your dream, someone else will hire you to help them build theirs.

– Dhirubhai Ambani, founder, Reliance Industries[1]

Mississippi is the poorest of the 50 US states: one person in five lives in poverty and it has the highest infant mortality rate in America. Yet, if the UK were the fifty-first state, it would be, by some estimates, poorer than Mississippi and certainly among the poorest five or six US states.[2]

By contrast, incomes in the neighbouring state of Arkansas are significantly higher, partly because the city of Bentonville is home to Walmart, the biggest retailer in the US. The company has brought both prosperity and full employment to the city with its 14,000 staff and about the same number of employees in suppliers' offices: it is a thriving place and one with a purpose. This demonstrates the 'home-town advantage' and applies to towns and cities hosting large and medium-sized companies all across America. In Bentonville, Alice Walton, daughter of Walmart founder Sam Walton, has spent hundreds of millions of dollars of her $64 billion fortune to create one of the best museums of American art. Her Crystal Bridges Museum of American Art employs 300 staff and houses important artworks and architecture from all over the US. In one case the museum bought a Frank Lloyd Wright house from New Jersey on the East Coast, dismantled it, drove the components 1,200 miles west, and reassembled the building in the museum grounds.

Company-supported towns follow a long-established tradition in the US. In 1900, 3 per cent of Americans lived in one of the hundreds of these towns, usually mining or logging settlements.[3] Later on, towns were established by individual companies for dam-building, mineral extraction or weapons manufacturing, and many of them flourished over extended periods. One such was Midland in Michigan, which has been the home of Dow Chemical Company since 1897; Dow has built libraries, gardens, parks, a museum of science and art, a tennis centre with 32 courts, and an Olympic-size ice rink in the city. These endowments are not just from the company: individual Dow family members have contributed, demonstrating the double advantage for a town of playing host to both the company and its shareholders.

Headquarters offices are usually good employers, paying above-average salaries, supporting nearby suppliers and often sponsoring local colleges. In Redmond City, Washington State, the median household income is about twice the US national average – mostly because it is the headquarters of Microsoft. Here the company has built 15 million square feet of office space – more than the total in the whole of Bristol or Glasgow. Even the smaller multinationals have a big impact on their home town: Nike's headquarters in Beaverton, Oregon, has 75 buildings spread over more than 300 acres, and, since 1990, when it settled there, the town's population has almost doubled to 100,000.[4] The local prosperity results from Nike's worldwide reach, including its 8 million UK customers.

Another north-western US town, Issaquah in Washington State, has boomed on the back of a business model that is transforming how people shop. Costco relocated there in 1995, and since then the population has quadrupled. In the UK, Costco has 29 stores, which already account for more sales than John Lewis, and they plan to increase the size of their UK business by 50 per cent over the next two years.[5] The company has strong ethical principles and its filed accounts show that, unlike many large corporations, it always pays its tax in full without using tax-avoidance tactics.[6] Naturally, the after-tax profit is sent back to Issaquah.

In these towns there is usually a symbiotic relationship between the company and the local council: together they build a community that attracts new employees. Such partnerships are seen in the West Coast towns of Mountain View (Google's headquarters) and Cupertino (Apple's headquarters), which have prosperous communities. This pattern runs right across the country, with IBM in Armonk outside New York, DuPont in Wilmington, Delaware, Eli Lilly in Indianapolis, Indiana, 3M in Maplewood, Minnesota, and thousands of others. This book often mentions a US company's home town as well as its home state to acknowledge the importance of location to Americans and the significance of the home-town advantage. The attraction of having headquarters in your city or town was shown in 2017 with the stampede created by Amazon's announcement that it was planning to establish a new hub, 'HQ2'. Reportedly, 238 cities in North America spent millions of dollars on bids offering tax breaks and promises of rapid permits for new building.[7] Amazon tantalisingly dangled the suggestion that it would be creating 50,000 highly paid jobs and investing $5 billion. US real estate agent Javier Vivas fully understood the advantages of winning: 'The city that gets selected will immediately see a boost to jobs and wages, pushing home values up and triggering new construction.'[8]

Dozens of US towns and cities also have a military home-town advantage. With 1.4 million Americans serving in the US armed forces, all across the country there are army, navy and air force bases supporting local economies. Fayetteville in North Carolina, San Diego in California and Norfolk in Virginia each have about 50,000 military personnel. In contrast, Britain has very few such towns, after slashing the size of its military over the last 30 years.

This home-town advantage was until recently the engine at the heart of many British communities. In the nineteenth century numerous towns and cities across the country flourished because of the wealth their inhabitants generated. Impressive classically styled art galleries and concert halls were established in cities such as Huddersfield, Bradford and Halifax. Almost all the industry that funded them has died away, leaving many buildings to stand sentry through the decline.

In other British towns the home-town advantage lasted longer. In 1824, Cadbury was established in Bournville, a suburb of Birmingham, where it went on to provide a stream of local bene- fits for 186 years: civic amenities, high-quality housing and good jobs for managers and researchers. That flow was stopped abruptly when it was taken over by Kraft in 2010 and its headquarters was moved to Chicago. Critics also claim that Kraft's takeover saw Cadbury tear up its formal commitments to fair trade, and it faced further allegations of failing to prevent child labour in its supply chain in 2022.[9]

No similar buyout has affected confectionery company Hershey, based on East Chocolate Avenue in an eponymous town in Pennsylvania.[10] Its founder used profits from the choco- late business to set up a nationally important school for orphans, and it continues to support its local community with golf courses, a stadium and several museums. Apart from Cadbury, scores of other headquarters have moved away from Britain and across to the US through acquisitions, such as that of Worldpay, which moved its operation from London to Cincinnati after being purchased in 2018. These takeovers tend to shift new directors' jobs out of the UK and into American home towns. In other cases the headquarters officially remains in the UK but critical functions are moved to the US. This happened with Inmarsat, the satellite company bought by California's Viasat in 2023, and Meggitt, the defence contractor, bought by Parker Hannifin of Cleveland, Ohio in 2022.[11]

Taking people as well as companies

Although the most important jobs are usually at the head office, American businesses do not just recruit locally: for top roles they want the best talent. To find it they have developed human resources departments focused on efficient recruitment. Gone are the gentlemanly arrangements of 30 years ago, when Oxford and Cambridge hosted annual 'milk rounds' for the largest UK employers to present their company and discreetly interview final-year students. In recent years this talent search process in the UK has been taken over by US companies, who adopt a more ruthless approach to finding the best students. They catch high-flyers early on, find the eager ones and select through internships as extended interviews.

One student, now in her early twenties, explains it: 'I couldn't see why my fellow students were so anxious to become officers of the Economics Society in their first year at university. They virtually climbed over each other to get nominated and elected. I soon discovered that this wasn't about love of the subject. Getting elected meant that you would almost certainly be given a "Spring Week" by one of the big US financial organisations.'[12]

A Spring Week is a short internship in the Easter holidays that often leads to a summer internship and then to a highly paid job.[13] This process gives US banks early access to students who are smart, ambitious and studying a relevant subject. This 'go get 'em' attitude to recruitment means that employers can start early, sift carefully and make themselves look attractive to work for. Three-quarters of US banks and finance companies who are hunting for graduates will offer second-year internships, and a good chunk of them even offer Spring Weeks to first-year students. Over half of their graduate vacancies are filled by those who have done an internship. Transplanted from the US, this shows the mindset of the multinationals: if it works in the homeland it will work for the offshore offices. European companies have tried to copy this approach, but they lag behind.

Among those offering Spring Weeks to British students are Goldman Sachs, Blackstone, BlackRock, Citibank and Morgan Stanley – all US companies expanding their European operations. Of course, the flip side is that it has turned many university societies into competitive job clubs, and the traditional 'milk round' of big employers pitching up late in the day for third-year students has been replaced by a scramble to latch on to good students as early as possible. Another recent graduate described how many of his contemporaries went off to join law firms or big accountancy firms fully intending to jump ship after two or three years to work for a US private equity house, which, they believe, is 'where you make the big money'.[14] Hearing about the possibility of a Spring Week is, for many students, the first time they have thought about employment, and it makes students 'think finance'. The universities themselves have been recruited as willing conduits to draw more graduates into the orbit of major US financial institutions.

It is not just company recruitment that has been affected. American universities are poachers of both academics and undergraduates. One senior lecturer at Oxford told me that she was attracted by an offer to move to Harvard because she would double her pay, receive much more administrative support, get free housing and have a higher social status. US universities are far better funded, as demonstrated by the imbalance between two prominent institutions: together Oxford and its 44 colleges have endowment funds of $7 billion, whereas Harvard alone has $53 billion.[15] Funding for research is similarly one-sided, with an army of philanthropic organisations supporting US universities. This funding has its own extractive dimension, with many US research funds seeking to generate IP which will usually become US-owned. And it goes further: US universities have set up satellite institutions in the UK to give their students a taste of Britain and of what Europe has to offer: for instance, at NYU London, 500 students can, according to the university's website, experience a semester of learning about UK business and international relations.[16]

Joe Spence, the master of Dulwich College, one of the top public schools in the UK, explained the university application process to me.

> We send many boys to the top universities in this country and across the world. Oxbridge has a tendency to act as though it has a monopoly on excellence. Its tutors seldom meet with us, which contrasts with the big US universities, who fly over to London and invite me to workshops, dinners and breakfasts, where their top people outline what's on offer, including paying the fees and living costs for British students, awarded on the basis of talent and/or need, including their flights to and from the US, as well as helping them find work experience or service engagement opportunities.

Last year I got two letters, coincidentally on the same day, each about one of our boys who had just accepted a university offer. One very warm letter was from Yale in Connecticut which said how excited they were to have our pupil join them and here was a book they'd like me to award him at our Speech Day on their behalf. They also offered a list of contacts and resources he could access while preparing for his course. The other was a far more formal letter from a Cambridge college about a second pupil who had accepted a place there. It asked if I had anything to report on his progress, told me to draw his attention to the college's expectations and they added they would be sending him a list of the books he'd have to read by October. The implication was that he was lucky to have secured a place, whereas US institutions thank their incoming undergraduates for choosing them. The contrast in tone could not have been sharper.[17]

The American hunger to find the best and be the best, coupled with Britain's economic decline, contributes to the decision by many astute people to make their lives in the US, and if they do ever return to the UK, they usually do so as American employees. The US has pulled gifted Brits across the Atlantic with powerful magnets: the pulse of the internet flows from Silicon Valley, the energy industry has its heart in Houston and the world's financial capital is New York. In addition, there is the international commodity centre in Chicago and the globe's film-making focal point in Hollywood. Each of these hubs drags many of the most talented people in their fields away from the UK.

Take the case of Cal Henderson, born in 1981, who grew up in Bedfordshire and went to university in Birmingham to study computing. He then emigrated to California, where he co-founded Flickr, and later built up Slack, the platform for programmers and other professionals to talk to each other.

Slack was sold to Salesforce for $28 billion, giving Henderson a personal payday of £500 million in 2020, but, he laments: 'It probably would have been impossible to start Slack in the UK... Because of the way we built the company, and the money that starting the kind of company like Slack requires, it's just not possible anywhere outside of [Silicon] Valley.'[18] His English eccentricities have not done him any harm: one of his early websites, www.cansleepwith.com, which tells people how old their ideal partner should be, is still running. He is known for wearing shorts whatever the weather, and invented all sorts of popular and unusual features on Slack. Cal is one of thousands of talented British economic migrants in Silicon Valley, many of whom work for tech companies like Slack.

Carting off the treasure

While the flight of talented individuals diminishes the UK's human capital, there has also been a steady transfer of historical treasures packed off in crates heading west. To staunch this flow, a legal mechanism was put in place to block exports of important artworks. It is a temporary pause and creates a chance for UK institutions to step in and buy at the market value – if they can afford it. In 2019, the J. Paul Getty Museum in Los Angeles agreed to pay £3.5 million for *Two Boys with a Bladder* (*c.*1769), an iconic work by the eighteenth-century painter Joseph Wright of Derby.[19] Painted during the Enlightenment, it shows two boys studying an inflated bladder and uses light and dark to remarkable effect. Helen Whately, the government's arts minister, claimed it was of 'paramount importance' that Wright's works be kept in the UK, and stated that she hoped a buyer could be found 'to save this masterpiece'.[20] Despite such statements and much publicity, however, no British institution had enough cash, and the painting was duly shipped off to California.

A similar fate seemed likely for Joshua Reynolds's masterpiece *Portrait of Omai* (*c.*1776), a painting of a young man in flowing white Tahitian dress who came back from Polynesia to Britain in 1774 with Captain Cook's second expedition. It is valued at £50 million. The National Portrait Gallery was able to raise only half the money needed, despite experts begging the government and others to contribute. In an unusual and face-saving manoeuvre the painting was bought jointly with that same Californian Getty Museum, and in 2026 it will be shipped over there in time for the 2028 Los Angeles Olympics.[21] These pictures are just two among thousands of artworks extracted from the UK every year, bought up by Britain's economic masters. For the last decade an annual haul of £5 billion worth of artworks has been bought by Americans and shipped across to the US.[22]

Moving the high street onto US platforms

Some British assets do not need to be bought up: they can simply be replaced by new ways of doing business. For many restaurants, the pandemic forced them to do business differently, and they followed their customers in signing up to the Deliveroo platform, paying commissions of between 25 and 35 per cent.[23] That rake-off was painful enough, but the delivery model undermines the viability of the high-street restaurants. It works like this: these platforms are the first stop for anyone ordering a takeaway meal, and the power to guide the customer, or supply them directly, has moved to the platforms. The restaurants can be sidestepped altogether: the platforms have created their own delivery-only food preparation factories, or 'dark kitchens', with a wide choice of meals being made on an industrial scale and delivered straight to the customer.[24] Now they own the relationship with the customer and no longer need to pay cycle couriers to schlep around to lots of different small restaurants cooking food in cramped conditions in congested city centres. As a result, many restaurants are going out of business, with the profits from the front end (ordering) and the back end (cooking) both moving to the takeaway-food platforms Deliveroo and Uber Eats. The pandemic period more than doubled the size of Deliveroo; its American founder and CEO, William Shu, confirms they are rapidly expanding their 'dark kitchens'. Amazon jumped into the mix by investing $575 million to buy a sixth of the company – a move originally blocked on competition grounds, but later approved by the UK's Competition and Markets Authority (CMA), on the basis that the business needed Amazon's support during the pandemic.[25]

In a similar way, Amazon, eBay and online shopping in general have driven many high-street shops into bankruptcy. Department stores have mostly disappeared. While it was inevitable that technology would change how people buy their goods and food, it was surely conceivable that the new suppliers would be British businesses. Travel agents have also mostly vanished, with their fate sealed by technology, but it was not inevitable that online travel bookings would predominantly be made through foreign companies Expedia (of Seattle), Airbnb (of San Francisco) and Booking.com (of Amsterdam).

In work, but also in poverty

In parallel with this continuing loss of high-street outlets, and the extraction of national artworks and talented people, the position of the broader population has become more perilous. Journalist

James Bloodworth went undercover for six months to experience what it is like to be one of the 2 million people who earn the minimum wage.[26] He worked sequentially as a carer, as an Uber driver, in a call centre and as a stock-picker in one of Amazon's warehouses. In every case he experienced a precarious lifestyle of zero-hours contracts at the minimum wage with insecure work, no work if he was ill, long days and tough conditions, and he described the misery of many he met who did not have any margin for error or any leeway to cope with unforeseen events. Bloodworth's conclusion is that 'our entire political vocabulary – *social mobility, bright but poor kids, grammar schools* – is geared towards pulling a few people out of the soup without changing its basic ingredients'. He is following the sentiments of the Scottish teacher and socialist John McLean, who said: 'Rise with your class, not out of it.'[27] Bloodworth's concern is not just about how a few can be pulled out of the soup, but about how many of them will become the packhorses for US multinationals. The question for the UK's low-pay workers is this: how can politics and negotiation effectively improve their position when the people in charge are distant – based on another continent – but with ever more influence over their jobs?

Britain's chancellors must wrestle with the same issue. On a macro scale, the UK economy has been transformed by the growth of the US multinationals, which are experts at minimising their tax contribution. And yet the UK's liabilities are large. In addition to official state borrowing, huge unfunded pension promises have been made to government employees and pension claimants. If both public service pensions and the state pension are treated as liabilities, the outstanding pension promises add up to more than £7 trillion, or £250,000 for each British household.[28] This enormous liability does not touch US corporations or Washington. It remains an entirely British problem, made harder to address for many reasons, including the low tax contribution from the US multinationals.

It has been received wisdom for several years that the number of Brits working for American firms matches the number of Americans with British bosses – about 1 million in each case. Indeed, in my interview with former Chancellor Philip Hammond in December 2020, he asserted exactly this equivalence. His claim was echoed three years later by the new US ambassador to London, Jane Hartley, who alighted on the 1 million figure. But the official IRS numbers contradict this, and if you include recent US acquisitions of UK businesses and the effect of the gig economy the numbers are far higher. The 2020 IRS statistics – the latest available – show that, on an official basis, the largest US multinationals employ 1,333,727 British workers, but that doesn't include the Brits working for the many smaller US employers.[29] And 2022 saw an extra 110,000 workers added by a single take-over, when US private equity won the bidding for Morrisons supermarkets.[30] On top of this, there are at least 400,000 gig economy workers, of whom more than 100,000 are making deliveries working through platforms like Amazon Flex.[31] Added to these are the 70,000-plus Uber drivers who were nominally self-employed until 2021.[32] It is reasonable to extrapolate that more than 2 million Brits work for US organisations, or about twice the figure casually estimated by establishment figures on both sides of the Atlantic. Beyond this, there are also all those Brits working for enterprises whose contracts depend on US firms. This illustrates the degree to which US dominance in employment is underplayed by the Westminster government, which has made no effort to work out the true numbers, or how rapidly they are growing. What we do know is that the British government pays many billions to US suppliers every year to buy back the labour of its own citizens.

For anyone doubting the US focus on the UK, they could look at the IRS statistics for other European countries, which show that American companies employ more Brits than the total of all of those whom they employ in France, Germany, Italy and Spain combined.[33] As well as a loss of control, British workers are significantly less well paid than German or French workers.[34]

While the number of workers being paid at or below the minimum wage is growing (14 per cent in 2021), the real value of the minimum wage is being eroded by inflation and higher taxes. Inflation has been crueller to lower-paid workers because the prices of essentials such as food and energy have risen most, while the tax-free allowance and minimum wage have not risen in line with living costs. Easing the position of the low paid will be harder with a tax base diminished by foreign ownership, and with so little influence over the US corporations that employ so many who are both working and living in poverty.

Inevitably a relationship in which one party holds almost all the power becomes asymmetric in many ways. Britain feels poorer in many ways, and is losing control of its people, its businesses, its assets, its data and its destiny. Despite this, our politicians tell us that we are 'world-beating'.

11

THE AMERICAN WAY

After all, the chief business of the American people is business. They are profoundly concerned with producing, buying, selling, investing and prospering in the world.

– Calvin Coolidge, 1925[1]

Whisky, Scotch beef and lamb, 'Test and Trace' Covid-19 testing, and even company registry services are all fields in which British politicians say their nation is 'world-beating'.[2] British government statements chant it and Labour's economic proposals brandish it because, we are told, the UK is a nation rich with 'world-beating innovators and entrepreneurs' – but, even if British creativity is written across the face of civilisation, Britain is not 'beating' the world.[3] America is.

Even in sectors with thriving British companies, America is usually winning. And, more tellingly, when British businesses are genuinely successful, that success is often underpinned by American money and acumen: transatlantic cash runs thick through the UK economy, almost everything operates on American software, and Amazon Web Services (AWS) underpins our 'world-beating' company registry.

There is urgency in shrugging off political boasts about British pre-eminence because they disguise what a 'world-beating' nation really looks like in the twenty-first century: it is one where just 4 per cent of the world's population own a quarter of the world's assets. And UK consumers love American products: iPhones, Teslas, Coke, Disney and Instagram. How does America do it?

Hard work and working in systems

One ingredient of US success is certainly demographic: the workforce has increased by 30 per cent in only 30 years, and the people are, on average, six years younger than those in Europe: in a very literal sense, Britain is part of the 'old world'. Americans are also more than twice as likely to relocate for work.

Sheer hard work is also a factor in America's achievements. A typical US worker puts in 200 more hours annually than a European. The commitment to getting the job done is also demonstrated by how much paid holiday employees take: typically, 75 per cent of British staff use up all their paid holidays, while only about 50 per cent of American workers do.

Fanatical working is encouraged by the titans of US business. Michael Bloomberg, the New York-based media entrepreneur who transformed the world of financial information, says: 'I am not smarter than anybody else but I can out-work you – and my key to success for you, or anybody else is make sure you are the first one in there every day and the last one to leave. Don't ever take a lunch break or go to the bathroom, you keep working.'[4] In the same vein, Jeff Bezos of Amazon used to tell new employees: 'You can work long, hard or smart, but at Amazon you can't choose two out of three.'[5] Elon Musk demands commitment and inspires by example, sleeping in his factories and often working a 120-hour week, explaining: 'However hard it was for them, I would make it worse for me.'[6]

Musk goes further. In 2022, he talked admiringly of the even more demanding work culture in China: 'There is just a lot of super talented hardworking people in China who strongly believe in manufacturing,' he said. 'They won't just be burning the midnight oil, they will be burning the 3am oil, they won't even leave the factory type of thing, whereas in America people are trying to avoid going to work at all.'[7]

Not that it is necessary for all workers to travel to work any more. US technology has enabled the never-ending workday. Laptops and smartphones initially allowed work to be taken home, and then on holiday, and eventually everywhere. Leaving the workplace no longer means leaving work.

When the most successful people in the US tell others to work hard and then provide them with the technology to do it, workers listen. America's employment report on full-time work showed that they worked for 43 hours each week in 2022, while, in the UK, the average figure is 36.5 hours – hundreds fewer hours each year.[8] But there are additional drivers pushing people to work long hours: economic incentives, corporate culture, as well as deep psychological reasons, including guilt, ambition, greed and perhaps one other, namely, America's own culture of competition and success.[9]

Nearly half the nation has little or no reservation about embracing competition in all its forms – far more than Britain or the rest of Europe. Striving to be ever better runs so deeply in the nation's psyche that even Alexis de Tocqueville, in the 1830s, described the American in this way: 'Forever seeking – forever falling, to rise again – often disappointed, but not discouraged – he tends unceasingly towards that unmeasured greatness so indistinctly visible at the end of the long track which humanity has yet to tread.'[10]

He may not be Tocqueville, but Donald Trump was reaching for the same spring of thought when he told his prospective voters: 'If I'm President, we will win on everything we do.'[11] He received rousing cheers in South Carolina rather than the arched eyebrows with which the Brits would, at their most polite, respond. But the competition that America excels at, which cuts across political divides and is the source of the nation's power, is not politics, it is competitive business, and that is about more than long hours: it is about developing systems of success, which include innovation and risk-taking, efficiency, defending company rights and fostering customer loyalty.

'There's a better way to do it – find it' – Thomas Edison

With 1,093 patents to his name, including for the light bulb, recorded sound, radio and motion pictures, Thomas Edison is considered to be the most significant inventor and industrialist of all time. One estimate suggests that his inventions are still responsible for $8–12 trillion of global productivity today, and one reason is that his most critical invention was the modern industrial research laboratory.[12] Edison created 'R & D' and, with it, an R & D culture in America funded by public and private capital. Today, US innovators are surrounded by a supportive environment that can offer hard cash. Investment comes from venture capitalists as well as the US government: the National Institutes of Health (NIH) alone award annual grants of $45 billion towards R & D.[13]

Innovation through US defence spending has led to inventions that have both transformed modern life and powered the US multinationals. Military spending led to the early development of satellites, drones and night vision. And US defence spending also created Kevlar, Teflon, better weather forecasting and nuclear power, each of which has been used widely in civilian life. But that is tip-of-the-iceberg stuff: military research has also empowered the big US tech companies through the sponsorship by the Department of Defense (DoD) of high-capacity batteries, digital cameras, speech recognition, faster computers, virtual reality, biometrics and GPS.

Going back to 1969, military researchers also contributed to the ARPANET, the precursor to the internet. In 1983, the ARPANET was split into two networks: one for the military and one for civilian use, so that the word 'internet' had its first use as a way to describe the interlinking of these two early networks.

US institutions have been prolific innovators. Massachusetts Institute of Technology (MIT) is affiliated with 100 Nobel laureates and has made dozens of advances, including in radar technology and encryption. The Bell Labs research project, run for many decades by AT&T, the telecoms giant, was responsible for the development of transistors, lasers and solar cells, and was also the birthplace of 'information theory', which underpins all our digital computing and telecommunications.[14] Such organisations have contributed to a culture of enterprise linked to the commercial world and leading directly to new products and processes.

Many other government agencies allocate funding at scale, such as the National Science Foundation (NSF), but even so the bulk of applied R & D funding comes from commercial corporations.

US spending on R & D and its workforce

In total, the US spends 3.4 per cent of its GDP on R & D – which for many years was double the UK's rate. But the actual numbers are stark. In 2020, the US spent $717 billion, while the UK spent only a tenth of that – some $90 billion.[15] But it is not just about the money: it is structure and geography, too. The US has encouraged the creation of innovation hubs and clusters, where tech companies, venture capital firms and research institutions can create ecosystems for entrepreneurs. Apart from Silicon Valley and the cities of New York and Los Angeles, there are also major hubs growing in Boston, Seattle and Austin. And, while the UK is trying to follow suit in Cambridge and London, it has decades of catching up to do.

America also invests in developing its workforce. Compared to the average of all OECD countries, the US spends 37 per cent more on schooling, resulting in a workforce with a higher percentage of graduates (34 per cent), and its universities are the best in the world.[16] A typical ranking of the world's top universities suggests that a significant majority are American.[17] US financial heft has enabled the creation of universities for education and innovation, as demonstrated by the foundation of Stanford University. When the only son of Senator Leland Stanford and his wife Jane died of typhoid fever in 1884, at the age of 15, the family used their wealth to buy land on the San Francisco peninsula, eventually acquiring 8,000 acres, where they established a new university, with the idea that 'the children of California shall be our children'.[18] Stanford is now ranked third in the world, having produced 36 Nobel Prize winners and 18 Turing Award winners, and was the meeting place for the co-founders of Google. It has been a nursery for other enterprises too: its alumni and affiliates set up Netflix, Snapchat, Nike, Hewlett-Packard (HP), Sun Microsystems, Instagram, PayPal and Yahoo.

As well as educating workers, the US is determined to find innovative people and draw them to its shores using immigration policy. The 'American Competitiveness in the 21st Century Act'

(2000) allows up to 85,000 highly qualified employees each year to get visas to stay for three years, extendable to six.[19] Lawmakers are savvy about how to optimise this, and they make 20,000 of these visas available for foreign graduates of US universities. In all cases the permits (H-1B visas) are tied to a sponsoring employer. This also means wages can be kept under control: foreign employees, once in the US, cannot just go after a better-paid job. In total there are now over half a million highly qualified foreign workers relying on these visas.[20]

America takes a very different approach to risk too. Britain shames people who fail financially: there is a stigma attached to 'going skint', and the government is careful to publish the names of the insolvent in the *London Gazette*. But, early in their careers, Henry Ford and Walt Disney both went bankrupt, and so did several businesses of future president Donald Trump. Perhaps because America cherishes competition, it also understands failure. Edison certainly did. His biographer Leonard DeGraaf, who is also an archivist at the Thomas Edison National Historical Park, explains the difference in attitude: 'Edison's not a guy that looks back. Even for his biggest failures he didn't spend a lot of time wringing his hands and saying "Oh my God, we spent a fortune on that." He said, "we had fun spending it."'[21]

Like Edison, even after triumphing many of the most successful US entrepreneurs continue taking risks and investing in new enterprises and keep building their wealth – one reason that more than a quarter of the world's 2,700 billionaires are American.[22]

The American take on intellectual property

The patent laws are not now made to encourage monopolies of what before belonged to others, or to the public, which is the true idea of a monopoly, but the design is to encourage genius in advancing the arts, through science and ingenuity, by protecting its productions of what did not before exist, and of what never belonged to another person, or the public.

– Justice Charles L. Woodbury, 1845[23]

In summing up one of the early IP cases in US jurisprudence – which concerned cotton-weaving technology developed by one factory and used by another – Justice Woodbury neatly encapsulated how the defence of IP and R & D are closely linked in America. It would be unthinkable for companies to invest as they do in new technology if it could be adopted without cost by their competitors.

Today, whether as films made by Netflix, software that Snapchat relies on or the brands Nike promotes, US researchers and businesspeople will go to almost any lengths to protect their IP rights: their universities and companies claim the lion's share of the world's patents. Seventeen per cent of all patent applications worldwide are made by Americans.[24] Like all inventors they fear that others will steal their ideas, and they fight fiercely to protect their creative output and its potential to generate abnormal profits. For anyone doing business with Americans, non-disclosure agreements (NDAs) are a part of daily life – safeguarding ideas before they are even shared. An illustration of how American business values IP rights is the number of US patent lawyers: 37,000, against just 2,600 in the UK, so on a per-head basis about three times as many.[25]

The US multinationals make no secret of their ambition to use IP protection to sell their wares across the globe: company slogans often spell out the breadth of their ambition. IBM claims to be working for a 'smarter planet'; Procter & Gamble's mission statement is about improving the lives of 'the world's consumers'; and the storytellers at Disney claim they have created the 'Happiest Place on Earth'.[26]

There is a vital point about US business that is sometimes overlooked: the most profitable, high-margin businesses tend to be those in which, once the sale is made, the company still owns what it just sold. Films, media, software and online games are all like this. The company sells a copy – and the copying costs are virtually zero – and that is all the buyer gets, with no right to sell it on. Free of significant reproduction costs, these businesses are almost infinitely scalable and can grow at speed, and for all of them it is critical to have protection through strong IP rights.

A company like Disney is constantly creating new IP, but it also makes its older brands work hard. A former Disney executive in London, Paul Barber, described the power of brand ownership: 'At Disney we were mostly doing licensing deals so in a sense we didn't actually sell anything – but printing a Mickey Mouse or a *Toy Story* picture on a bag of sweets ratchets up the price the retailer can charge. Licensing is all about legal rights and Disney, like most US companies, is dominated by lawyers.'[27]

Before a new Disney film is even released, the licensing machine is cranked up and deals are done to generate royalty income. Visiting McDonald's, children have come to expect a free gift of a plastic toy, usually a Disney character – a symbiotic partnership that gives Disney millions in income and has helped to build customer loyalty for the fast-food chain. There is little space in these partnerships for small or local firms, and these tie-ins are often done across multiple 'territories', as countries outside the US are called. These deals will be between US multinationals, as with another McDonald's partnership: almost all of its drinks are supplied by Coca-Cola.[28] In creating new films and merchandising their characters, Disney looks for the holy grail of building 'evergreen' characters. Evergreens have generated tens of billions of dollars, and can either be home-grown, like Mickey Mouse, or bought in, like Winnie-the-Pooh, for whom Disney acquired the rights in 2001.[29] Other evergreens are *Star Wars*, the various princesses (Ariel from *The Little Mermaid*, Snow White – and officially eleven others), *The Lion King* and Marvel characters: in business terms, these are the gifts that keep on giving. Consumers want their old favourites: the persistence of the big American brands is matched by the loyalty of Disney's customers.

Authorities on both sides of the Atlantic have escalated copyright infringements into criminal offences and work tirelessly to protect the assets of the US multinationals. Beyond direct action, UK authorities apply resources to throttle any infringing websites by cutting off their lifeblood: in 2022, the City of London Police's 'Operation Creative' stopped advertisers from supporting websites that break copyrights.[30] The police asked the payment processors, such as Visa, Mastercard and PayPal, to withhold services for websites suspected of infringing copyrights, patents or trademarks.

The science of efficiency

> The principal object of management should be to secure the maximum prosperity for the employer, coupled with the maximum prosperity for each employee.
>
> – Frederick Winslow Taylor, 1911[31]

In reaching across the world to dominate the markets in goods and services, Americans have made efficient production into a science. This started with Frederick Winslow Taylor. As a young man in 1881, Taylor and his future brother-in-law Clarence Clark entered the first ever tennis doubles tournament of the US Open, and won it. Although it was only a hobby, Taylor said that becoming a tennis champion gave him a feel for efficient movement along with a taste for winning.

The pair went on to apply their skills to managing the steelworks at Midvale in Philadelphia, wrestling with the challenge of cutting costs and increasing output at the same time. It was here that Taylor developed his passion for working out how to improve efficiency, which he called 'scientific management'.

Later, working at Bethlehem Steel in Pennsylvania, Taylor noticed that workers used the same shovels for all materials, something he thought was inefficient. He proved that the most effective load for a shovel was 21.5 pounds, so he found a shovel for each material that would scoop up that exact amount. Other experiments led to training the workers to follow his guidelines on how to move their tools. This was based on a careful analysis, breaking down the way they moved into component parts. As the workers were paid by what they produced, they welcomed his ideas, which won over the managers too. His approach was widely praised and copied. He was, as the management consultant Peter Drucker commented, 'the first man in recorded history who deemed work deserving of systematic observation and study'.[32]

Drucker would push these ideas on, creating his own rules of management, which were influential across America in the post-war period of the 1950s and 1960s by emphasising decentralised task-setting, and creating common goals between workers and managers. Another Taylor disciple, Henry Gantt, used these ideas to develop the 'Gantt Chart', a graphical representation of activity against time, and Harvard offered a degree in business management whose first-year curriculum was based on Taylor's methods. In each sector, someone pursued the principles of scientific management: Frank Gilbreth applied them to construction and Harrington Emerson did the same in the railroad industry.

This way of thinking became further embedded when James McKinsey, a business professor at the University of Chicago, and the founder of consulting firm McKinsey & Company, advocated 'Taylorism', as it became known.

A typical set of experiments exploring how to increase productivity were the 'Hawthorne studies' of the late 1920s.[33] Intended to work out the optimum level of lighting in factories, these ended up proving something quite different: researchers found that productivity increased when lighting levels were turned up, but surprisingly also when the lights were turned down, revealing that workers' awareness of being tested was enough to push up their productivity. In another counter-intuitive study involving lighting, a group of workers was given the choice of the level of lighting, and this increased productivity significantly: being given some control over their environment was enough to improve their output.

The cat was out of the bag for treating work seriously and producing outsized returns in relation to effort. Right through the twentieth century America developed many new systems for better processes and management. 'Lean manufacturing' sought to streamline production and reduce waste; 'Six Sigma' was developed by Motorola to improve quality in a systematic way; and 'performance metrics' made sure that key performance indicators (KPIs) were measured.[34] American businesses developed a 'continuous improvement culture' encouraging all employees to look for opportunities to solve problems and improve efficiency, and 'agile methodologies' allowed iterative and incremental improvements to efficiency.[35] Other countries copied, but only very slowly, and they were almost always behind the US curve and forced to play catch-up.

Even when another country developed a good idea, such as Japan's 'just-in-time' stock management, the US drive for efficiency meant these new techniques were assimilated quickly and widely into American ways of working.[36] Productivity was being pursued in a second-order way: the US had even optimised the way in which its corporations adopted optimising strategies.

Building customer loyalty and walled gardens

Give the lady what she wants.

– Marshall Field

In his time, Marshall Field (1834–1906) was infamous for his tyrannical approach to the staff in his department store empire, but he is now remembered as the father of quality retailing. Patrons of his Chicago stores received a slew of customer service privileges, including standardised pricing and unconditional refunds. Field had moved to the city to make his fortune and, by the 1890s, was its richest man – because he offered better service.[37] And, even today, the best US businesses simply offer customers better products with more features and more reliability than they can receive anywhere else. But there is one difference between the 'customer is king' approach of Field, John Wanamaker and other nineteenth-century retailers and the likes of Amazon. Today, US businesses lock customers into relationships from which it is hard to escape.

We live in an age in which the notion of the 'loyalty scheme' has been developed to a point of near perfection. The first trading stamps were introduced in 1891 as the 'Blue Stamp Trading System'; then came cut-out carton lids from Betty Crocker, direct mail, frequent-flyer miles, loyalty cards and finally loyalty apps, which offer substantial discounts in exchange for hoovering up customer data. Online, users are forced to buy compatible services where competitors' offerings will not work. Word, Excel and

LinkedIn each draw users into the Microsoft world, and an owner of any Apple device will be pulled into an ecosystem of products controlled from Cupertino, California. As tech commentator John Battelle said when Facebook listed shares publicly in 2012: 'The old internet is shrinking and being replaced by walled gardens.'[38]

The same psychology that keeps customers in walled gardens also promotes the 'razor and blades' model on which many US vendors rely. A desirable piece of hardware – such as a razor or printer – is sold cheaply, sometimes below cost, so that consumers are forced to source the consumables, such as blades or cartridges, from the same supplier. On this basis, Gillette has built up high-margin, recurring revenues now worth over $6 billion a year.[39]

This system of locking people into buying consumables is now widespread, and US firms are always looking to establish this kind of dependency. The cost of recharging a Tesla car on a motorway is much more per kilowatt hour than charging it at home, in another version of the 'razor and blades' business model. With more than 1,000 superchargers spread across the UK and installations accelerating, Tesla's recurring income is speeding along.[40]

Lock-ins like this also generate streams of monopoly profits in many industrial markets. One businessman in London told me how his suppliers tie him in: 'If I buy a generator from Cummins, based in Indiana, I can't get it repaired by anyone else – it needs their software and spare parts. No one else will touch it and I end up paying many times the original cost. I'm a captive of my US suppliers – people just don't realise how much the Americans do business differently from the Europeans. It is ruthless. Personally they are friendly but you will get the dollars sucked out of you.'

A favourite strategy for US firms is the creation of 'category killers', in which an overwhelmingly dominant product is developed. Once established, these build momentum and many self-reinforcing characteristics. For instance, the Fitbit and the Kindle, both from the US West Coast, have become the leaders in their respective fields. Because of high sales volumes, manufacturing costs plummet, leading to higher margins, and in turn the sales throw off plenty of revenue to improve the products ahead of competitors. Other successful category killers are the GoPro and the iPhone. By 2023, the latter had captured more than 50 per cent of the UK's smartphone market.[41]

The American way, then, has a singular focus on competition and triumph in business. Staff work hard and are driven by competition, while the companies invest in ideas and people and ruthlessly defend their market position. Work is made to be efficient and, crucially, customers are entranced and then entrapped as far as possible in long-standing and profitable relationships. All this has been seeded and then grown in the British economy, where each US company has similar objectives: to find engines of profit and then pull them apart, merge them or supercharge them to create further growth. That is why Britain's new boss is not Bill Gates, Jeff Bezos or Mark Zuckerberg. It is not an individual or partnership, but the US corporation itself – an entity perfectly positioned to dominate any market in which it competes.

Backed by the largest economy in the history of the world, staffed by managers who train and compete for supremacy over decades, US corporations approach efficiency with scientific ruthlessness and patiently invest time and resources to dominate their competition. And British businesses have struggled to compete with these engineers of process and finance. Even when Britain's businesses achieve dramatic innovations and create popular products or services, US corporations can out-compete them, or are allowed to just buy them up.

They have found ways to build their profits with treadmills and inertia, with monopolies and mergers, and through borrowing and squeezing. While US corporations may not have consciously

planned to turn Britain into a vassal state, the effects of their commercial prowess, combined with UK policy-makers' open-armed
welcome, has produced exactly that result. As Denny Ludwell said
almost 100 years ago: 'Herbert Hoover saw the future America as
a new type of empire, an economic world empire, built on business
efficiency, held together by lines of trade and credit, penetrating
all nations and cutting under other empires.'[42]

Again and again, political language about success and identity
in the UK flatters to deceive or, in the case of 'world-beating', creates complacency and evades hard questions about what is going
on – about the rules and ideas that are shaping the UK's business culture, economic policies, work and investments. Successive
Westminster governments have allowed US corporations – and
Washington – to become the puppeteers while pretending that
the British remain autonomous.

12

PUPPET MASTERS

I've often been asked… 'What do they think of us over there?'
The answer, not very flattering to our pride, is that they scarcely
think about us at all.

— E. M. Forster[1]

Colin Cherry was a British scientist with ideas ahead of his time.
As professor of telecommunications at Imperial College in the
1950s, he anticipated the issues of a more connected world, raised
the possibility of 'world government by television' and lectured on
the issues of citizens losing control of their private information.[2]
One of his more unusual notions was that car accidents arose
because of poor communication between drivers, and in a 1963
newspaper article he advocated that all cars should be fitted with
radio transmitters with a range of 100 metres. However, Cherry's
great legacy was to work out how people pick out important
information from a background hubbub. He made a remarkable
discovery, known as the 'cocktail party effect', where he showed
that partygoers can focus their attention to hear only a single
discussion. They will tune into that conversation and be able to
ignore other chatter even when it is at louder volumes. But it turns

out that when certain words or ideas are expressed in other conversations, listeners cannot stop themselves from hearing what is said. This occurs when their own name is mentioned, or if there is anything overtly sexual or taboo. In the title of his seminal paper, Cherry refers to 'recognition of speech, with one and two ears'.[3] He ran his experiments by putting headphones on his subjects with different soundtracks running into each ear.

American politicians and officials must feel they are permanently at a noisy cocktail party, and most of the time they are listening with only one ear. But when anything is said that affects their vital interests, they hear loud and clear, with both ears, including when the UK discusses its foreign policy, its trade deals or how multinationals are taxed and regulated. In January 2020, President Trump heard about UK Treasury plans to introduce a Digital Services Tax (DST) to capture some of the profits made by US companies in the UK. He had previously stated: 'We tax our companies, they don't tax our companies.'[4] As we have seen, eventually the British dropped the DST entirely.

The 'cocktail party effect' was in play when President Biden heard about the Irish need to retain a soft border with Northern Ireland. American interests were at stake, not just because of the large Irish American population in the US, but also because Ireland is home to many US multinationals. Biden flexed his muscles by tweeting: 'Any trade deal between the US and the UK must be contingent upon respect for the agreement and preventing the returning of a hard border.'[5] He was straining against the principle of non-interference in the affairs of other sovereign nations but fully reinforcing the rule of paying attention to US interests, and then protecting them.

The US is listening more closely in the UK these days. The number of staff working at the US embassy in London has risen by more than 40 per cent since 2001, from 700 to more than 1,000 by 2023.[6] This is not because of simple diplomacy, but rather because Britain is home to an ever-growing list of US-owned businesses and, since the 1920s, the US government has worked hard to protect the interests of US commerce – as any American voter would hope and expect.

One hostile French perspective is that US diplomatic support for business extends much further than a growing roster of embassy staff. Former French government minister Arnaud Montebourg argues that Americans use pseudo-military tools to wage economic warfare:

> First of all, they use all the listening and intelligence systems that they built on after 9/11… they listen to foreign companies that compete with theirs… it became clear in 2014 when [Edward] Snowden revealed that there were 75 million conversations and emails that had been exploited by the NSA [National Security Agency] on France, on French companies… Second, they have a tool called extraterritorial law. The Americans are using a form of law, which is an imperialist law, which consists in declaring themselves competent for matters which in no way concern them… They declare themselves policeman of the world by undermining the sovereign interests. They do it in all fields, and especially the economic field.[7]

Montebourg claims the Americans use International Traffic in Arms Regulations (ITAR) to advance their economic interests. The US, he says, has set a list of 22,000 components whose export by a foreign power it has awarded itself the right to authorise – or block. If a French manufacturer buys a varnish made in the US to put on the wing of a French fighter plane, the Americans will limit the countries to which the plane can be exported. No export is allowed to any country which is an enemy of the US. 'Why,' asks Montebourg, 'should I care if [the buyer is] an enemy of the United States of America?'[8]

Montebourg should know that the answer to his question is four letters long: 'NATO', but he has other complaints, including about the Patriot Act of 2001.[9] According to him, this US law says that when a French company is bought by an American company, the US government has the unilateral power to request any and all information from the newly acquired company: about patents, technologies and people. This came to a head with the attempted takeover of Segault, the maker of valves for the French nuclear submarines. Montebourg was so outraged by the intelligence this law would transfer to the Americans that he blocked the takeover and insisted the company be sold to Canadians. 'It is not an issue to work with Canadians. But Americans are different because they are predators.'[10]

It is an incendiary viewpoint, heavy with political claims about predation and imperialism, but Montebourg can hardly argue the French government does not aggressively defend and advance its own interests at a cost to other nations. Britain has long tried to do the same; the problem is that, very often, its political leaders make such a mess of it.

The China problem

Consider the Huawei case. For some years, both Britain and the US relied on the Chinese telecoms giant to provide some of their underpinning mobile phone network hardware. And, for even longer, there have been serious concerns about Chinese espionage, and specifically the loss of intellectual property from both British and American industry to Chinese hacking, in accordance with China's policy of 'forced technology transfer' (FFT). This risk, which was real, was routinely considered but did not prevent the buying of Chinese products for critical infrastructure in both countries. Then, suddenly, things changed.

Elected on a policy of trade protectionism with particularly critical views on China, Donald Trump erected trade barriers against America's Far Eastern rival. Then, in 2020, with trade tensions rising, the US government announced that Chinese mobile telephony manufacturer Huawei was now a security threat and suggested to the British that they ban all its products, which put the UK government on the spot. Initially, UK justice secretary Robert Buckland declared: 'The decision we make will be based upon our own sovereign right to choose… We will make an informed decision based on the evidence, and we will do so in an autonomous way.'[11] Prime minister Boris Johnson pointed out that 'the British public deserves access to the best possible technology', and officials said a ban on Huawei would delay the UK's 5G roll-out by two to three years, increasing costs to consumers and harming economic growth.[12]

After a long meeting, the Cabinet decided it would stick with Huawei and just exclude Chinese kit from core parts of the telecoms network and from sensitive areas such as nuclear and military facilities. The establishment was happy: Nicky Morgan, Secretary of State for Digital, Culture, Media and Sport, announced that this was a 'UK-specific solution for UK-specific reasons' and that it allowed the UK to 'seize the huge opportunities of 21st-century technology'.[13] Ciaran Martin, chief executive of the National Cyber Security Centre (NCSC), chimed in: 'This package will ensure that the UK has a very strong, practical and technically sound framework for digital security in the years ahead.'[14]

So the Brits had made up their minds decisively: there was an acceptable level of risk in continuing to work with Huawei in this more limited way, just as the US had done previously. But what did the Americans think of it? On hearing the news of the British decision, Donald Trump phoned Boris Johnson and was reported to be 'apoplectic'.[15] In a tweet, former speaker of the US House of Representatives Newt Gingrich described it as a strategic defeat for his country.[16] This was a challenge to the Americans' authority; they set about reversing a very public decision, one that had been made at the highest level and fully endorsed by the British security establishment. They applied pressure at four points: the prime minister, Conservative MPs, the security services and British public opinion.

A few days after the British decision, the US ambassador to Germany spoke very publicly: 'Donald Trump just called me from AF1 [Air Force One] and instructed me to make clear that any nation who chooses to use an untrustworthy 5G vendor will jeopardise our ability to share intelligence and information at the highest level.'[17] This was sabre-rattling at its loudest and an implicit demand that the UK reverse its decision and comply with US wishes.

Tim Morrison, a US official, urged MPs to rebel: 'There is still time for backbenchers in both parties to save the special relationship and the privacy rights of Britons if they vote to block this mistake by the government.'[18] A group of 60 Conservative rebels were led by Iain Duncan Smith, who said: 'There's a lot more pressure to come.'[19] Another MP said: 'The fightback is on.' Even the normally discreet chair of Parliament's Defence Committee, Tobias Ellwood, acknowledged US interference: 'There is no doubt that we feel the pressure from the United States.'[20]

Within a short time, the Americans got what they wanted. In a humiliating U-turn the UK government left it to a junior minister, Oliver Dowden, to announce: 'Following US sanctions against Huawei and updated technical advice from our cyber experts, the government has decided it is necessary to ban Huawei from our

5G networks… No new [Huawei] kit is to be added from January 2021, and the UK 5G networks will be Huawei-free by the end of 2027.'[21]

While most US officials would have accepted their victory quietly, Donald Trump is not known for either modesty or subtlety, and he decided to spell it out: 'I talked many countries out of using [Huawei equipment]. If they want to do business with us, they can't use it.'[22]

In a sort of victory lap, the US Secretary of State, Mike Pompeo, then visited the UK in July 2020 to tell Boris Johnson to fall fully behind the US in the challenge to China, and he went out of his way to meet up with the group of Tory MPs who had supported the American position: the US might well need their help again. Having forced the UK's hand, Pompeo tried to pretend it had been Britain's idea all along: 'We support those sovereign choices. We think "well done".'[23]

There are, of course, credible reasons to be sceptical about Chinese state-linked technology companies, but these are not new. What the Huawei incident illustrates, however, is that these issues become decisive in Britain not when elected UK officials decide they matter, but when the US says so. A hard reality of US power was revealed by the incident: mostly, Washington is happy for the British to have their own conversations and make their own decisions, and there is no need for the US to show its teeth, but if the Brits act against perceived US interests, American diplomats go to work, even threatening 'the special relationship'. It demonstrated the language of partnership coupled with the actions of control.

The targeting of Chinese technology extends far beyond Huawei too. Debates about banning Chinese-owned TikTok are about markets as well as security: it has been calculated that by totally excluding TikTok from the US and UK the authorities would boost the value of TikTok's American competitors by as much as $400 billion (mostly helping Meta, Snap and YouTube).[24] The UK government tried to support the US by banning the app on official phones. Australia did the same, but the platform was so popular that politicians started using 'burner' phones to get access, and in the end the government gave up. More widely, the MAMAA companies – the big five of US tech – fear competition in markets such as the UK from the Chinese tech firms Tencent, Baidu, Alibaba and Xiaomi. By making the British toe the line over Huawei, the Americans have made it more likely that they can protect other markets against the Chinese. Britain is not just caught in the crossfire of an American trade dispute: it is obliged to make common cause against the Chinese. And, typically, it has got into a mess as a result.

One can see Britain's dilemma. It has warmly accepted Chinese investment since the 1990s, when the US initiated trade liberalisation with China. This culminated in not just the use of Huawei products in mobile infrastructure, but much more. Between 2010 and 2020, successive British governments brought Chinese technologies into the heart of the UK's critical infrastructure.[25] The China General Nuclear Corporation (CGN) was even permitted to take stakes in nuclear reactors under development. None of this was a problem in an era of liberal trade with China. Former prime minister David Cameron was even appointed vice chair of a £1 billion China–UK investment fund upon leaving office. Defenders of the British state's previous position might argue that risks were balanced, that the UK should not shun China and that, in any case, it was only following the lead of the US, where, for example, Westinghouse Corporation has been a long-time supplier of nuclear technology to China. Fast forward to 2024, however, and more than a decade of policy-making appears to have been made in complete error. Huawei is banned from the 5G network; the British government is increasingly nervous about

Chinese involvement in nuclear projects; and Cameron's investment fund is said by the Parliament's Intelligence and Security
Committee (ISC) to have been engineered by the Chinese state.[26]
Britain has been caught on the wrong side of a fractious, complex
and increasingly tense geopolitical reorganisation led by Sino-
American relations. Unable to plot a coherent and independent
course, it is forced to backpedal frantically.

Trade policy, and sucking businesses out of Europe

Where the US flexes its muscles most visibly is in trade policies:
much of Donald Trump's protectionism has been fully adopted by
his successor Joe Biden. The latter's so-called Inflation Reduction
Act of August 2022 has very little to do with inflation: even
the Congressional Budget Office (CBO) said it would have no
measurable effect on inflation.[27] Instead, it has everything to do
with subsidising American industry at the expense of the UK
and Europe: the $400 billion of energy and climate measures
will suck yet more industry towards the US. It offers irresist-
ible subsidies, but only to firms which manufacture in North
America. As a result, in early 2023 Tesla decided to move its
new battery plant from Europe to the US, and Volkswagen, with
an incentive of at least €9 billion, has put on hold its plans for a
battery factory in Eastern Europe, deciding instead to focus on
production in the US.[28] The *Financial Times* reported a similar
subsidy that drove Northvolt to move a battery-making facility
from Germany to the US.[29] It has also affected other important
emerging green energy industries where Joe Biden has created
a magnet to draw companies across the Atlantic: in the clean
hydrogen sector, HydrogenOne Capital has decided to relocate
much of its work from London to the US, and new subsidies will

ensure that carbon capture will mostly be developed in the US. These are the spoils of wealth being used determinedly to ensure that America controls the future. With incentives on this scale at work, Britain can only look on with envy.

Straining the 'partnership'

America's power is also demonstrated in the law itself. The Anglo-US extradition arrangements can force UK citizens into American courts in a one-sided way. David Davis, a former Conservative government minister, calls the relationship 'asymmetric, ineffective and fundamentally unfair on British citizens'. The government, he says, approved the Extradition Act 2003 'as though their duty was first and foremost to support the wishes of our American friends, not to safeguard the rights of UK citizens'.[30] The numbers who are extradited confirm his point: in the decade up until 2019, the UK allowed 135 UK citizens to be extradited to the US, whereas only 11 Americans were brought in the other direction. The imbalance is more pronounced if you take account of the relative sizes of the countries. As David Davis says: 'The US has the power to reach out around the world and, provided there is even a very, very tenuous connection with the US, it has the power to prosecute... This asymmetry is not an inevitable outcome of being an ally of the US – it's a policy choice.'[31]

And once British citizens have been extradited they face a criminal system in which the odds seem stacked against them. They cannot easily find witnesses to support their case because those individuals must travel to the US and risk being charged themselves. All this is before the accused gets to court and faces an agonising choice because of the plea bargain system. According to Davis, 97 per cent of cases in the US are settled with a plea bargain, whereby the defendant admits guilt in exchange for a much reduced sentence. The choice for the British citizen in the American legal system can be between the certainty of a plea bargain with, for example, one year spent in jail, or the risk of taking on an expensive and protracted legal battle with the possibility of spending 20 years behind bars.[32]

The case of 19-year-old Harry Dunn shows how extradition works with this power imbalance. On the evening of 27 August 2019, Harry was riding his motorcycle near the entrance to RAF Croughton in Northamptonshire, a US listening station. He was hit by an oncoming car driving on the wrong side of the road and died from his injuries later that night in the major trauma centre of Oxford's John Radcliffe Hospital. The driver, Anne Sacoolas, was working for the US intelligence community and claimed diplomatic immunity, with US support. British barristers later declared that there was no such immunity, but it was too late: Sacoolas had fled the country and attempts to extradite her to face trial were unsuccessful. The bereaved family vowed in a statement to continue protesting until 'common sense prevails and the US government agrees not to abuse their power again'.[33] On the advice of the US government, she refused to return to the UK. Three years after the incident a compromise was reached and she pleaded guilty by video link from the US. She was not in court to hear that she had been given a suspended prison sentence, despite the court's request for her to attend. The judge also remarked that whatever sentence was passed would not be enforceable.

US power is hiding in plain sight

Usually, the puppet master works quietly, behind the scenes. But the US president sometimes visits the UK, and his sheer power becomes clear. While journalists may treat it like the visit of any other head of state, it is anything but. Routinely, host countries weld down manhole covers along the route to improve security and the president travels in a cavalcade of up to 50 cars.[34] Although the president travels in Cadillac 1, commonly called 'the Beast', there are always at least two identical 'Beasts' so that an attacker can never be certain where to find the commander-in-chief of the US military. The car is said to be fitted with pump-action shotguns, has five-inch-thick bullet-proof glass, can create a smokescreen or an oil slick, carries reserves of blood which matches the president's and only does four miles to the gallon because it weighs ten tons. It also carries high-frequency jamming equipment to block the airwaves, which protects privacy and prevents the use of any bomb-activation signals, as well as the 'nuclear football', which is really a briefcase.

Despite these occasional flashes of raw power, influence is usually exerted more subtly and the public often do not notice how much US interests are being promoted. When Rishi Sunak first hinted in September 2023 that the northern leg of the HS2 rail project might be abandoned, due to the difficulty of paying for it, the *Financial Times* front-page headline demonstrated this deference: 'Scrapping HS2 will damage trust in Britain, warn US buyers of Birmingham City.'[35] Birmingham City is, of course, only a football club, but it is minority-owned by the American Tom Brady, an NFL legend and seven-time Super Bowl winner.[36]

Fig leaf of partnership hides dependence on US leadership

Although the actions of US diplomats are those of control, the words used are always about 'partnership'. However, the British are only partners in the sense that they go along with it, not in the sense that they fully share the decision-making or the rewards.

This highlights the risks on the horizon: America's leadership is increasingly unpredictable. And, as Tudor courtiers knew, capricious kings can be deadly. It was off to the Tower for efficient but unpopular tax collectors, chancellors who pressed their arguments too earnestly and wives who did not provide suitable heirs. The court is fraught with dangers because the monarch's desires can change on a sixpence.

In early 2024, reports describing exactly that change emerged when Thierry Breton, a French EU commissioner, reported an exchange between US president Donald Trump and the German defence minister Ursula von der Leyen. Mr Trump said: 'You need to understand that if Europe is under attack we will never come to help and support you... And by the way, you owe me $400 billion, because you didn't pay, you Germans, what you had to pay for defence.'[37]

Should America once again elect a capricious leader, even what little ground remains on which the British can move will no longer be solid. The cultural, diplomatic and ethical ties which bind the nations together will disappear, but domination will remain and the consequences for the UK could be even bleaker.

This analysis indicates that the US will continue to reap huge dividends from a compliant UK, but on matters where the US hears a conversation which affects its vital interests it will act with force to ensure conformity.

13

THE ULTIMATE CHALLENGE

If tragedy is upon us the final act has yet to be written. In any case, this is not a history book, but, with a little luck, a call to action.

– Jean-Jacques Servan-Schreiber[1]

It does not have to be like this. Strong political and business leadership could prevent Britain's state of vassalage from getting worse, and maybe reverse some of its most damaging excesses. Much more is needed than the resolve of Boxer, the workhorse in Orwell's *Animal Farm* (1945), who repeats the mantra that he must 'work harder'. Boxer is described as 'faithful and strong'; he has a blind belief in his leaders, who always get their way. Eventually, in the saddest scene in the book, Boxer dies from overwork and his body is taken unceremoniously to the knacker's yard to be turned into glue. Instead of toiling for others with a mistaken mindset, the British should reassess what has happened to them and overturn three core beliefs that have formed the bedrock of recent policy and led them astray so disastrously.

1. Stop the sell-offs

The first and biggest of these is the idea that Foreign Direct Investment (FDI) is good in all its forms and that sales of businesses to foreign owners should be accepted without question. Indifference about who owns British businesses and who gets government contracts is badly misguided: these policies should be reversed at speed.

Like Boxer the horse, Britain's leaders have been naively devoted to an idea that is spelling disaster. That idea – of buyer-blind globalisation – has led them to allow the selling off of many of the UK's most productive and innovative businesses. Meanwhile, as this book has shown, our closest trading partner, America, as well as China and many European nations, has long tipped the scales of global trade, tax and investment in its own interests where it can. The UK should do the same and as much as possible and try to have its cake and eat it.

In contrast to the UK, both France and Germany try to resist takeovers of their existing companies, and they work to protect their employees. The 'Loi Florange' (2014) in France covers buy-outs of quoted companies and requires the buyer to guarantee jobs and investment. It also means that unions and works councils have to be consulted during a takeover. Both France and Germany have laws to stop takeovers in the strategic sectors of defence, energy and telecoms.

To protect their companies, the French have even been willing to move the goalposts. When PepsiCo tried to buy Danone, France's biggest milk products company, in 2005, the authorities hurriedly passed the 'Danone Law', which allowed the yogurt maker to be defined as a strategic business. The list of protected sectors was subsequently extended by the 'Montebourg Decree' of 2014. This reflects not only French nationalism but an awareness that Danone has long traditions, is central to many communities and so needed extra defences against foreign buyers with plenty of capital and raw profit-maximising objectives.

Another protection against opportunistic US takeovers has been the Agence des Participations de l'État (APE), the French Government Shareholdings Agency, which holds chunks of nationally important industries such as Française des Jeux (FDJ), the operator of France's national lottery, and Renault, as well as an 85 per cent holding in EDF (a company which also supplies energy to 25 million retail customers, including 5 million British households).[2] The APE also orchestrates strategic reorganisations to create national or European champions, as it did when arranging the union of Air France and the Dutch airline KLM. This statism extends to making banks and insurance companies support French enterprises. Nicolas Dufourcq, as head of the Banque Publique d'Investissement (literally, the 'public investment bank'), said: 'France doesn't have pension funds so we are doing the job.'[3] Through this bank, the French government controls more than €100 billion of assets in 1,500 businesses across France, which are therefore protected against business predators.

2. Government should actively support innovation

The second pillar of recent thinking which needs to be abandoned is the notion that private capital alone will deliver sufficient innovation and investment throughout the economy. Even with a large tax incentive for companies, the UK still spends less on R & D than either the US or the E27 average.[4] Other countries' governments have never acted in accordance with this doctrine. In the case of the US, it has used state support for innovation that has nurtured its corporations as they grow. The Apollo space missions and the myriad inventions which NASA conceived and supported were not funded by private enterprise, even though many of these have been developed further by private capital. This backing includes funding the launch of 4,000 satellites by SpaceX, where even now state support continues: SpaceX has received $15 billion in US government contracts since 2003, and through Starlink has enabled worldwide internet access.[5]

3. Invest in people

Thirdly, the British should protect their people and invest in them. By contrast, the US invests heavily in its citizens, including new arrivals. US immigrants are more likely to gain degrees than those in other OECD countries, and the US is a world leader in adult education. Lifelong learning is deeply embedded in the mindset of Americans.[6]

Measure, diagnose and increase autonomy

In practical terms, the basic requirement is to start measuring. Throughout this account we have seen the UK government's wilful refusal even to ask questions about who owns assets and who runs parts of the economy. Numbers which should have been readily available have had to be painstakingly unearthed and deciphered, often from sources outside the UK.

To reverse the country's vassalage, Britain's leaders need to recognise just how dependent the country has become and to set out a clear objective of increasing autonomy. British politicians must properly grip the extent of foreign ownership, the over-whelming stake held by one nation – America – in the UK, and then assess how to respond. They could choose to call for ever closer union with the US with the attendant loss of sov-ereignty, and impose a culture with greater inequalities in the UK. Alternatively, they may seek to move away from growing dependency and to plot their own course. Either way, they should no longer pretend that the issue simply does not exist by failing to measure it. The logic of this analysis is not anti-American; rather, it is pro-British: it is not arguing for nationalism but against abject dependency. It is about cultivating our strengths and building our independence.

Core challenges overlooked or denied

Long before his dispirited resignation as prime minister, Lord Cameron once talked of a 'global race' between nations. As this book shows, there has been no systematic attempt by government to assess the position of this country in that race. At present, no voice in UK politics or public life questions the growing American dominance, and there is a perverse unwillingness to identify suppliers and buyers by their nationality – as if doing so would be somehow offensive or politically insensitive. The multi-nationals are constantly referred to collectively without any rec-ognition that the great majority of them are American (59 of the world's 100 largest[7]). Measuring who owns what and identifying the nationality of government suppliers would be cheap to organ-ise, and would pinpoint the areas of highest US concentration in business and in government spending. It would also provide the evidence base and springboard from which the government could start to act.

That action would go to the core of the UK's economic strategy. It would entail a radical review of how suppliers are chosen, of business regulation, of industry lobbying, of which takeovers are allowed and, crucially, of how the taxation system works. There should be no shame in having, in common with other countries, including the US, an explicit preference for locally owned suppliers and a policy of retaining British ownership of companies which operate principally in the UK. At present, the UK has no such policy, unlike much of Europe and the US itself.

Once one starts to look through this lens at US corporate power, the UK's true predicament comes into focus. But it could be worse. Foreign owners of British companies are overwhelmingly from the US. The buyer-blind approach that Whitehall has taken means that buyers of British businesses could easily have been from, say, Russia or China, and the consequences might have been even more problematic.

As we have seen, US mastery has predominantly resulted in the takeover of whole companies and market sectors, but it extends to art treasures and recruiting some of Britain's most talented individuals. Far from being one-off acquisitions, these takings represent an ongoing extraction of wealth. Britain has allowed its systems to be moulded, in business and education, into a conveyor belt that makes it certain that, without change, many successful firms, our best innovations and workers will continue to be drawn into US ownership and employment.

Meanwhile, Britain's chronic problem of unfunded government liabilities is growing, meaning that there are several trillion pounds' worth of pension promises and other commitments. If the UK government is to honour these, it will, of course, have no recourse to the American investors who have often and indirectly benefited from the build-up of liabilities. The pension burden will fall exclusively on British workers and savers.

The struggle for values

British people have been forced to respond to the overmighty corporation before. In the past our answer to unchecked corporate power has involved collective action – not just by unions, but involving the cooperative movement, building societies, mutual ownership and civil society. But this history, while briefly invoked by prime minister David Cameron's 'Big Society' in 2010, has been wiped from our memories again. Cooperatives and collectives are in decline, and new solutions, such as pension-savings schemes, are individual rather than shared.

The analysis of this book also forces us to reinterpret the historical significance of Margaret Thatcher, an ardent Atlanticist. While she is mostly credited with reducing the role of the state, cutting the power of trade unions and promoting private enterprise, her more lasting legacy is the wholesale transfer of British assets to new American owners, something she instigated. If she were alive today, Thatcher would be shocked by just how much of the economy is US-owned and how servile the UK government has become, yet it was she who made it all possible through her strong advocacy of privatisations that were blind to the nationality of the buyers, and her general non-interventionist stance. She might also be horrified to see how her idea of 'popular capitalism', with citizens as shareholders, has collapsed, with private shareholdings shrinking year by year. In her second full year in office, 1981, only 3.6 per cent of UK shares were owned overseas. By 2020 that number was more than 56 per cent.[8]

Vassals in a vassal state

The vassalage of the UK as a whole has been mirrored by the way in which sections of the population have become vassals. Britain is now the second most economically unequal of the larger developed countries, after the US: 50 years ago it was one of the most equal.[9] As the UK mimics the US in becoming a high-inequality nation, it drives whole swathes of the population into a precarious existence. The result is that a higher percentage of Britons live below the poverty line than in Poland.[10] This is not directly the fault of the US: it has been our choice to run our economy this way. And it is our choice to copy the Americans in how we cut our barely growing cake.

Multinationals are by their nature amoral. Corporate managers state correctly that they have a fiduciary duty to their shareholders to maximise profits, which leaves no hope of an appeal to a founder or founding family who might moderate the relentless drive for profit. There is no one to challenge the ethics of the marketing department, and no one to restrain the finance department's tax-minimising contortions. And their ability to shift location makes such corporations extremely hard to regulate. While Environmental, Social and Governance (ESG) measures have given a nod towards non-financial objectives, these initiatives are often concentrated in the countries where the corporations are headquartered, very often on the other side of the Atlantic.

Selling out is incentivised

The British tax system is tilted heavily in favour of transatlantic encroachment. Even though US corporations typically pay UK tax of just 5 per cent on their profits, the UK government has surrendered to US demands by abandoning the digital tax on the tech giants and supporting a 15 per cent global tax rate. And in other ways, too, the tax regime is shaped for US interests: freedom to deduct interest payments from profits before paying tax creates a powerful motivation to borrow excessively and helps, in particular, the hordes of private equity buyers who have bought up so much of Britain. For private business owners, the tax regime incentivises selling out: a business sale will attract a maximum tax rate of only 20 per cent, whereas ongoing profits are taxed at more than double that: they are taxed at 25 per cent corporation tax, and then a further income tax of up to 45 per cent when the money is paid out of the company to the individual owner. And for public companies, a US acquirer will often shed much of the tax burden by moving profits offshore, making purchases more attractive.

Consequently, if the British want to retain local ownership of their remaining businesses they must radically and swiftly reform their tax regime. Without changes to tax and policy on acquisitions, a further raft of companies is likely to be taken over by US predators – such as BP, BAE Systems, GSK, AstraZeneca, Rio Tinto, Reckitt, Shell, Smith & Nephew, Unilever, Britvic, Diageo, Vodafone and the high-street banks.

Many of Britain's problems have stemmed from a failure to measure, and a thoughtless drift into the arms of the Americans. More conscientious leadership would define and enable a distinctive British capitalism that is neither European nor American. This would be an approach that resists the financialisation of the economy and reduces the pressure on firms to pursue short-term profit maximisation or to sell out for short-term gain.

Learn from the Europeans too – structure and attitudes

Continental Europe consciously stands against foreign incursions, a stance which contrasts with the warm reception the Americans have received in the UK. In resisting, Europe's businesses are often helped by the way they are owned and integrated into the community. Some 60 per cent of the German economy is represented by the *Mittelstand* companies.[11] The rough equivalent in Britain are the SMEs (small and medium-sized enterprises), but the *Mittelstand* is a much bigger group and accounts for two-thirds of German exports. Usually these enterprises are family-owned, and were often set up after the Second World War with the expectation that they would be handed down the generations. By their nature they are fiercely independent and locally integrated: a sale to a US firm would usually be seen as both short-termist and socially unethical. Employees have an emotional attachment to these companies, and the owners' sense of social responsibility and local loyalty would usually stop them from even entertaining takeover discussions.

Often *Mittelstand* companies have grown by doing one thing really well, with a focus on innovation and excellence. Their managers plan for long-term profitability, even at the cost of lower short-term profits. To varying extents, a similar *Mittelstand* of companies exists in France, Italy and Spain, where family ownership and community integration protect them from predators. Despite this, a few have succumbed, especially when there is a succession issue. After the death of Detlev Louis in 2012, there were no obvious family members to take on his Hamburg-based motorcycle clothing business. It was exactly what a US buyer would want: an established niche supplier, low borrowing, expansion possibilities and, with its 90 outlets, a presence across Europe. Berkshire Hathaway snapped it up for $450 million in

2015 in what CEO Warren Buffett called his 'elephant hunt', and he trumpeted the fact that he wanted more businesses like this: 'The US is my first love, but I see terrific possibilities for us in Europe.'[12] Despite the hopes of Buffett and other acquirers, there have been few similar subsequent purchases. The Europeans have restrained American influence, and have kept growth in US businesses below 4 per cent each year (as against 9 per cent a year in the UK).

Technology moves too fast for Westminster

The years since 2010 have been almost unbelievably good for US corporations, which enjoyed a combination of low interest rates and a migration of trade and social life into an online world of digital platforms. Many traditional businesses reaped some digital benefit, but the true winners were US software corporations.

Meta/Facebook, Apple, Microsoft, Amazon and Alphabet/Google (MAMAA) represent a sort of perfection of the US corporation, taking payments instantly, selling products with zero marginal cost and building vast customer bases in weeks, not years. They are often freed from manufacturing timetables, the constraints of stock control and the need to source raw materials, with many of their products being infinitely scalable and replicable. And they are so cash rich that executives at the firms need not even spend time arranging borrowing. The prospect now is that, over the next 20 years, US companies will also be the winners from the rapid spread of AI and robotics: the British must develop plans to respond to, and adopt, these technologies.

Even at this stage, though, the Brits could still do something about their economic precariousness and start to build independence, rather than follow the submissive stance of current

British leaders who appease and concede. Some crucial issues are simply ignored, such as the balance-of-payments deficit and the hidden iceberg of unfunded liabilities. Instead of countering US domination, politicians endlessly debate the tax-and-spend dilemma, giving the public an exaggerated impression of their authority.

The British establishment appears to underestimate how poor and indebted its country has become. This may be partly because most policy-makers are based in London, which is in many ways an island of wealth. More than a million Londoners are dollar millionaires, mostly through the value of their homes; Londoners own over half the UK's wealth, and average income per person in the capital is double that of the rest of the country.[13] Inevitably, such cocooning means that those in London can identify with the words of the American astronaut Roger Chaffee, who said: 'Problems look mighty small from 150 miles up.'[14]

What now?

In 2016, Britain opted to 'take back control' from Europe, but the nation's paymasters and providers turned out to be on an entirely different continent. As a consequence, choosing Brexit has in practice meant reducing European influence while welcoming greater American ownership and control of Britain.

As part of the EU, Britain was party to regulations limiting anti-competitive behaviour by all corporations – including those based in the US. The EU exacted fines against global firms, including Microsoft, for monopolistic practices. Outside the union but ever more dependent on supplies from US corporations, the UK economy is now vulnerable in just the manner its friends have warned it about since the 1950s. How much power will Britain have to curb the flow of US commercial dominance in a decade's time?

Others have been here before. In 1968, continental Europe was facing a crisis of industrial management and was also at risk of being subsumed by American interests. The French thinker Jean-Jacques Servan-Schreiber warned: 'We are witnessing the prelude to our own historical bankruptcy.'[15]

The French responded to that call by integrating with Europe, acting strategically and plotting a path to prosperous economic independence from the US, at the same time as maintaining strong political and military links with it.

In a similar predicament almost 60 years later, what will we choose to do?

Acknowledgements

I struggle to write. Fortunately two very smart writers came to the rescue: Ed Howker and my editor Mark Richards, each marshalling my words into line, like little soldiers, and adding reinforcements of their own. Ed voiced many ideas and sparked mine, as did Meryl Dahlitz, Matt Hitchens, Sarah Hewin, Ashley Seager, Felicity Lawrence, Matt Bullard, Isaac Castella McDonald, Rosalind Arden, Alec Hagland, Angie Barrow, Jim Belben, John Samson and Susan Wolton.

Melissa Knight pushed me into writing this book, offering remarkable help and insisting that what really matters is how the American influence affects ordinary people. Her namesake, Melissa Bui, has been a dogged and perceptive researcher, along with smart sleuths Adam Dilizia and Andrew Bennett. Invaluable help has come from the Swift team, including Ruth Killick, Diana Broccardo and Rachel Nobilo. More namesakes, Alex Billington and Alex Middleton have been skilful and sharp-eyed shepherds.

Inevitably with moving targets such as business and the economy, adjustments and updates are constantly needed: in this, Paul Barber and Morgan Gabereau have had their eyes on the horizon for me, and both Antony Mason and Jon Thornton have been generous and thoughtful proofreaders.

Second to none is my friend and literary agent, Andrew Lownie, who took a chance on me despite the fact that we had lost touch for 40 years. His stature is such that another author told me he would have 'given his right ball' to have Andrew as his agent.

Several relatives have helped, such as my nephew, Peter Campbell, who writes for the *FT*, and my wife Fabienne, along with our boys, my siblings and Victoria Hanton. I also got suggestions from my late father, Alastair, who visited America only once – as a young man – and was always in awe of the country, and of its chocolate milkshakes.

Yet there are two other collaborators who asked me not to mention their names because they fear recrimination: people's willingness to speak publicly is often constrained by the views of those who hold power over them.

One of the most important influences was that of my American cousins and my many American friends, who are unwaveringly kind and have demonstrated to me the strengths and variety of America, and have helped me to understand more about the UK's economic overlords.

Unsurprisingly, all mistakes are mine in a work that is essentially an expression of my opinion.

Notes

Introduction

1 'SOI tax stats – country by country report', IRS [website], https://www.irs.gov/statistics/soi-tax-stats-country-by-country-report [updated annually].
2 'Direct investment by country and industry, 2022', Bureau of Economic Analysis [website] (20 July 2023), https://www.bea.gov/news/2023/direct-investment-country-and-industry-2022. See Chapter 2 for an analysis of this data.

1. Thundering Herd: Charging into All Corners of the Kingdom

1 Alessandra Malito, 'Grocery stores carry 40,000 more items than they did in the 1990s', MarketWatch [website] (17 June 2017), https://www.marketwatch.com/story/grocery-stores-carry-40000-more-items-than-they-did-in-the-1990s-2017-06-07.
2 Jessica Ransom, 'Weetabix makes supermarket own-brand cereal that is nearly HALF the price', *Woman & Home* [website] (28 April 2017), https://www.womanandhome.com/life/news-entertainment/supermarket-own-brand-weetabix-ludicrously-similar-to-branded-product-206515/.
3 'UK household paper products market report 2023', Mintel [website], https://store.mintel.com/report/uk-household-paper-products-market-report; Jimmy Nicholls and Daniel Selwood, 'Household paper products 2022: tissues grow by £33m as post-Covid sniffles surge', *The Grocer* (16 December 2022), https://www.thegrocer.co.uk/top-products/household-paper-products-2022-tissues-grow-by-33m-as-post-covid-sniffles-surge/674596.article.

4 Calculated using statistics available at 'Tissue & hygiene paper – United Kingdom', Statista [website], https://www.statista.com/outlook/cmo/tissue-hygiene-paper/united-kingdom.

5 'Brands of tampons ranked by number of users in Great Britain from 2018 to 2021', Statista [website] (28 February 2023), https://www.statista.com/statistics/305057/leading-brands-of-tampons-in-the-uk/.

6 'Charlie Munger' [podcast interview], Acquired [website] (29 October 2023), https://www.acquired.fm/episodes/charlie-munger.

7 Quoted in 'Krispy Kreme boss shrugs off UK's tightening anti-obesity rules', *Financial Times* (15 May 2023), https://www.ft.com/content/fccf5ae7-6cbb-4ea5-87e9-46ac6d10a112.

8 See 'Our company', Pilgrim's [website], https://sustainability.pilgrims.com/our-company/ and Avara Foods [website], https://www.avarafoods.co.uk.

9 'Pilgrim's acquires largest pork producer in the UK', *National Hog Farmer* [website] (28 August 2019), https://www.nationalhogfarmer.com/pork-market-news/pilgrim-s-acquires-largest-pork-producer-in-the-uk.

10 'Completed acquisition by NCR Corporation of Cardtronics plc: decision on relevant merger situation and substantial lessening of competition' [PDF] (10 August 2021), Gov.uk [website], http://tinyurl.com/ff5565ma.

11 Caffè Nero is owned by US businessman Gerry Ford, who holds it through a complex corporate structure.

12 'Amazon annual report 2022' [PDF], p.2, https://s2.q4cdn.com/299287126/files/doc_financials/2023/ar/Amazon-2022-Annual-Report.pdf.

13 'Hermes Parcelnet's turnover in the United Kingdom in 2019 and 2022 (in million GBP)', Statista [website] (31 August 2023), https://www.statista.com/statistics/1280772/hermes-parcelnet-turnover-uk/.

14 On the number of UK subscribers, see Rob Binns, 'Netflix statistics 2023: subscriber amount, time watched, and platform growth', *Independent* (3 August 2023), https://www.independent.co.uk/advisor/vpn/netflix-statistics/.

15 On the gender balance among gamers, see 'Player diversity & demographics', Ukiepedia [website], https://ukiepedia.ukie.org.uk/index.php/Player_Diversity_%26_Demographics and 'Gender challenge in the video games industry', *Financial Times* (25 June 2015), https://www.ft.com/content/4778b356-1409-11e5-9bc5-00144feabdc0.

16 See 'Steam game release summary', SteamDB [website], https://steamdb.info/stats/releases/.

17 'Is Valve trying to evade taxes?' [post on community discussion page], Steam [website] (30 December 2019), https://steamcommunity.com/discussions/forum/0/1747892655526380525/.

18 Grant Prior, 'Skanska installs giant aquarium in Heron Tower', Construction Enquirer [website] (11 August 2010), https://www.constructionenquirer.com/2010/08/11/skanska-installs-europes-largest-private-aquarium/.

19 'The national balance sheet and capital stocks, preliminary estimates, UK: 2022', Office for National Statistics [website] (5 May 2022), https://www.ons.gov.uk/economy/nationalaccounts/uksectoraccounts/bulletins/thenationalbalancesheetandcapitalstockspreliminaryestimatesuk/2022#.

20 'Mergers and acquisitions involving UK companies, annual overview: 2018', Office for National Statistics [website] (5 March 2019), https://www.ons.gov.uk/businessindustryandtrade/changestobusiness/mergersandacquisitions/articles/ukmergersandacquisitionsactivityincontext/2018.

21 Grace Maral Burnett, 'Cross-border M&A held market share amid pandemic', Bloomberg Law [website] (14 January 2021).

22 Bethan Darwin, 'What new solicitors need to do get £160,000 salaries', BusinessLive [website] (21 February 2022), https://www.business-live.co.uk/opinion-analysis/what-new-solicitors-needs-160000-23164926.

23 'McKinsey fact sheet' [PDF], McKinsey [website] (31 May 2023), https://www.mckinsey.com/~/media/mckinsey/about%20us/media%20center/mckinseymediafactsheet_31-may-2023.pdf.

24 'Data is the new oil' was the title of a talk given by the British mathematician and entrepreneur Clive Humby at the Association of National Advertisers conference in 2006.

25 See https://www.ancestry.co.uk/c/dna/.

26 Peter Flanagan, 'Genealogy giant sold for €1.2bn months after Dublin move', *Irish Independent* (23 October 2012), https://www.independent.ie/irish-news/genealogy-giant-sold-for-12bn-months-after-dublin-move/28822300.html.

27 Oliver Mark, 'Top 10 best-selling tractor brands in the UK revealed', *Farmers Weekly* (19 January 2022), https://www.fwi.co.uk/machinery/tractors/top-10-best-selling-tractor-brands-in-the-uk-revealed.

28 'YouGov – vegan-only in January' [PDF], YouGov [website], https://d3nkl3psvxxpe9.cloudfront.net/documents/YouGov_-_Vegan-only_January.pdf.

29 'ADM 2022 proxy statement / 2021 form 10-K' [PDF], https://s1.q4cdn.com/365366812/files/doc_financials/2021/ar/2022-Letter-to-Stockholders-and-Proxy.pdf.

30 'CF Fertilisers' "monopoly producer" status questioned by UK farming body', *City A.M.* (14 June 2022), https://www.cityam.com/cf-fertilisers-monopoly-producer-status-questioned-by-uk-farming-body/.

31 '3M United Kingdom public limited company', Endole [website], https://suite.endole.co.uk/insight/company/01123045-3m-united-kingdom-public-limited-company.

32 CFM is US-based, but a joint venture between GE Aerospace and Safran Aircraft Engines of France.

33 'Petroleum refining in the United Kingdom', Wikipedia [website], https://en.wikipedia.org/wiki/Petroleum_refining_in_the_United_Kingdom.

34 For the $700 billion figure, see 'Table 1A' (2020 figures), column 4 ('Total'), line 154 ('United Kingdom') at 'SOI tax stats – country by country report', IRS [website], https://www.irs.gov/statistics/soi-tax-stats-country-by-country-report. The figure is probably higher now, and this excludes the very significant sales coming through Ireland and the Netherlands. For UK GDP, see D. Clark, 'Gross domestic product of the United Kingdom from 1948 to 2022', Statista [website] (28 November 2023), https://www.statista.com/statistics/281744/gdp-of-the-united-kingdom/.

35 US sales are from the latest IRS figures. See 'SOI tax stats – country by country report', IRS [website], https://www.irs.gov/statistics/soi-tax-stats-country-by-country-report [updated annually]. GDP is taken from UN figures, summarised at 'List of countries by GDP (nominal)', Wikipedia [website], https://en.wikipedia.org/wiki/List_of_countries_by_GDP_(nominal). The percentage of the workforce employed by US multinationals is calculated using the figures in 'Table 1A' (2020 figures), column 10 ('Number of employees'), at 'SOI tax stats – country by country report', divided by the total workforce, available at 'Labor force, total – European Union', The World Bank [website], https://data.worldbank.org/indicator/SL.TLF.TOTL.IN?locations=EU (for EU countries), and at Brigid Francis-Devine, Isabel Buchanan and Andrew Powell, 'UK labour market statistics' [PDF], Parliament.uk [website] (12 December 2023), https://researchbriefings.files.parliament.uk/documents/CBP-9366/CBP-9366.pdf (for the UK).

36 For the $88 billion figure, see 'Table 1A' (2019 figures), column 5 ('Profit (loss) before income tax'), line 154 ('United Kingdom') at 'SOI tax stats – country by country report', IRS [website], https://www.irs.gov/statistics/soi-tax-stats-country-by-country-report.

37 This is based on the 2022 figures from the US government's Bureau of Economic Analysis (BEA), which adds up the dividends paid to US companies from Europe. $31 billion is transferred direct from the UK; in addition, there is the UK's share of the $140 billion which goes through European tax havens. I estimate that this is at least 30 per cent, based on the percentage of US employees in Europe who worked in the UK in 2020 (IRS statistics). That number has since increased.

38 For the $3 trillion figure, see 'Market capitalization of Apple (AAPL)', CompaniesMarketCap.com [website], https://companiesmarketcap.com/apple/marketcap/. The top 350 UK listed companies are worth £2.2 trillion, equivalent to $2.8 trillion. See 'FTSE 350', London Stock Exchange [website], https://www.londonstockexchange.com/indices/ftse-350.

39 See Table 1 and Figure 9 at 'Ownership of UK quoted shares: 2020', Office for National Statistics [website] (3 March 2022), https://www.ons.gov.uk/economy/investmentspensionsandtrusts/bulletins/ownershipofukquotedshares/2020, which show that more than 56 per cent of UK-quoted shares are foreign-owned and that, of this, 46 per cent are US-owned, but in addition the European holdings include US ownerships through Luxembourg and the Netherlands.

40 See Table 1A, column 1 ('Number of reporting multinational enterprise groups'), line 154 ('United Kingdom') at 'SOI tax stats – country by country report'.

41 Denny Ludwell, *America Conquers Britain: A Record of Economic War* (New York: A. A. Knopf, 1930).

2. Grim and Grimmer: Welcoming the Buyers

1 On the way in which familiarity can overpower rationality, see 'Illusory truth effect', Wikipedia [website], https://en.wikipedia.org/wiki/Illusory_truth_effect.

2 'Spring Budget 2023 speech', Gov.uk [website] (15 March 2023), https://www.gov.uk/government/speeches/spring-budget-2023-speech.

3 'Nissan Motor Manufacturing UK', Wikipedia [website], https://en.wikipedia.org/wiki/Nissan_Motor_Manufacturing_UK; David Mullen, 'Nissan issues warning over future of Sunderland car plant', *Sunday Times* (7 February 2023), https://www.driving.co.uk/news/business/nissan-issues-warning-over-future-of-sunderland-car-plant/.

4 Macmillan was referring to the Conservatives' 1980s policy of privatisation under Margaret Thatcher. His actual words, delivered in a speech to the Tory Reform Group on 8 November 1985, were as follows: 'First of all the Georgian silver goes, and then all that nice furniture that used to be in the saloon. Then the Canalettos go.' See 'Harold Macmillan giving a speech on Margaret Thatcher's privatisation policies' [video], YouTube [website] (8 December 2010), https://www.youtube.com/watch?v=G1ssGrq5S3w.

5 Walter Ellis, 'Europe's stealth invasion of British industry', CapX [website] (4 March 2016), https://capx.co/europes-stealth-invasion-of-british-industry/.

6 Wales Tech Week, 'Fireside chat with Lord Gerry Grimstone and Avril Lewis' [video], YouTube (28 June 2021), https://www.youtube.com/watch?v=hVgiBTuSki0&ab_channel=WalesTechWeek, from exactly six minutes in.

7 'Telegraph.co.uk: some privatisations for Gerry Grimstone to consider', Adam Smith Institute [website] (28 August 2008), www.adamsmith.org/news/news/telegraph-co-uk-some-privatisations-for-gerry-grimstone-to-consider.

8 UNCTAD Investment, 'Statement by H.E. Lord Gerry Grimstone, minister of investment UK' [video], YouTube [website] (8 December 2020), http://tinyurl.com/4xy7923v.

9 Quoted in Tom Pyman, 'British firms perform BETTER when owned by foreigners says business minister Lord Grimstone as he insists there is nothing to fear in overseas bids for Morisons [*sic*] and other UK giants', *Daily Mail* (25 August 2021), https://www.dailymail.co.uk/news/article-9925871/British-firms-perform-BETTER-owned-foreigners-says-Business-Minister-Lord-Grimstone.html.

10 Quoted in Larry Elliott, 'Blair soothes captains of industry', *Guardian* (6 November 2001), https://www.theguardian.com/politics/2001/nov/06/uk.labour.

11 Quoted in Graeme Wearden, 'Gordon Brown: UK still good investment opportunity', *Guardian* (22 February 2010), https://www.theguardian.com/business/2010/feb/22/uk-good-investment-brown.

12 'Foreign direct investment involving UK companies: 2021', Office for National Statistics [website] (23 January 2023), https://www.ons.gov.uk/economy/nationalaccounts/balanceofpayments/bulletins/foreigndirectinvestmentinvolvingukcompanies/2021.

13 'Direct investment by country and industry, 2022', Bureau of Economic Analysis [website] (20 July 2023), https://www.bea.gov/news/2023/direct-investment-country-and-industry-2022.

14 The total agricultural acreage in England is about 42 million acres, worth £10,600 per acre, making a total value of £445 billion or $560 billion.

15 Myners and Macpherson quoted in Kaye Wiggins, Harriet Agnew and Daniel Thomas, 'Private equity and the raid on corporate Britain', *Financial Times* (11 July 2021), https://www.ft.com/content/315a02d1-6606-433e-b6f4-1989f2fad27d.

16 Quoted ibid.

17 Quoted in 'Foreign ownership of UK assets volume 767: debated on Thursday 19 November 2015', Parliament.uk [website] (19 November 2015), https://hansard.parliament.uk/lords/2015-11-19/debates/15111930000822/ForeignOwnershipOfUKAssets.

18 Quoted ibid.

19 Ian King, 'Thames Water aiming to sluice away bad reputation', Sky News [website] (29 November 2017), https://news.sky.com/story/thames-water-aiming-to-sluice-away-bad-reputation-11147571.

20 *Barbarians at the Gate: The Fall of RJR Nabisco* was the title of a 1989 account, by Bryan Burrough and John Helyar, of the first large hostile takeover (then called a 'leveraged buyout', or LBO) by private equity.

21 'Exon–Florio Amendment', Wikipedia [website], https://en.wikipedia.org/wiki/Exon%E2%80%93Florio_Amendment#.

22 'Presidential economic address' [video], C-SPAN [website] (17 February 1993), https://www.c-span.org/video/?38055-1/presidential-economic-address.

23 'Global advisory board', Pimco [website], https://www.pimco.co.uk/en-gb/global-advisory-board; 'Alistair Darling elected to Morgan Stanley board of directors', Morgan Stanley [website] (8 December 2015), https://www.morganstanley.com/press-releases/alistair-darling-elected-to-morgan-stanley-board-of-directors.

24 'George Osborne', 9Yards Capital [website], https://theorg.com/org/9yards-capital/org-chart/george-osborne.

25 Mark Sweney, 'Former chancellor Sajid Javid takes new role at JP Morgan', *Guardian* (18 August 2020), https://www.theguardian.com/business/2020/aug/18/former-chancellor-sajid-javid-role-jp-morgan-adviser-us-bank-mp-conservative.

26 'Kwasi Kwarteng', Wikipedia [website], https://en.wikipedia.org/wiki/Kwasi_Kwarteng.

27 Annabelle Dickson, 'Boris Johnson's parting shot: "Stay close to the Americans"', Politico [website] (20 July 2022), https://www.politico.eu/article/stay-close-americans-boris-johnson-parting-shot/.

28 'Chancellor Rishi Sunak held US green card until last year', BBC News [website] (8 April 2022), https://www.bbc.co.uk/news/uk-politics-61044847.

29 Peter Walker et al., 'Akshata Murty may have avoided up to £20m in tax with non-dom status', *Guardian* (7 April 2022), https://www.theguardian.com/politics/2022/apr/07/rishi-sunaks-wife-says-its-not-relevant-to-say-where-she-pays-tax-overseas.

30 Rupert Neate, 'Rishi Sunak and Akshata Murty join UK rich list with combined £730m fortune', *Guardian* (20 May 2022), https://www.theguardian.com/business/2022/may/20/sri-and-gopi-hinduja-named-uk-richest-people-james-dyson.

31 Kiran Stacey, 'Labour accuses Rishi Sunak of angling for job after Elon Musk interview', *Guardian* (3 November 2023), https://www.theguardian.com/politics/2023/nov/03/labour-accuses-rishi-sunak-of-angling-for-job-after-elon-musk-interview.

32 Tomas Malloy, 'Tata Somerset gigafactory: UK government's huge "£500m" battery plant subsidy explained', SomersetLive [website] (22 July 2023), https://www.somersetlive.co.uk/news/somerset-news/tata-somerset-gigafactory-uk-governments-8616044.

33 House of Commons International Trade Committee, 'Inward foreign direct investment: third report of session 2021–22' [PDF], Parliament.uk [website] (21 September 2021), https://publications.parliament.uk/pa/cm5802/cmselect/cmintrade/124/report.html.

34 House of Commons International Trade Committee, 'UK investment policy: seventh report of session 2017–19' [PDF], Parliament.uk [website] (24 July 2019), https://publications.parliament.uk/pa/cm201719/cmselect/cmintrade/998/998.pdf, quoted ibid.

35 David Ricketts, 'City stalwart Lord Grimstone lands Bain advisor role', Financial News [website] (28 September 2023), https://www.fnlondon.com/articles/city-stalwart-lord-grimstone-lands-bain-advisor-role-20230928.

36 Joanna Partridge, 'Behold London's "landscraper"! Google's new UK HQ – as long as the Shard is tall', *Guardian* (1 July 2022), https://www.theguardian.com/business/2022/jul/01/behold-londons-landscraper-googles-new-uk-hq-as-long-as-the-shard-is-tall.

37 '2022 investment climate statements: United Kingdom', US Department of State [website], https://www.trade.gov/country-commercial-guides/united-kingdom-investment-climate-statement.

38 Ibid.

39 Quoted in House of Commons International Trade Committee, 'Inward foreign direct investment: third report of session 2021–22'.

40 Gordon Brown, 'The special relationship is going global', *Sunday Times* (1 March 2009), https://www.thetimes.co.uk/article/the-special-relationship-is-going-global-07l0jq0pvnb.

41 Alice Miles, 'Humiliated, hopeless, paralysed. Time to go', *Times* (4 March 2009), https://www.thetimes.co.uk/article/humiliated-hopeless-paralysed-time-to-go-7jnt8t6qg7z.

42 Quoted in Eleanor Hayward and Jack Doyle, '"Special relationship" was seen as a joke by US diplomats, claims former presidential adviser: aide also admits slipping Malvinas references into press conferences in bid to "spoil it"', *Daily Mail* (9 October 2017), https://www.dailymail.co.uk/news/article-4964236/Special-relationship-seen-joke-diplomats.html.

43 'Joe Biden to remain tough on trade while re-embracing partners', *Financial Times* (16 November 2020), https://www.ft.com/content/c4e1c0e3-ba5b-46f8-87c7-9a56ca7a0a1a.

44 Patrick Wintour, 'Joe Biden warning dashes UK hopes of early US trade deal', *Guardian* (2 December 2020), https://www.theguardian.com/politics/2020/dec/02/uk-hopes-of-early-us-trade-deal-dashed-by-biden-warning; Luke McGee, 'The UK will never get the US trade deal it wants', CNN Business [website] (6 November 2019), https://edition.cnn.com/2019/11/06/business/brexit-us-uk-trade-donald-trump-boris-johnson-intl-gbr/index.html.

45 Interview with the author, 29 December 2020. Hammond expressed a similar sentiment on LBC: 'Post-Brexit UK–US trade deal will be "incredibly difficult": Lord Philip Hammond', LBC [website] (4 November 2020), https://www.lbc.co.uk/radio/presenters/nick-ferrari/post-brexit-uk-us-trade-deal-will-be-incredibly-difficult-to-strike/.

46 Quoted in Alistair Smout, 'Britain to set up investor concierge service in fight for FDI', Reuters [website] (22 November 2023), https://www.reuters.com/world/uk/britain-set-up-investor-concierge-service-fight-fdi-2023-11-22/.

3. Island of the Tech Giants

1 Bezos was speaking at a press conference held in Van Horn, Texas, on 20 July 2021, following the return to earth of the Blue Origin *New Shepard* space vehicle, on which he was a passenger. See CNBC Television, 'Jeff Bezos on spaceflight: this achievement was a team effort' [video], YouTube [website] (20 July 2021), https://www.youtube.com/watch?v=En3k20odNPQ&ab_channel=CNBCTelevision (40 seconds in).

2 See the video embedded in the following tweet: Richard Branson, 'I was once a child with a dream looking up to the stars. Now I'm an adult in a spaceship looking down to our beautiful Earth. To the next generation of dreamers: if we can do this, just imagine what you can do [...]' [Twitter post] (11 July 2021), https://twitter.com/richardbranson/status/1414289206717865984?lang=en.

3 CNBC Television, 'Jeff Bezos on spaceflight: this achievement was a team effort' (from 2 minutes, 15 seconds in).

4 'Paul Allen to spend $200 million to build world's largest airplane', *Seattle Business Magazine* (13 December 2011), https://seattlebusinessmag.com/paul-allen-spend-200-million-build-worlds-largest-airplane/.

5 Barry Pickthall, 'Allen vs. Ellison', *Yachting Magazine* (4 October 2007), https://www.yachtingmagazine.com/allen-vs-ellison/.

6 Sarah Butler, 'Amazon's main UK division pays no corporation tax for second year in a row', *Guardian* (1 June 2023), https://www.theguardian.com/technology/2023/jun/01/amazon-uk-services-main-division-pay-no-corporation-tax-for-second-year-in-row-tax-credit-government-super-deduction-scheme.

7 'Blue Origin Jeff Bezos post-flight press conference transcript', Rev [website] (20 July 2021), https://www.rev.com/blog/transcripts/blue-origin-jeff-bezos-post-flight-press-conference-transcript.

8 'The history of Uber', Uber [website], https://www.uber.com/en-gb/newsroom/history/.

9 Quoted in Stuart Dredge, 'MySpace – what went wrong: "The site was a massive spaghetti-ball mess"', *Guardian* (6 March 2015), https://www.theguardian.com/technology/2015/mar/06/myspace-what-went-wrong-sean-percival-spotify.

10 The 1997 letter is quoted in full at '2020 letter to shareholders', Amazon [website] (15 April 2021), https://www.aboutamazon.com/news/company-news/2020-letter-to-shareholders.

11 'Blue Origin Jeff Bezos post-flight press conference transcript'.

12 '10 ways we're making the UK the best place for tech businesses', Gov.uk [website] (13 June 2023), https://www.gov.uk/government/news/10-ways-were-making-the-uk-the-best-place-for-tech-businesses.

13 Nicky Godding, 'UK hits milestone of 100 UK tech companies valued at $1bn or more', *Business Magazine* (18 June 2021), https://thebusinessmagazine.co.uk/technology-innovation/uk-hits-milestone-of-100-uk-tech-companies-valued-at-1bn-or-more/.

14 Poppy Watson, 'You've heard of a tech unicorn but here come the "futurecorns" – Scotland's next generation of tech talent', *Futurescot* (19 May 2021), https://futurescot.com/youve-heard-of-a-tech-unicorn-but-here-come-the-futurecorns-scotlands-next-generation-of-tech-talent/.

15 Author's workings, based on Andrea Murphy and Hank Tucker, 'The global 2000', Forbes [website] (8 June 2023), https://www.forbes.com/lists/global2000/#4e5977015ac0.

16 GSK was formed from a merger of nineteenth-century pharmaceutical manufacturers, Unilever from a merger of Lever Brothers (founded in 1885) and a Dutch margarine business. HSBC was founded in 1830.

17 In 1984, General Electric, Racal Electronics, Plessy and Ferranti, as well as Standard Telephones and Cables (STC) all featured.

18 'I.C.L. agrees to be acquired', *New York Times* (17 August 1984), https://www.nytimes.com/1984/08/17/business/icl-agrees-be-acquired-london-aug-16-international-computers-ltd-plc-largest.html.

19 'Tech Nation: expenditure: question for Department for Digital, Culture, Media and Sport', Parliament.uk [website] (18 January 2021), https://questions-statements.parliament.uk/written-questions/detail/2021-01-18/138964.

20 'The future UK tech built: Tech Nation report 2021' (21 January 2022), archived at https://web.archive.org/web/20220121030356/https://technation.io/report2021/#key-statistics.

21 Ian Hogarth, 'AI nationalism', Ian Hogarth [blog] (13 June 2018), https://www.ianhogarth.com/blog/2018/6/13/ai-nationalism.

22 Quoted in John Cumbers, 'Global investor Hermann Hauser warns: your country may be about to lose technological sovereignty', Forbes [website] (31 March 2021), http://tinyurl.com/yv3dvusy. Hauser has tried to help solve the scale problem at an EU and a UK level, advising UK Labour and Coalition governments to establish catapult centres across the UK to help businesses grow. See Sebastian Klovig Skelton, 'Government R&D funding fails to maximise "catapult" potential', Computer Weekly [website] (5 February 2021), https://www.computerweekly.com/news/252495926/Government-RD-funding-fails-to-maximise-catapult-potential.

23 John Brownlee, 'This is how ARM saved Apple from going bust in the 90s', Cult of Mac [website] (25 May 2011), https://www.cultofmac.com/97055/this-is-how-arm-saved-apple-from-going-bust-1990s/.

24 Hermann Hauser, 'Letter: Arm sale will hit Europe's technological sovereignty', *Financial Times* (24 August 2020), https://www.ft.com/content/4970848d-7821-45dc-b8cb-211036be5d30.

25 EIT Digital, 'Hermann Hauser on venture capital for deep tech competitiveness and EU tech sovereignty' [video], YouTube [website] (20 December 2021), https://www.youtube.com/watch?v=17kULzySxCI.

26 Quoted in Mark Sweney, 'UK chip designer Arm chooses US-only listing in blow to Rishi Sunak', *Guardian* (3 March 2023), https://www.theguardian.com/business/2023/mar/03/uk-chip-designer-arm-chooses-us-only-listing-in-blow-to-rishi-sunak.

27 Author's research, mostly based on reviewing companies' 10-K Securities and Exchange Commission (SEC) filings.

28 A. J. Chavar, 'Why you keep using Facebook, even if you hate it', Vox [website] (11 April 2018), https://www.vox.com/videos/2018/4/11/17226430/facebook-network-effect-video-explainer.

29 Quoted in Brad Stone, *The Everything Store: Jeff Bezos and the Age of Amazon* (London: Transworld, 2013).

30 'How much is Amazon Web Services worth on a standalone basis?', Forbes [website] (28 February 2019), https://www.forbes.com/sites/greatspeculations/2019/02/28/how-much-is-amazon-web-services-worth-on-a-standalone-basis/.

31 Ted Weschler, speaking to the German publication *Manager Magazin* (21 October 2016), quoted in Jacob Wolinsky, 'Biting to the core of Apple', ValueWalk [website] (20 August 2021), https://www.valuewalk.com/nasdaq-aapl/.

32 Ciaran Driver, Anna Grosman and Pasquale Scaramozzino, 'Dividend policy and investor pressure', *Economic Modelling* 89 (July 2020), pp. 559–76, doi: 10.1016/j.econmod.2019.11.016.

33 'Aviva plc: half year report 2023' [PDF], Aviva [website] (16 August 2023), https://static.aviva.io/content/dam/aviva-corporate/documents/investors/pdfs/results/2023/aviva-plc-half-year-report-2023.pdf. See also 'Aviva confirms 2023 profit and dividend guidance amid "momentum"', Morningstar [website] (16 November 2023), http://tinyurl.com/ycxssxmn.

34 Quoted in Akin Oyedele, 'Here's what Wall Street is saying about Netflix's blowout subscriber growth last quarter', Business Insider [website] (19 January 2017), https://www.businessinsider.com/netflix-earnings-analyst-notes-comments-subscriber-growth-2017-1?r=US&IR=T.

35 Quoted in Oli Ballard, 'Jeff Bezos: "If you're a shareowner in Amazon, you may want to take a seat because we're not thinking small"', Business Leader [website] (1 May 2020), https://www.businessleader.co.uk/jeff-bezos-if-youre-a-shareowner-in-amazon-you-may-want-to-take-a-seat-because-were-not-thinking-small/.

36 Quoted in Cumbers, 'Global investor Hermann Hauser warns'.

4. A Slice of Everything: Payments, Publicity and Platforms

1 Quoted in John Huber, 'Warren Buffett 1997 email exchange on Microsoft', Saber Capital Management [website] (19 December 2019), https://sabercapitalmgt.com/warren-buffett-1997-email-exchange-on-microsoft/.

2 'Card use soars to 90% of retail spending', British Retail Consortium [website] (9 December 2022), https://brc.org.uk/news/corporate-affairs/card-use-soars-to-90-of-retail-spending/.

3 Quoted in 'Who needs cash (or borders)?', *New York Times* (16 October 2010), https://www.nytimes.com/2010/10/17/business/global/17banga.html.

4 Quoted in AnnaMaria Andriotis, 'Visa takes war on cash to restaurants', *Wall Street Journal* (12 July 2017), https://www.wsj.com/articles/visa-takes-war-on-cash-to-restaurants-1499853601.

5 Patrick Collinson, 'Hundreds of cash machines close as UK turns to contactless payments', *Guardian* (29 June 2018), https://www.theguardian.com/money/2018/jun/29/hundreds-of-cash-machines-close-as-uk-turns-to-contactless-payments.

6 Lorna Booth, 'Statistics on access to cash, bank branches and ATMs'[PDF], Parliament.uk [website] (1 September 2023), https://researchbriefings.files.parliament.uk/documents/CBP-8570/CBP-8570.pdf.

7 Ibid.

8 Salman Haqqi, 'Credit card facts and statistics: 2023', Money [website] (26 October 2023), https://www.money.co.uk/credit-cards/credit-card-statistics.

9 Helena Young, 'Credit card processing fees & rates for UK merchants 2023', Startups [website] (16 November 2023), https://startups.co.uk/payment-processing/credit-card-processing-fees/.

10 Grace Witherden, 'More people could turn to cash to help budget as cost of living rises', Which? (6 May 2022), https://www.which.co.uk/news/article/more-people-could-turn-to-cash-to-help-budget-as-cost-of-living-rises-aada54Q9HEAk.

11 'Access to cash', UK Finance [website], https://www.ukfinance.org.uk/our-expertise/personal-banking/access-cash.

12 Quoted in Witherden, 'More people could turn to cash to help budget as cost of living rises'.

13 'Payments survey 2022' [PDF], British Retail Consortium [website], https://brc.org.uk/media/681273/payment-survey-2022_final.pdf.

14 Quoted in Martha Southall, 'How UK retailers can tackle card fees as inflation soars', British Retail Consortium [website] (30 August 2022), https://brc.org.uk/news/associate-insight/how-uk-retailers-can-tackle-card-fees-as-inflation-soars/.

15 Joshua M. Frank, 'Priceless or just expensive? The use of penalty rates in the credit card industry', Center for Responsible Lending [website] (16 December 2008), https://www.responsiblelending.org/research-publication/priceless-or-just-expensive-use-penalty-rates-credit-card-industry.

16 Quoted in Mayur Shetty, 'I've declared war on cash: Ajay Banga', *Economic Times* (1 October 2010), https://economictimes.indiatimes.com/wealth/personal-finance-news/ive-declared-war-on-cash-ajay-banga/articleshow/6661561.cms?from=mdr.

17 Grace Witherden, 'Amazon credit card closure: when will your card stop working?', Which? [website] (16 September 2022), https://www.which.co.uk/news/article/amazon-credit-card-closure-when-will-your-card-stop-working-a0ADB3r8kJy5.

18 Kaye Wiggins and Silvia Sciorilli Borrelli, 'How the private equity industry stole a march in European payments', *Financial Times* [website] (20 November 2020), https://www.ft.com/content/e5756da3-e040-4f41-9849-9bfdd17a8a69. Peter Morris was the author of *Private Equity, Public Loss?*, published by the think tank the Centre for the Study of Financial Innovation (CSFI) in 2010.

19 Antoine Gara and Ortenca Aliaj, 'FIS sells majority stake in Worldpay to buyout group at $18.5bn valuation', *Financial Times* (6 July 2023), https://www.ft.com/content/b133fa58-5ef2-4cc4-972b-8271f749779e.

20 Quoted in Wiggins and Borrelli, 'How the private equity industry stole a march in European payments'.

21 'Alfred Kelly Jr net worth & insider trades', Benzinga [website] (4 December 2023), https://www.benzinga.com/sec/insider-trades/v/ALFRED-KELLY%20 JR; 'Ajay Banga – net worth and insider trading', GuruFocus [website], https:// www.gurufocus.com/insider/3836/ajay-banga.

22 Charlotte Tobitt and Aisha Majid, 'National press ABCs: *FT* stays steady while *Evening Standard* falls below 300,000 for first time since going free', *Press Gazette* (15 November 2023), https://pressgazette.co.uk/media-audience-and-business-data/media_metrics/most-popular-newspapers-uk-abc-monthly-circulation-figures-2/.

23 'UK ad spend grew 8.8% in 2022 to reach £34.8bn', Advertising Association [website] (27 April 2023), https://adassoc.org.uk/our-work/uk-ad-spend-grew-8-8-in-2022-to-reach-34-8bn-inflationary-pressures-persist-with-minimal-growth-forecast-for-2023/.

24 'Nobody reads terms and conditions: it's official', Pinsent Masons [website] (19 April 2010), https://www.pinsentmasons.com/out-law/news/nobody-reads-terms-and-conditions-its-official.

25 'It pays to read license agreements (7 years later)', PC Matic [website] (12 June 2012), https://www.pcmatic.com/blog/it-pays-to-read-license-agreements-7-years-later/.

26 Gina Hall, 'San Jose area has world's third-highest GDP per capita, Brookings says', The Business Journals [website] (23 January 2015), https:// www.bizjournals.com/sanjose/news/2015/01/23/san-jose-has-worlds-third-highest-gdp-per-capita.html.

27 'Investing in American dynamism (with Katherine Boyle)' [transcript of podcast interview with embedded video], Acquired [website] (5 June 2022), https://www.acquired.fm/episodes/american-dynamism-with-katherine-boyle.

28 David Curry, 'Etsy revenue and usage statistics (2023)', Business of Apps [website] (8 November 2023), https://www.businessofapps.com/data/etsy-statistics/.

29 Krystal Hu, 'ChatGPT sets record for fastest-growing user base – analyst note', Reuters [website] (2 February 2023), https://www.reuters.com/technology/chatgpt-sets-record-fastest-growing-user-base-analyst-note-2023-02-01/.

30 For 'privacy zuckering', 'roach motel' and 'confirmshaming', see 'Dark pattern', Wikipedia [website], https://en.wikipedia.org/wiki/Dark_pattern. For WinRed, see 'How Trump steered supporters into unwitting donations', *New York Times*

(7 August 2021), https://www.nytimes.com/2021/04/03/us/politics/trump-donations.html.

31 'The ultimate guide to Airbnb service fees (3%, 14%, 15%, 17%)', Uplisting [website], https://www.uplisting.io/blog/guide-to-airbnb-service-fees.

32 Alex Baggott, 'Every Apple App Store fee, explained: how much, for what, and when', AppleInsider [website] (8 January 2023), https://appleinsider.com/articles/23/01/08/the-cost-of-doing-business-apples-app-store-fees-explained.

33 Simon Sinek, 'How great leaders inspire action' [video], TED [website] (September 2009), https://www.ted.com/talks/simon_sinek_how_great_leaders_inspire_action?language=en.

34 'HP Garage', Wikipedia [website], https://en.wikipedia.org/wiki/HP_Garage.

35 The World Uncovered, 'Google: from garage to global dominance – the extraordinary life story' [video], YouTube [website] (1 August 2023), https://www.youtube.com/watch?v=oME2I09Pzpg&ab_channel=TheWorldUncovered.

36 Ali Montag, 'Jeff Bezos' first desk at Amazon was a door with four-by-fours for legs – here's why it still is today', CNBC Make It [website] (23 January 2018), https://www.cnbc.com/2018/01/23/jeff-bezos-first-desk-at-amazon-was-made-of-a-wooden-door.html.

37 'Elon Musk: no change to Twitter moderation policy yet', BBC News [website] (29 October 2022), https://www.bbc.co.uk/news/business-63428848.

38 'How to create a pitch deck in one day', Founders Network [website], https://foundersnetwork.com/blog/how-to-create-a-pitch-deck-in-one-day/.

39 'Competition is for losers with Peter Thiel (how to start a startup 2014: 5)' [video], YouTube [website] (22 March 2017), https://www.youtube.com/watch?v=3Fx5Q8xGU8k&ab_channel=YCombinator.

40 Marc Andreessen, 'Why software is eating the world', Andreessen Horowitz [website] (20 August 2011), https://a16z.com/why-software-is-eating-the-world/.

41 'Seven ways platform workers are fighting back' [PDF], TUC [website], p. 3, https://www.tuc.org.uk/sites/default/files/2021-11/PlatformEssaysWithPollingData2.pdf.

42 Robert Booth, 'Gig economy threatens government finances, says May adviser', *Guardian* [website] (30 November 2016), https://www.theguardian.com/business/2016/nov/30/gig-economy-threatens-government-finances-says-may-adviser.

5. Life-as-a-Service: The Twin Treadmills of Subscriptions and Debt

1 'Trip Adler', Quote.org [website], https://quote.org/author/trip-adler-49853.

2 For more on Benioff, see Marc Benioff and Carlye Adler, *Behind the Cloud: The Untold Story of How Salesforce.com Went from Idea to Billion-Dollar Company – and Revolutionized an Industry* (San Francisco: Wiley-Blackwell, 2009).

3 Marilyn Much, 'How Salesforce's Marc Benioff revolutionized the software industry', Investor's Business Daily [website] (11 February 2019), https://www.investors.com/news/management/leaders-and-success/how-salesforces-marc-benioff-revolutionized-the-software-industry/.

4 Phil Wainewright, 'Microsoft CEO to business: your future as a SaaS provider', Diginomica [website] (16 March 2015), https://diginomica.com/microsoft-ceo-business-future-saas-provider.

5 Erik Bullard, 'The escalating costs buried in your Salesforce agreement', UpperEdge [website] (26 February 2020), https://upperedge.com/salesforce/the-escalating-costs-buried-in-your-salesforce-agreement/.

6 Mario Grunitz, 'Everything-as-a-service: a look into the subscription-based model', WeAreBrain [website] (30 August 2022), https://wearebrain.com/blog/everything-as-a-service/.

7 Quoted in Catrin Jones, 'Caterpillar release cloud-based system to boost performance', Construction Briefing [website] (23 November 2022), https://www.constructionbriefing.com/news/caterpillar-release-cloud-based-system-to-boost-performance/8024919.article.

8 'Power by the hour (PBH)', AJW Group [website], https://www.ajw-group.com/services/supply-chain-management/power-by-the-hour/.

9 'The Princess of Wales rents a gown for the Earthshot Prize ceremony in Boston', *Harper's Bazaar* (3 December 2022), https://www.harpersbazaar.com/uk/fashion/fashion-news/a42139785/kate-middleton-rents-green-dress-earthshot-prize/; Rebecca Cohen and Madison Hall, 'AOC only paid for her Met Gala outfit and other possible "impermissible gifts" after investigators asked about it, ethics agency finds', Business Insider [website] (2 March 2023), https://www.businessinsider.com/aoc-ethics-prove-paid-met-gala-outfit-house-report-2023-3?r=US&IR=T.

10 'The story of Zipcar', Zipcar [website], https://www.zipcar.com/en-gb/about#:~:text=We're%20on%20a%20mission,vehicles%20that%20support%20environmental%20sustainability.

11 Richard Thaler, *Nudge: Improving Decisions about Health, Wealth, and Happiness* (New Haven, CT: Yale University Press, 2008).

12 Daniel Kahneman, *Thinking, Fast and Slow* (New York: Farrar, Straus & Giroux, 2011).

13 Quoted in Tim Bradshaw, 'Apple aims to double service revenues by 2021', *Financial Times* (31 January 2017), https://www.ft.com/content/a3e00a3a-4372-3f96-b8d6-d673ac4a5d57.

14 Quoted in 'Apple paid subscriptions top 1 billion, doubling in three years', Pymnts [website] (2 November 2023), https://www.pymnts.com/apple/2023/apple-paid-subscriptions-top-1-billion-doubling-in-three-years/.

15 'Media nations UK 2023' [PDF], Ofcom [website] (3 August 2023), https://www.ofcom.org.uk/__data/assets/pdf_file/0029/265376/media-nations-report-2023.pdf.

16 Quoted in 'Pain of paying – everything you need to know', InsideBE [website], https://insidebe.com/articles/pain-of-paying/.

17 Florent Geerts, 'The jam experiment – how choice overloads makes consumers buy less', Medium [website] (17 August 2017), https://medium.com/@FlorentGeerts/the-jam-experiment-how-choice-overloads-makes-consumers-buy-less-d610f8c37b9b.

18 Barry Schwartz, *The Paradox of Choice: Why More Is Less* (New York: Harper Perennial, 2004). See also Barry Schwartz, 'The tyranny of choice' [PDF], *Scientific American* (1 December 2004), https://bschwartz.domains.swarthmore.edu/Sci.Amer.pdf.

19 'Why do we value items purchased in a bundle less than those purchased individually?', The Decision Lab [website], https://thedecisionlab.com/biases/bundling-bias.

20 'Everything included in Prime', Amazon [website], https://www.amazon.co.uk/b?ie=UTF8&node=14917073031.

21 'CMA issues directions to NatWest about bundling products', Gov.uk [website] (31 August 2022), https://www.gov.uk/government/publications/cma-issues-directions-to-natwest-about-bundling-products.

22 'FTC takes action against Amazon for enrolling consumers in Amazon Prime without consent and sabotaging their attempts to cancel', Federal Trade Commission [website] (21 June 2023), https://www.ftc.gov/news-events/news/press-releases/2023/06/ftc-takes-action-against-amazon-enrolling-consumers-amazon-prime-without-consent-sabotaging-their.

23 Quoted in Stefania Palma and Patrick McGee, 'Amazon "tricked and trapped" customers with Prime service, FTC claims', *Financial Times* (21 June 2023), https://www.ft.com/content/a0a3791d-71d6-42f8-9da2-49c7c2dde78f.

24 Ben Stevens, 'PerfectHome ordered to pay £2.1m back to customers by FCA', Retail Gazette [website] (21 March 2018), https://www.retailgazette. co.uk/blog/2018/03/perfecthome-ordered-pay-2-1m-back-customers-fca/.

25 David Curry, 'Candy Crush revenue and usage statistics (2023)', Business of Apps [website] (9 January 2023), https://www.businessofapps.com/data/candy-crush-statistics/.

26 'Consumer "inertia" boosts subscription firms' revenues by 200%', Pymnts [website] (9 October 2023), https://www.pymnts.com/subscription-commerce/2023/study-consumer-inertia-boosts-subscription-firms-revenues-by-200/.

27 'Half a billion pounds spent on subscriptions that rolled over without people realising during the cost-of-living crisis', Citizens Advice [website] (1 December 2022), http://tinyurl.com/4k8yxpns.

28 'Introducing Snapchat+', Snap [website] (29 June 2022), https://newsroom. snap.com/en-GB/snapchatplus.

29 Quoted in 'Over 2 million have problems cancelling subscriptions on credit or debit cards', Citizens Advice [website] (8 March 2016), https://www. citizensadvice.org.uk/cymraeg/amdanom-ni/about-us1/media/press-releases/2-million-have-problems-cancelling-subscriptions/.

30 'Financial Lives 2022: key findings from the FCA's financial lives May 2022 survey', Financial Conduct Authority [website] (26 July 2023), https://www. fca.org.uk/publication/financial-lives/financial-lives-survey-2022-key-findings. pdf.

31 'UK households waste almost £170 on average each year on unused subscriptions', Swansea Bay News [website] (27 June 2022), https:// swanseabaynews.com/2022/06/27/uk-households-waste-almost-170-on-average-each-year-on-unused-subscriptions/.

32 'The money statistics December 2023', The Money Charity [website], https:// themoneycharity.org.uk/money-statistics/; 'Household credit: a visual summary', Bank of England [website] (31 January 2023), https://www.bankofengland. co.uk/statistics/visual-summaries/household-credit.

33 'The money stats – October 2022 – rising household bills drive financial resilience epidemic for UK consumers', The Money Charity [website] (27

October 2022), https://themoneycharity.org.uk/the-money-stats-october-2022-rising-household-bills-drive-financial-resilience-epidemic-for-uk-consumers/.

34 Quoted in Vicky Shaw, 'Scale of problem debt at "epidemic levels", says Archbishop of Canterbury', *Independent* (21 March 2018), https://www.independent.co.uk/news/business/news/uk-debt-levels-archbishop-of-canterbury-credit-cards-cap-a8266131.html.

35 Welby and Barlow quoted in Vicky Shaw, 'Problem debt is at "epidemic levels" – the help that's out there', *Daily Mirror* (17 May 2018), https://www.mirror.co.uk/money/problem-debt-epidemic-levels-helps-12224220.

36 'Financial Lives 2022: key findings from the FCA's financial lives May 2022 survey'.

37 Martyn James, 'How to cancel subscriptions and save a fortune', *Times* (12 December 2023), https://www.thetimes.co.uk/money-mentor/coronavirus-crisis/consumer-rights/how-to-cancel-subscriptions-and-save-a-fortune.

38 'Barclaycard data shows lockdown has made us a "subscription society"', InsightDIY [website] (26 August 2020), https://www.insightdiy.co.uk/news/barclaycard-data-shows-lockdown-has-made-us-a-subscription-society/8832.htm.

39 'Household debt', OECD [website], https://data.oecd.org/hha/household-debt.htm.

40 Jake Attfield, 'Shame, upbringing and burdening others: why do 29 million UK adults feel uncomfortable talking about money despite feeling worried about it?', LinkedIn [website] (13 November 2020), https://www.linkedin.com/pulse/shame-upbringing-burdening-others-why-do-29-million-uk-jake-attfield/.

41 'Household debt'.

42 'About us', Klarna [website], https://www.klarna.com/uk/about-us/.

6. Private Equity: The Extraction Machines

1 Quoted in Kaye Wiggins, Harriet Agnew and Daniel Thomas, 'Private equity and the raid on corporate Britain', *Financial Times* (11 July 2021), https://www.ft.com/content/315a02d1-6606-433e-b6f4-1989f2fad27d.

2 Bess Levin, 'Populist hero Stephen Schwarzman's birthday blowout included fireworks, acrobats, and live camels', *Vanity Fair* (13 February 2017), https://www.vanityfair.com/news/2017/02/stephen-schwarzmans-birthday-blowout-included-fireworks-acrobats-and-live-camels.

3 'Stephen Schwarzman's 2007 birthday party', Guest of a Guest [website], https://guestofaguest.com/new-york/nyc-society/inside-the-biggest-billionaire-bashes&slide=1.

4 James B. Stewart, 'The birthday party', *New Yorker* (4 February 2008), https://www.newyorker.com/magazine/2008/02/11/the-birthday-party-2?verso=false.

5 'University announces unprecedented investment in the humanities', University of Oxford [website] (19 June 2019), https://www.ox.ac.uk/news/2019-06-19-university-announces-unprecedented-investment-humanities.

6 Quoted in Robin Pogrebin, 'Stephen A. Schwarzman gives $150 million for Yale cultural hub', *New York Times* (12 May 2015), https://www.nytimes.com/2015/05/12/arts/design/stephen-a-schwarzmangives-150-million-for-yale-cultural-hub.html.

7 Patrick Range McDonald, 'Modern-day robber baron: the sins of Blackstone CEO Stephen Schwarzman', Housing Is a Human Right [website] (29 July 2020), https://www.housingisahumanright.org/modern-day-robber-baron-the-sins-of-blackstone-ceo-stephen-schwarzman/; Kai Ryssdal and Sarah Leeson, 'How private equity creates a "circle of pain" in the US economy', Marketplace [website] (27 April 2023), https://www.marketplace.org/2023/04/27/how-private-equity-creates-a-circle-of-pain-in-the-us-economy/.

8 On raising prices, see 'Private equity investors raising U.S. medical prices, study says', *Washington Post* (10 July 2023), https://www.washingtonpost.com/business/2023/07/10/private-equity-raising-prices-doctors-practices-private-equity-doctors/.

9 Stephen A. Schwarzman, *What It Takes: Lessons in the Pursuit of Excellence* (New York: Simon & Schuster, 2019).

10 'Portfolio operations', Blackstone [website] https://www.blackstone.com/our-businesses/portfolio-operations/.

11 Quoted in 'First on CNBC: Blackstone's Stephen Schwarzman speaks with CNBC following his appointment as chair of Trump's "President's Strategic & Policy Forum"', CNBC [website] (2 December 2016), https://www.cnbc.com/2016/12/02/first-on-cnbc-blackstones-stephen-schwarzman-speaks-with-cnbc-following-his-appointment-as-chair-of-trumps-presidents-strategic-policy-forum.html.

12 'Leon Black', Forbes [website], https://www.forbes.com/profile/leon-black/?sh=2bb7372b1629.

13 Quoted in Antoine Gara, 'Buyout firm Thoma Bravo goes from niche to big league', *Financial Times* (6 December 2021), https://www.ft.com/content/456f2fd7-f868-4ea6-abd7-fce34e783333.

14 Michael Novinson, 'Sophos undertakes company restructuring, staff cuts due to COVID-19: reports', CRN [website] (9 June 2020), https://www.crn.com/news/security/sophos-to-cut-staff-by-up-to-16-percent-due-to-covid-19-reports.

15 'List of private equity firms', Wikipedia [website], https://en.wikipedia.org/wiki/List_of_private_equity_firms.

16 Steven J. Davis et al., 'The economic effects of private equity buyouts' (8 July 2021), doi: 10.2139/ssrn.3465723.

17 For 'swarm of locusts', see Luke Harding, 'German industrialist hopping mad at "locust" accusation', *Guardian* (3 May 2005), https://www.theguardian.com/world/2005/may/03/germany.lukeharding.

18 'S.3022 – Stop Wall Street Looting Act', Congress.gov [website], https://www.congress.gov/bill/117th-congress/senate-bill/3022/actions.

19 Quoted in 'Warren, Baldwin, Brown, Pocan, Jayapal, colleagues unveil bold legislation to fundamentally reform the private equity industry', Elizabeth Warren [website] (18 July 2019), http://tinyurl.com/2pd9hrcx.

20 Tim Shipman, 'Sharks who made a killing out of "care": how City predators destroyed firm caring for 31,000 old people', *Daily Mail* (2 June 2011), https://www.dailymail.co.uk/news/article-1393294/Southern-Cross-Healthcare-destroyed-Stephen-Schwarzmans-private-equity-firm-Blackstone.html.

21 Quoted in 'Southern Cross, Orchid View September 2009–October 2011' [PDF], Care Quality Commission [website] (June 2014), http://tinyurl.com/2e3cw2hv.

22 Simon Goodley, 'Southern Cross care fiasco sheds light on secretive world of private equity', *Guardian* (3 June 2011), https://www.theguardian.com/business/2011/jun/03/southern-cross-care-private-equity.

23 For the quotation from Buchan, see 'The *Guardian* view on the care home sector: trouble looms as rents rise', *Guardian* (2 February 2023), https://www.theguardian.com/commentisfree/2023/feb/02/the-guardian-view-on-the-care-home-sector-trouble-looms-as-rents-rise.

24 Blackstone, 'Mondays at Blackstone' [video], YouTube [website] (7 May 2015), https://youtu.be/k8iZe9NsGto?si=I-Dtxe7wpj3jg0Og.

25 Quoted in Wiggins, Agnew and Thomas, 'Private equity and the raid on corporate Britain'.

26 'UK investors sound alarm over London exchange rule changes', *Financial Times* (3 May 2023), http://tinyurl.com/y9mwma5h.

27 Quoted in Wiggins, Agnew and Thomas, 'Private equity and the raid on corporate Britain'.

28 Ibid.

29 Quoted in 'Private equity steps in where others fear to tread during pandemic', *Financial Times* (17 June 2020), https://www.ft.com/content/912929f7-7366-45d0-90ce-4467b9fec7f0.

30 Joice Alves and Sujata Rao, '"UK for sale": Britain's year of private equity buyouts', Reuters [website] (16 August 2021), https://www.reuters.com/business/uk-sale-britains-year-private-equity-buyouts-2021-08-16/.

31 'Shell explored quitting Europe and moving to the US', *Financial Times* (27 February 2023), http://tinyurl.com/bd7cr98k.

32 Robin Wigglesworth, 'The private capital industry's "dry powder" has hit $4tn', *Financial Times* (12 December 2023), https://www.ft.com/content/cb161f56-de60-4a4d-bdf9-b0b3e0e62174.

33 Quoted in Landon Thomas Jr, 'Stephen Schwarzman of Blackstone feels the agony of victory', *New York Times* (4 September 2015), https://www.nytimes.com/2015/09/06/business/dealbook/stephen-schwarzman-of-blackstone-feels-the-agony-of-victory.html.

34 Aime Williams and Josh Spero, 'Blackstone in £1.5bn deal for UK's Victorian railway arches', *Financial Times* (10 September 2018), https://www.ft.com/content/cd64a3c0-b50b-11e8-bbc3-ccd7de085ffe.

35 Quoted in Tom White, 'Railway arch shops face eviction after rent rises of up to 85%', *Guardian* (1 June 2019), https://www.theguardian.com/business/2019/jun/01/railway-arch-shops-uk-face-eviction-rent-increases-network-rail.

36 Ibid.

37 'Network Rail's sale of railway arches', National Audit Office [website] (2 May 2019), https://www.nao.org.uk/reports/network-rails-sale-of-railway-arches/.

38 Interview with the author, 29 December 2020.

39 Stephen A. Schwarzman, 'Lawmakers' rush to punish banks threatens recovery', *Washington Post* (12 February 2010), https://www.washingtonpost.com/wp-dyn/content/article/2010/02/11/AR2010021102206.html.

40 Claire Ruckin and Andrew Berlin, 'More banks joining $14 billion debt for Blackstone's TR unit buy', Reuters [website] (14 February 2018), https://www.reuters.com/article/us-tr-unit-leveraged-loans-idUSKCN1FY2BV.

41 'Sanctions against KPMG and former partner in relation to Silentnight', Financial Reporting Council (5 August 2021), https://www.frc.org.uk/news/august-2021/sanctions-against-kpmg-and-former-partner-in-relat.

42 Pension Protection Fund, 'Providing security, building sustainable futures: annual report and accounts 2022/23' [PDF] (13 July 2023), https://assets.publishing.service.gov.uk/media/64ae63eb8bc29f000d2ccb15/ppf-annual-report-and-accounts-2022-2023.pdf.

43 Ludovic Phalippou, 'An inconvenient fact: private equity returns and the billionaire factory' [University of Oxford, Said Business School, working paper] (10 June 2020), doi: 10.2139/ssrn.3623820.

44 Nicholas Shaxson, *The Finance Curse: How Global Finance Is Making Us All Poorer* (London: Bodley Head, 2018).

45 Interview with the author, 29 December 2020.

46 'Public company takeovers in the UK: a guide for us private equity acquirers' [PDF], Squire Patton Boggs [website] (August 2012), https://www.squirepattonboggs.com/en/insights/publications/2012/08/public-company-takeovers-in-the-united-kingdom-a__.

47 Blackstone, 'Mondays at Blackstone'.

48 'Zoopla.co.uk – revolutionary new online property venture launched by successful internet entrepreneurs and backed by leading venture capital firm', Zoopla [website] (15 January 2008), https://www.zoopla.co.uk/press/releases/003/zoopla-revolutionary-new-online-property-venture-launched-by-successful-internet-entrepreneurs-and-backed-by-leading-venture-capital-firm/.

49 For the figure of £2.2 billion, see Rahul B. and Paul Sandle, 'Britain's Zoopla, PrimeLocation bought by Silver Lake for $3 billion', Reuters [website] (11 May 2018), https://www.reuters.com/article/us-zpg-m-a-silver-lake-idUSKBN1IC0I0.

50 Kalyeena Makortoff, 'The Restaurant Group to go private after accepting £506m takeover bid', *Guardian* (12 October 2023), https://www.theguardian.com/business/2023/oct/12/the-restaurant-group-to-go-private-after-accepting-506m-takeover-bid.

7. Why You Cannot Milk an Eagle

1 Quoted in 'G.E.'s strategies let it avoid taxes altogether', *New York Times* (24 March 2011), https://www.nytimes.com/2011/03/25/business/economy/25tax.html.

2 'List of countries by GDP (nominal)', Wikipedia [website], https://en.wikipedia.org/wiki/List_of_countries_by_GDP_(nominal); 'SOI tax stats – country by country report', IRS [website], https://www.irs.gov/statistics/soi-tax-stats-country-by-country-report.

3 Bobby Allyn, 'Apple does not owe Ireland nearly $15 billion in back taxes, court rules', NPR [website] (15 July 2020), https://www.npr.org/2020/07/15/891383815/apple-does-not-owe-ireland-nearly-15-billion-in-back-taxes-court-rules.

4 'Paradise Papers: Apple's secret tax bolthole revealed', BBC News [website] (6 November 2017), https://www.bbc.co.uk/news/world-us-canada-41889787.

5 Quoted in Shane Walton, 'Where next for Apple shares as $14B tax order set to be challenged?', IG Bank [website] (17 September 2019), https://www.ig.com/en-ch/news-and-trade-ideas/where-next-for-apple-shares-as--14b-tax-order-set-to-be-challeng-190917.

6 'Labour force survey quarter 1 2021', Central Statistics Office [website], https://www.cso.ie/en/releasesandpublications/ep/p-lfs/labourforcesurveyquarter12021/labourforce/, combined with the statistics for 2020 at 'SOI tax stats – country by country report'.

7 Cain Burdeau, 'Apple suffers setback as it fights colossal tax penalty in EU courts', Courthouse News Service [website] (9 November 2023), https://www.courthousenews.com/apple-suffers-setback-as-it-fights-colossal-tax-penalty-in-eu-courts/.

8 'Bermuda black hole', Wikipedia [website], https://en.wikipedia.org/wiki/Bermuda_Black_Hole.

9 Gabriel Zucman et al., 'The missing profits of nations' [PDF], Gabriel Zucman [website] (June 2018), https://gabriel-zucman.eu/files/TWZ2018.pdf.

10 Katarzyna Anna Bilicka, 'Comparing UK tax returns of foreign multinationals to matched domestic firms', *American Economic Review* 109/8 (2019), pp. 2921–53, doi: 10.1257/aer.20180496.

11 The figure of 10 per cent is based on the official IRS numbers available at 'SOI tax stats – country by country report'.

12 Nicky Burridge, 'Government to spend £8.6bn on 119,000 affordable homes', Zoopla [website] (1 September 2021), https://www.zoopla.co.uk/discover/property-news/government-to-spend-gbp8-6bn-on-119-000-affordable-homes/.

13 Quoted in Richard Murphy, 'Starbucks avoiding tax has a knock-on effect on homegrown business', *Guardian* (16 October 2012), https://www.theguardian.com/commentisfree/2012/oct/16/starbucks-tax-british-business.

14 Tom Bergin, 'UK committees to examine Starbucks tax strategies', Reuters [website] (15 October 2012), https://www.reuters.com/article/us-britain-starbucks-tax-idUSBRE89E0EX20121015.

15 Tom Bergin, 'Starbucks's European tax bill disappears down $100 million hole', Reuters [website] (1 November 2012), https://www.reuters.com/article/us-starbucks-tax-europe-idINBRE8A00DP20121101.

16 'Special report – how Starbucks avoids UK taxes', Reuters [website] (15 October 2012), https://www.reuters.com/article/idUSBRE89E0F4/.

17 Andrew Goodall, 'Starbucks paid no corporation tax on "profitable" UK business', *Tax Journal* (16 October 2012), https://www.taxjournal.com/articles/starbucks-paid-no-corporation-tax-profitable-uk-business-16102012.

18 Alex Dunnagan, 'US set to raise $8.5bn from four tech companies following global tax deal', TaxWatch [website] (7 October 2021), https://www.taxwatchuk.org/tag/apple/.

19 Alex Cobham and Petr Jansky, 'Global distribution of revenue loss from corporate tax avoidance: re-estimation and country results: global corporate tax avoidance', *Journal of International Development* 30/2 (March 2018), pp. 206–32, doi:10.1002/jid.3348.

20 Felicity Lawrence, *Not on the Label: What Really Goes into the Food on Your Plate* (London: Penguin, 2004).

21 'New ranking reveals corporate tax havens behind breakdown of global corporate tax system; toll of UK's tax war exposed', Tax Justice Network [website] (28 May 2019), https://taxjustice.net/press/new-ranking-reveals-corporate-tax-havens-behind-breakdown-of-global-corporate-tax-system-toll-of-uks-tax-war-exposed/.

22 'European stocks vs US stocks portfolio comparison', Lazy Portfolio ETF [website], https://www.lazyportfolioetf.com/comparison/european-stocks-vs-us-stocks/.

23 For Luas, see 'Luas', TII [website], https://www.tii.ie/public-transport/luas/.

24 Quoted in 'The most influential person in the tax world', *NYU Law Magazine* 23 (2013) [PDF], https://issuu.com/nyulaw/docs/complete_law_school_magazine_2013/36?e=1606929/4742059.

25 For the 'Harvard of tax departments', see Tabby Kinder and Emma Agyemang, '"It's a matter of fairness": squeezing more tax from multinationals', *Financial Times* (7 July 2020), https://www.ft.com/content/40cffe27-4126-43f7-9c0e-a7a24b44b9bc.

26 'Around the world with $5bn – HMRC's allegations of tax fraud at General Electric revealed', TaxWatch [website] (4 August 2020) https://www.taxwatchuk. org/ge_hmrc_tax_fraud_allegations/.

27 'MPs accuse HMRC of "sweetheart" tax settlement with GE', *Financial Times* (16 September 2021), https://www.ft.com/content/31e01fdd-7a10-4985-9b37-3793662bda47.

28 The ONS states that, of the £7.6 billion of relief, the majority goes to larger companies and in the sectors where the US presence is largest. See Figure 7 at 'Research and development tax credits statistics: September 2023', Gov.uk [website] (28 September 2023), https://www.gov.uk/government/statistics/ corporate-tax-research-and-development-tax-credit/research-and-development-tax-credits-statistics-september-2023. Other research shows that over 50 per cent of such claims are from foreign-owned companies. See David Connell, 'Is the UK's flagship industrial policy a costly failure?', University of Cambridge Judge Business School [website] [PDF] (May 2021), https://www.jbs.cam.ac.uk/wp-content/uploads/2021/05/cbr-report-uk-flagship-industrial-policy-2021.pdf.

29 N. Grassano et al., 'The 2022 EU industrial R&D investment scoreboard', European Commission [website] (13 December 2022), https://iri.jrc.ec.europa. eu/scoreboard/2022-eu-industrial-rd-investment-scoreboard.

30 Quoted in Paul Sandle, 'Britain to target online giants with new "digital services tax"', Reuters [website] (30 October 2018), https://www.reuters.com/ article/us-britain-budget-digital-tax-idUSKCN1N3265.

31 Quoted in Aaron Lorenzo, 'Wyden threatens U.S.–U.K. trade agreement over digital services tax', Politico Pro [website] (11 July 2019), https://subscriber. politicopro.com/article/2019/07/wyden-threatens-us-uk-trade-agreement-over-digital-services-tax-1585556.

32 Quoted in Sam Fleming et al., 'US upends global digital tax plans after pulling out of talks with Europe', *Financial Times* (17 June 2020), https://www. ft.com/content/1ac26225-c5dc-48fa-84bd-b61e1f4a3d94.

33 Brian Fung, 'US threatens 100% tariffs on French cheese and champagne', CNN Business [website] (3 December 2019), https://edition.cnn.com/2019/12/02/ tech/french-tariffs-digital-services-tax/index.html.

34 'The government tax break worth £100m+ for Heathrow', Tax Watch [website] (20 February 2019), https://www.taxwatchuk.org/reports/2-2/.

35 Eloise Walker, 'New UK restriction on corporate interest tax relief', Pinsent Masons [website] (5 Jun 2017), https://www.pinsentmasons.com/out-law/ legal-updates/new-uk-restriction-on-corporate-interest-tax-relief.

36 Ross Lydall, 'Revealed: US government owes over £12m in unpaid congestion charge', *Evening Standard* (4 June 2019), https://www.standard. co.uk/news/london/us-government-owes-over-ps12m-in-unpaid-congestion-charge-a4158936.html.

37 Quoted in Patrick Wintour, 'Boris Johnson among record number to renounce American citizenship in 2016', *Guardian* (9 February 2017), https:// www.theguardian.com/politics/2017/feb/08/boris-johnson-renounces-us-citizenship-record-2016-uk-foreign-secretary.

38 See the answer to the first question ('I'm a US citizen living and working outside of the United States for many years. Do I still need to file a US tax return?') at 'Frequently asked questions (FAQs) about international individual tax matters', IRS [website], http://tinyurl.com/54nwj4rf.

39 'Obama goes after overseas tax cheats' [video], YouTube [website] (4 May 2009), https://www.youtube.com/watch?v=PMEInTNsacg. See also 'Leveling the playing field: curbing tax havens and removing tax incentives for shifting jobs overseas', The White House: President Barack Obama [website] (4 May 2009), https://obamawhitehouse.archives.gov/the-press-office/leveling-playing-field-curbing-tax-havens-and-removing-tax-incentives-shifting-jobs.

40 'Where does the government get its money?', Taxlab [website], https://ifs. org.uk/taxlab/taxlab-key-questions/where-does-government-get-its-money.

41 For New Jersey, see 'NJ maintains highest combined corporate taxes in the US', New Jersey Business & Industry Association [website] (27 September 2022), https://njbia.org/nj-maintains-highest-combined-corporate-taxes-in-the-us/.

42 Leigh Thomas, 'Explainer: what is the global minimum tax deal and what will it mean?', Reuters [website] (8 October 2021), https://www.reuters.com/business/finance/what-is-global-minimum-tax-deal-what-will-it-mean-2021-10-08/.

43 'Global minimum tax will put the squeeze on investors' returns', *Financial Times* (12 January 2024), https://www.ft.com/content/53d7140a-88e4-4c70-8a55-1649d3d629c3.

44 George Turner, 'G7 tax deal represents a tax cut for big tech in the UK – new analysis', TaxWatch [website] (27 September 2021), https://www.taxwatchuk. org/g7_tax_deal/.

45 'Exposed: Amazon's enormous and rapidly growing plastic pollution problem', Oceana [website] (December 2021), https://oceana.org/reports/amazon-report-2021/.

46 'The road to full fibre', BT [website], https://www.bt.com/about/bt/policy-and-regulation/keeping-the-uk-connected/fibre-for-all.

47 Quoted in Anna Gross, 'Campaign to make big tech pay for telecoms networks gathers pace', *Financial Times* (10 October 2022), https://www.ft.com/content/cb8d8dfa-5e8c-4dd7-b9c7-7535a52be5a0.

48 Matthew Keep, 'Tax statistics: an overview' [PDF], Parliament.uk [website] (5 June 2023), https://researchbriefings.files.parliament.uk/documents/CBP-8513/CBP 8513.pdf.

8. The NHS Cash Cow

1 Quoted in Aubrey Allegretti and Jessica Elgot, 'Covid: "greed" and capitalism behind vaccine success, Johnson tells MPs', *Guardian* (24 March 2021), https://www.theguardian.com/politics/2021/mar/23/greed-and-capitalism-behind-jab-success-boris-johnson-tells-mps.

2 For the 40 new pharma billionaires, see Giacomo Tognini, 'Meet the 40 new billionaires who got rich fighting Covid-19', Forbes [website] (6 April 2021), https://www.forbes.com/sites/giacomotognini/2021/04/06/meet-the-40-new-billionaires-who-got-rich-fighting-covid-19/.

3 Sarah Marsh, 'The history of Covid vaccine development', *Guardian* (8 December 2021), https://www.theguardian.com/world/2021/dec/08/the-history-of-covid-vaccine-development.

4 For Honeywell, see '70 million face masks for NHS and care workers through new industry deal', Gov.uk [website] (15 May 2020), https://www.gov.uk/government/news/70-million-face-masks-for-nhs-and-care-workers-through-new-industry-deal. For Hologic, see David Wilcock and Connor Boyd, 'PPE providers, the firm behind school meal vouchers and the NHS locum medic bank among big winners making millions as government pays private firms £6.5 BILLION during COVID crisis', *Daily Mail* (20 August 2020), https://www.dailymail.co.uk/news/article-8646941/Government-paid-private-firms-6-5BILLION-COVID-crisis-services-struggled.html. For Thermo Fisher, see 'Thermo Fisher agrees to supply UK coronavirus tests', *Financial Times* (10 April 2020), https://www.ft.com/content/a08688a9-6936-432b-a5b2-f900962c6497. For Sitel, see Josh Halliday, 'Outsourcing firms miss 46% of Covid contacts in England's worst-hit area', *Guardian* [website] (21 August 2020), https://www.theguardian.com/world/2020/aug/21/outsourced-firms-miss-46-of-covid-test-contacts-in-englands-worst-hit-areas. For TransUnion, see Stephen Delahunty, 'Government silent on involving credit firm in COVID-19 testing', *Byline Times* (22 May 2020), https://bylinetimes.com/2020/05/22/government-silent-on-involving-credit-firm-in-covid-19-testing/. For Brake Bros, see Sam Baker, 'Government awards £1billion in state contracts to companies including French-owned Edenred, a healthcare firm advised by a Tory MP and US-run Brake Bros WITHOUT public tender in fast-tracked deals amid coronavirus pandemic', *Daily Mail* (16 May 2020), https://www.dailymail.co.uk/news/article-8325925/Government-awards-1billion-fast-tracked-state-contracts-firms-WITHOUT-public-tender.html.

5 See listing for Brake Bros at David Barmes, Danisha Kazi and Simon Youel, 'The Covid Corporate Financing Facility' [PDF], Positive Money [website] (July 2020), p. 9, https://positivemoney.org/wp-content/uploads/2020/07/CCFF-Final-version.pdf.

6 Francesco Guarascio, 'Tougher terms: why the EU is paying more for new COVID shots', Reuters [website] (3 August 2021), https://www.reuters.com/world/europe/tougher-terms-why-eu-is-paying-more-new-covid-shots-2021-08-03/.

7 'AstraZeneca says it will start profiting from its vaccine', *New York Times* (12 November 2021), https://www.nytimes.com/2021/11/12/business/astrazeneca-vaccine-profit.html.

8 For 150 nurses, see Gemma Mitchell, 'Covid-19: new nurse death figures prompt call for investigation', *Nursing Times* (25 January 2021). For 50 doctors, see 'Remembering them: the doctors who died fighting COVID', BMA [website] (12 April 2022), https://www.bma.org.uk/news-and-opinion/remembering-them-the-doctors-who-died-fighting-covid.

9 'Coroner rules that Covid-19 is an industrial disease, in first case of its kind', Doughty Street Chambers [website] (16 January 2023), https://www.doughtystreet.co.uk/news/coroner-rules-covid-19-industrial-disease-first-case-its-kind.

10 Both doctors quoted in Tim Tonkin, 'Let down', British Medical Association [website] (19 May 2022), https://www.bma.org.uk/news-and-opinion/let-down.

11 Channel 4 News, 'Revealed: PPE stockpile was out-of-date when coronavirus hit UK' [video], YouTube [website] (7 May 2020), https://www.youtube.com/watch?v=Piie71tf_bU.

12 See David Conn, 'UK government ordered to reveal firms awarded "VIP" Covid contracts', *Guardian* (18 October 2021), https://www.theguardian.com/uk-news/2021/oct/18/uk-government-told-reveal-firms-given-vip-covid-contracts-ppe.

13 Tristan Kirk, '"Murky dealings": UK government told PPE deals were lined up with "bribes" in China', *Evening Standard* (19 May 2021), https://www.standard.co.uk/news/uk/ppe-bribes-china-uk-government-pestfix-b936043.html.

14 Tevye Markson, 'Tory peer "secretly involved" with firm that won £200m in PPE contracts after she referred it to "VIP lane"', Civil Service World [website] (7 January 2022), https://www.civilserviceworld.com/professions/article/tory-peer-secretly-involved-with-ppe-firm-which-won-200m-in-government-contracts-through-vip-lane.

15 Channel 4 News, 'Revealed: PPE stockpile was out-of-date when coronavirus hit UK'.

16 Harry Davies, 'Revealed: private firm running UK PPE stockpile was sold in middle of pandemic', *Guardian* (22 April 2020), https://www.theguardian.com/world/2020/apr/22/revealed-private-firm-running-uk-ppe-stockpile-was-sold-in-middle-of-pandemic.

17 Jack Serle, 'Chief exec of NHS agency resigns', *Health Service Journal* (19 September 2020), https://www.hsj.co.uk/workforce/chief-exec-of-nhs-agency-resigns/7028487.article.

18 'Curriculum vitae of Simon Stevens, NHS Privatiser' [PDF], Sell Off [website], https://selloff.org.uk/nhs/CVforSimonStevens260516.pdf.

19 Hélène Mulholland, 'Blair welcomes private firms into NHS', *Guardian* (16 February 2006), https://www.theguardian.com/society/2006/feb/16/health.politics.

20 Quoted in David Leigh, Rob Evans and Ed Harriman, 'US firm gets results for NHS – but soft sell masks an expensive truth', *Guardian* (30 September 2004), https://www.theguardian.com/uk/2004/sep/30/politics.freedomofinformation.

21 Ibid.

22 'Prescribing costs in hospitals and the community 2019–2020', NHS [website], https://digital.nhs.uk/data-and-information/publications/statistical/prescribing-costs-in-hospitals-and-the-community/2019-2020. The number will have gone up significantly from this date and only covers England.

23 For the top pharma companies worldwide, see 'Pharmaceutical industry', Wikipedia [website], https://en.wikipedia.org/wiki/Pharmaceutical_industry.

24 Six per cent of NHS sending is on diagnostics, which is almost £10 billion a year. See Charlotte Wickens, 'Why do diagnostics matter? Maximising the potential of diagnostics services', The King's Fund [website] (13 October 2022), https://www.kingsfund.org.uk/publications/why-do-diagnostics-matter.

25 For Abbott, see 'Abbott announces contract to supply millions of IGG lab-based antibody tests to the UK government', Abbott [website] (21 May 2020), https://abbott.mediaroom.com/2020-05-21-Abbott-Announces-Contract-to-Supply-Millions-of-IgG-Lab-Based-Antibody-Tests-to-the-UK-Government. For BD, see Beth Timmins, 'NHS blood tube shortage: supplier ramps up imports', BBC News [website] (31 August 2021), https://www.bbc.co.uk/news/business-58394899.

26 'Pathology facts and figures', Royal College of Pathologists [website], https://www.rcpath.org/discover-pathology/news/fact-sheets/pathology-facts-and-figures-.html.

27 'Ian Donald', Wikipedia [website], https://en.wikipedia.org/wiki/Ian_Donald.

28 'GE Healthcare offices in UK', GE Healthcare [website], https://www.gehealthcare.co.uk/about/ge-healthcare-offices-in-uk.

29 'Outsourced: the role of the independent sector in the NHS' [PDF], British Medical Association [website], https://www.bma.org.uk/media/5378/bma-nhs-outsourcing-report-march-2022.pdf.

30 Denis Campbell and Anna Bawden, 'NHS paying £2bn a year to private hospitals for mental health patients', *Guardian* (24 April 2022), https://www.theguardian.com/society/2022/apr/24/nhs-paying-2bn-pounds-a-year-to-private-hospitals-for-mental-health-patients.

31 Quoted in Julia Kollewe, 'US healthcare giant's takeover of GP practices lands in high court', *Guardian* (2 February 2022), https://www.theguardian.com/business/2022/feb/01/us-healthcare-giants-takeover-of-uk-gp-practices-lands-in-high-court.

32 'Investors take a bite into the UK and European dentistry markets', Lincoln International [website] (January 2020), http://tinyurl.com/mvc55hf6.

33 'New investment group buys out Mydentist', Dentistry [website] (28 May 2021), https://dentistry.co.uk/2021/05/28/new-investment-group-buys-out-mydentist/.

34 'Acquisition of Portman Dental Care', Core Equity Holdings [website] (27 June 2018), https://www.coreequityholdings.com/acquisition-portman-dental-care/.

35 '£1.7 bn tender opened for future NHS workforce tech', HTN [website] (31 August 2022), https://htn.co.uk/2022/08/31/1-7-bn-tender-opened-for-future-nhs-workforce-tech/.

36 Quoted in Arwa Mahdawi, 'Palantir, the all-seeing US tech company, could soon have the data of millions of NHS patients. My response? Yikes!',

Guardian (14 June 2022), https://www.theguardian.com/commentisfree/2022/jun/14/palantir-the-all-seeing-us-tech-company-could-soon-have-the-data-of-millions-of-nhs-patients-my-response-yikes.

37 Helen Cahill, 'US tech firm Palantir "to handle data for millions of NHS patients"', *Times* (21 November 2023), https://www.thetimes.co.uk/article/us-tech-firm-palantir-to-handle-data-for-millions-of-nhs-patients-cnm7nk6hj.

38 'The cost of sequencing a human genome', NHGRI [website], https://www.genome.gov/about-genomics/fact-sheets/Sequencing-Human-Genome-cost.

39 'Introducing Amazon Clinic, a virtual health service that delivers convenient, affordable care for common conditions', Amazon [website] (15 November 2022), https://www.aboutamazon.com/news/retail/what-is-amazon-clinic.

40 James Le Fanu, *Too Many Pills: How Too Much Medicine Is Endangering Our Health and What We Can Do about It* (London: Little, Brown, 2018).

41 For Gadsden's comments to *Fortune* magazine, see Alan Cassels and Ray Moynihan, 'US: selling to the worried well', *Le Monde diplomatique* (May 2006), https://mondediplo.com/2006/05/16bigpharma.

42 Michael Savage and Toby Helm, 'Britain is "recklessly exposed" to new pandemics, expert warns', *Guardian* (10 June 2023), https://www.theguardian.com/world/2023/jun/10/uk-recklessly-exposed-to-new-pandemics-expert-warns.

43 'Catalent acquires facility in Oxfordshire to expand biologics capabilities in the UK and across Europe', Catalent [website] (6 April 2022), https://www.catalent.com/catalent-news/catalent-acquires-facility-in-oxfordshire-to-expand-biologics-capabilities-in-the-uk-and-across-europe/.

44 Nicky Godding, 'Progress at Harwell's Vaccine Manufacturing and Innovation Centre slows after purchaser profit warning', *Business Magazine* (28 November 2022), https://thebusinessmagazine.co.uk/technology-innovation/progress-at-harwells-vaccine-manufacturing-and-innovation-centre-slows-after-purchaser-profit-warning/.

45 Laith Al-Khalaf, 'Moderna to build £150m vaccine centre in UK after NHS deal', *Sunday Times* (5 March 2023), https://www.thetimes.co.uk/article/moderna-to-build-150m-vaccine-centre-in-uk-after-nhs-deal-jfflbmxmn; 'Moderna selects Harwell as UK home', Harwell Science and Innovation Campus [website] (5 March 2023), https://www.harwellcampus.com/moderna/.

46 Quoted in Savage and Helm, 'Britain is "recklessly exposed" to new pandemics, expert warns'.

9. Suppliers of Choice to HM Government

1 'United Kingdom – country commercial guide: selling to the public sector', International Trade Administration [website] (3 November 2023), https://www.trade.gov/country-commercial-guides/united-kingdom-selling-public-sector.

2 'DataCentred commits to 200 jobs', Manchester Digital [website] (3 October 2014), https://www.manchesterdigital.com/post/manchester-digital/datacentred-commits-to-200-jobs.

3 James Graham, 'The tech pioneer with his head in the cloud', The Business Desk [website] (5 January 2015), https://www.thebusinessdesk.com/northwest/news/708007-the-pioneer-with-his-head-in-the-cloud.

4 Quoted in Sebastian Moss, 'DataCentred is shutting down after losing HMRC as a customer', Data Center Dynamics [website] (24 October 2017), https://www.datacenterdynamics.com/en/news/datacentred-is-shutting-down-after-losing-hmrc-as-a-customer/.

5 'AWS is utterly dominating UK gov't cloud spend', The Stack [website] (24 June 2022), https://www.thestack.technology/uk-government-cloud-spend-digital-suppliers/.

6 Fatima Attarwala, 'Amazon, Microsoft, and Google face investigation into cloud services by UK regulators', Investopedia [website] (5 October 2023), https://www.investopedia.com/amazon-microsoft-and-google-face-investigation-into-cloud-services-by-uk-regulators-8347946.

7 'AWS is utterly dominating UK gov't cloud spend'.

8 For the Passport Office, see 'Her Majesty's Passport Office: delivery partner for online passport application services', Gov.uk [website], https://www.digitalmarketplace.service.gov.uk/digital-outcomes-and-specialists/opportunities/2400. For the Land Registry, see Mark Say, 'Land Registry signs Kainos as tech partner', UKAuthority [website] (5 August 2020), https://www.ukauthority.com/articles/land-registry-signs-kainos-as-tech-partner/.

9 Mark Say, 'Passport Office agrees new deal with Kainos', UKAuthority [website] (11 August 2021), https://www.ukauthority.com/articles/passport-offices-agrees-new-deal-with-kainos/.

10 'Kainos secures £8m contract with HM Land Registry', Irish News (13 August 2020), https://www.irishnews.com/business/2020/08/13/news/kainos-secures-8m-contract-with-hm-land-registry-2034171/.

11 'Frameworks for the UK public sector', Bytes [website], https://www.bytes.co.uk/customers/verticals/government-frameworks.

12 'Softcat plc annual report and accounts 2022' [PDF], Softcat [website], https://www.softcat.com/3616/6799/2880/Softcat_plc_Annual_Report_and_Accounts_2022_-_Website.pdf.

13 For Hewlett Packard, see Gavin Clarke, 'Hewlett-Packard paid £1.7bn by UK.gov in 2 years – report', The Register [website] (27 June 2014), https://www.theregister.com/2014/06/27/institute_for_government_hp_dominates_gov_spending/. For DXC, see 'Crown Prosecution Service for England and Wales taps DXC Technology for workplace transformation', DXC Technology [website] (3 October 2023), https://dxc.com/us/en/about-us/newsroom/press-releases/10032023. For AWS, see Georgia Butler, 'AWS wins £94m contract with UK Gov's DWP', Data Center Dynamics [website] (8 January 2024), https://www.datacenterdynamics.com/en/news/aws-wins-94m-contract-with-uk-govs-dwp/.

14 House of Commons Public Administration Select Committee, 'Government and IT – "a recipe for rip-offs": time for a new approach: twelfth report of session 2010–12' [PDF], Parliament.uk [website] (18 July 2011), https://publications.parliament.uk/pa/cm201012/cmselect/cmpubadm/715/715i.pdf.

15 'Overseas suppliers to the UK public sector report', Tussell [website], https://www.tussell.com/overseas-suppliers-report-2021-2.

16 Ibid.

17 For the figure of £733 million, see section 5 at 'MOD trade, industry and contracts: 2023', Gov.uk [website] (28 September 2023), https://www.gov.uk/government/statistics/mod-trade-industry-and-contracts-2023/mod-trade-industry-and-contracts-2023. See also Louisa Brooke-Holland, 'Defence procurement reform' [PDF], Parliament.uk [website] (10 June 2022), https://researchbriefings.files.parliament.uk/documents/CBP-9566/CBP-9566.pdf.

18 'Department of Defense unveils comprehensive recommendations to strengthen foreign military sales', US Department of Defense [website] (13 June 2023), https://www.defense.gov/News/Releases/Release/Article/3425963/department-of-defense-unveils-comprehensive-recommendations-to-strengthen-forei/.

19 George Allison, 'British Army "no plans" to increase deployable divisions', UK Defence Journal [website] (14 March 2022), https://ukdefencejournal.org.uk/british-army-no-plans-to-increase-deployable-divisions/.

20 Jamie Merrill Friday, 'Royal Navy relied on Nato to protect British waters 20 times in 2015', Independent (12 February 2016), https://www.independent.co.uk/news/uk/home-news/royal-navy-relied-on-nato-to-protect-british-waters-20-times-in-2015-a6870686.html.

21 Jake Wallis Simons, 'How Washington owns the UK's nukes', Politico [website] (30 April 2015), https://www.politico.eu/article/uk-trident-nuclear-program/.

22 'KBR selected to support UK MOD defense training estate', KBR [website] (1 May 2020), https://www.kbr.com/en/insights-news/press-release/kbr-selected-support-uk-mod-defense-training-estate.

23 'United Kingdom – aerospace', Export.gov [website] (1 August 2019), https://www.export.gov/apex/article2?id=United-Kingdom-Aerospace.

24 'Aerospace & defense', CA.gov [website], https://business.ca.gov/industries/aerospace-and-defense/.

25 'Aircraft projects (cancellation) HC deb 13 April 1965 vol 710 cc1171–297', Parliament.uk [website], https://api.parliament.uk/historic-hansard/commons/1965/apr/13/aircraft-projects-cancellation.

26 Quoted in David Dimbleby and David Reynolds, *An Ocean Apart: The Relationship between Britain and America in the Twentieth Century* (New York: Random House, 1988).

27 'Brake Bros', Wikipedia [website], https://en.wikipedia.org/wiki/Brake_Bros.

28 Aditya Chakrabortty, 'How Boots went rogue', *Guardian* (13 April 2016), https://www.theguardian.com/news/2016/apr/13/how-boots-went-rogue.

29 Robert Booth and Nick Hopkins, 'Olympic security chaos: depth of G4S security crisis revealed', *Guardian* (13 July 2012), https://www.theguardian.com/sport/2012/jul/12/london-2012-g4s-security-crisis.

30 Alan Travis, 'G4S faces fraud investigation over tagging contracts', *Guardian* (12 July 2013), https://www.theguardian.com/business/2013/jul/11/g4s-investigated-overcharging-millions-pounds.

31 Jamie Grierson and Jessica Elgot, 'Failings at Birmingham Prison reflect broader crisis, MOJ is warned', *Guardian* (20 August 2018), https://www.theguardian.com/society/2018/aug/20/failings-of-hmp-birmingham-reflect-broader-prison-crisis-moj-warned.

32 'Riot officers enter HMP Birmingham amid disturbances', BBC News [website] (16 December 2016), https://www.bbc.co.uk/news/uk-england-birmingham-38341924.

33 'The worst ever prison', InsideTime [website] (31 August 2018), https://insidetime.org/the-worst-ever-prison/.

34 Joanna Partridge, 'G4S agrees to £3.8bn takeover by US rival Allied Universal', *Guardian* (8 December 2020), https://www.theguardian.com/business/2020/dec/08/g4s-agrees-to-38bn-takeover-by-us-rival-allied-universal.

35 Calum Rosie, 'Private prisons have shown a lax approach to human rights', EachOther [website] (26 April 2021), https://eachother.org.uk/private-prisons-have-shown-a-lax-approach-to-human-rights/.

36 For HS2, see also Ailie MacAdam, 'It's all about the people', *Transport Times* (September 2014), https://www.bechtel.com/getmedia/f805ed68-8315-446f-aa96-4912e97c810e/bechtel-its-all-about-the-people-times-hs2-sept-14.

37 'Number of satellites in orbit by major country as of April 30, 2022', Statista [website], https://www.statista.com/statistics/264472/number-of-satellites-in-orbit-by-operating-country/.

38 Cristina Gallardo, 'UK scraps Brexit alternative to EU's Galileo satellite system', Politico [website] (24 September 2020), https://www.politico.eu/article/uk-scraps-plan-to-build-global-satellite-navigation-system-to-replace-galileo/.

39 For Lord Young's review, see 'Government procurement in the United Kingdom', Wikipedia [website], https://en.wikipedia.org/wiki/Government_procurement_in_the_United_Kingdom. For the FSB, see 'FSB welcomes political consensus to tackle procurement scandal', FSB [website] (31 August 2020), https://www.fsb.org.uk/resources-page/fsb-welcomes-political-consensus-to-tackle-procurement-scandal.html.

40 'Crown Commercial Service annual report and accounts 2022 to 2023', Gov.uk [website] (17 July 2023), https://www.gov.uk/government/publications/crown-commercial-service-annual-report-and-accounts-2022-to-2023.

41 'Build America Buy America', Office of Acquisition Management [website], https://www.commerce.gov/oam/build-america-buy-america.

42 'Made in America', Made in America [website], http://tinyurl.com/5dpmrsc6.

43 Victoria Waldersee, 'Tesla scales back German battery plans, won over by US incentives', Reuters [website] (22 February 2023), https://www.reuters.com/technology/tesla-scales-back-german-battery-plans-won-over-by-us-incentives-2023-02-21/.

44 'Viridor', Plasteurope.com [website] (15 July 2020), https://www.plasteurope.com/news/VIRIDOR_t245521/.

45 Quoted in Kaye Wiggins, 'Private equity steps in where others fear to tread during pandemic', *Financial Times* [website] (18 June 2020), https://www.ft.com/content/912929f7-7366-45d0-90ce-4467b9fec7f0.

46 'Energy Capital Partners (ECP) completes acquisition of Biffa', Energy Capital Partners [website] (27 January 2023), https://www.ecpgp.com/insights/energy-capital-partners-ecp-completes-acquisition-of-biffa.

47 'Offer for Biffa plc', London Stock Exchange [website] (27 September 2022), https://www.londonstockexchange.com/news-article/market-news/offer-for-biffa-plc/15645553.

48 The average over recent years. See 'Table 1A' at 'SOI tax stats – country by country report', IRS [website], https://www.irs.gov/statistics/soi-tax-stats-country-by-country-report. For 2020: column G, line 154 (£12.8 billion). For 2019: column G, line 154 (£10.6 billion). For 2018: column G, line 155 (£10.9 billion). For 2017: column G, line 155 (£9.3 billion).

49 Robert Wood Johnson, 'Don't let smears about US farms trap Britain into the EU's Museum of Agriculture', *Daily Telegraph* (1 March 2019), https://www.telegraph.co.uk/environment/2019/03/01/dont-let-smears-us-farms-trap-britain-eus-museum-agriculture/.

50 Quoted in 'UK–US trade deal: envoy attacks "myths" about US farming', BBC News [website] (2 March 2019), https://www.bbc.co.uk/news/uk-47426138.

51 Deborah Summers, 'Gordon Brown's "British jobs" pledge has caused controversy before', *Guardian* (30 January 2009), https://www.theguardian.com/politics/2009/jan/30/british-jobs-british-workers.

52 Michael Wilkinson, 'Amber Rudd vows to stop migrants "taking jobs British people could do" and force companies to reveal number of foreigners they employ', *Daily Telegraph* (4 October 2016), https://www.telegraph.co.uk/news/2016/10/04/jeremy-hunt-nhs-doctors-theresa-may-conservative-conference-live/.

10. Consequences: Why Does US Dominance Matter?

1 Quoted in Hamish McDonald, *The Polyester Prince: The Rise of Dhirubhai Ambani* (St Leonards, NSW: Allen & Unwin, 1998).

2 'Average household income, UK: financial year ending 2022', Office for National Statistics [website], http://tinyurl.com/46un3zde; 'Quick facts: Mississippi', United States Census Bureau [website], https://www.census.gov/quickfacts/fact/table/MS/BZA115221. The UK figures show a median household disposable income of £32,300, which at the 2023 year-end exchange rate was $41,021. The Mississippi median income figure is $52,985. The tax rate for such Mississippians (at the fiftieth percentile) would be 13.9 per cent, so after tax they would have $45,620, which is still more than 10 per cent above the UK median household disposable income. Even those who concentrate on other ways of measuring poverty agree that the UK is on a par with Mississippi. See 'Is Britain really as poor as Mississippi?', *Financial Times* (10 August 2023), https://www.ft.com/content/e5c741a7-befa-4d49-a819-f1b0510a9802.

3 'Company town', https://en.wikipedia.org/wiki/Company_town.

4 'Beaverton, Oregon', Wikipedia [website], https://en.wikipedia.org/wiki/Beaverton,_Oregon.

5 Aoife Morgan, 'Costco eyes 14 new stores as it ramps up expansion drive', Retail Gazette [website] (17 August 2023), https://www.retailgazette.co.uk/blog/2023/08/costco-store-expansion/.

6 For Costco's principles, see 'Our mission / our code of ethics' [PDF], Costco [website] (March 2010), https://www.costco.com/wcsstore/CostcoUSBCCatalogAssetStore/feature-pages/Attachment/16w0604-sustainability-ethics.pdf. For its accounts, see 'Costco Wholesale UK Limited', Gov.uk [website], https://find-and-update.company-information.service.gov.uk/company/02635489/filing-history.

7 'Amazon draws 238 bids from cities vying to host new headquarters', *Financial Times* (24 October 2017), https://www.ft.com/content/bc35267e-b881-11e7-8c12-5661783e5589.

8 Quoted in 'Where Amazon's HQ2 may help housing most', iPro [website] (19 January 2018), https://blucoveic.iprore.com/news/where-amazons-hq2-may-help-housing-most.

9 Severin Carrell, 'Cadbury takeover raises doubts over Kraft's business ethics', *Guardian* (20 January 2010), https://www.theguardian.com/business/2010/jan/20/cadbury-kraft-takeover-fair-trade. On Cadbury and fair trade, see also Maryam Zakir-Hussain, 'Customers urged to avoid buying from leading chocolate firms over "inadequate" ethical standards', *Independent* (2 December 2023), https://www.independent.co.uk/news/uk/home-news/chocolate-companies-cadbury-inadequate-ethical-standards-b2457369.html. On Cadbury and child labour, see Jon Ungoed-Thomas, 'Cadbury faces fresh accusations of child labour on cocoa farms in Ghana', *Guardian* (3 April 2022), https://www.theguardian.com/law/2022/apr/03/cadbury-faces-fresh-accusations-of-child-labour-on-cocoa-farms-in-ghana.

10 'The Hershey Company', Wikipedia [website], https://en.wikipedia.org/wiki/The_Hershey_Company.

11 For Inmarsat, see 'Viasat completes acquisition of Inmarsat', Inmarsat [website] (31 May 2023), https://www.inmarsat.com/en/news/latest-news/

corporate/2023/viasat-completes-acquisition-inmarsat.html. For Meggitt, see 'Parker completes acquisition of Meggitt plc', Parker [website] (13 September 2022), https://shorturl.at/hwCG1.

12 Interview with the author, 18 August 2021.

13 The Clockwork Apple, 'Guide: how to land Spring Week offers' [post], The Student Room [website] (2017), https://www.thestudentroom.co.uk/showthread.php?t=4560486.

14 Interview with the author, 18 August 2021.

15 'Colleges of the University of Oxford', Wikipedia [website], https://en.wikipedia.org/wiki/Colleges_of_the_University_of_Oxford; 'Harvard University endowment', Wikipedia [website], https://en.wikipedia.org/wiki/Harvard_University_endowment.

16 'NYU London', NYU [website], https://www.nyu.edu/london.html.

17 From a transcription of a face-to-face interview with the author, edited slightly by Spence and sent via email on 25 June 2023.

18 Quoted in 'Silicon Valley Brits: "We had to leave the UK behind"', BBC News [website] (21 September 2016), https://www.bbc.co.uk/news/technology-37417758.

19 'Getty Museum intends to acquire a painting by Joseph Wright of Derby and a sculpture by Veit Stoss', Getty Center [website] (4 June 2019), https://www.getty.edu/news/getty-announces-intent-to-acquire-painting-by-joseph-wright-and-sculpture-by-veit-stoss/.

20 Quoted in 'US gallery banned from purchasing Joseph Wright painting', BBC News [website] (18 October 2019), https://www.bbc.com/news/uk-england-derbyshire-50097028.

21 Mark Brown, 'Joshua Reynolds' *Portrait of Omai* acquired by National Portrait Gallery', *Guardian* (25 April 2023), https://www.theguardian.com/artanddesign/2023/apr/25/joshua-reynolds-portrait-of-omai-jointly-acquired-by-the-national-portrait-gallery-and-getty.

22 'Value of works of art, collectors' pieces, and antiques exported from the United Kingdom (UK) from 2008 to 2022', Statista [website], https://www.statista.com/statistics/477951/uk-united-kingdom-art-antiques-exports/. See also spreadsheet downloadable at 'UK trade in goods, year in review: 2022', Office for National Statistics [website] (17 February 2023), https://www.ons.gov.uk/economy/nationalaccounts/balanceofpayments/articles/uktradeingoodsyearinreview/2022. Column CS, row 221 gives a figure of only about £2.5 billion for 2022, but I take that to be an effect of Covid.

23 Shane Hickey, 'Hard to swallow: the 30% price hike that gets delivered with your meal', *Guardian* (11 July 2022), https://www.theguardian.com/money/2022/jul/11/hard-to-swallow-the-30-price-hike-that-gets-delivered-with-your-meal.

24 Jack Shenker, '"They're stealing our customers and we've had enough": is Deliveroo killing restaurant culture?', *Guardian* (25 April 2021), https://www.theguardian.com/global-development/2021/apr/25/deliveroo-tech-delivery-restaurant-service-dark-kitchens.

25 'CMA clears Amazon's 16% investment in Deliveroo', Gov.uk [website] (4 August 2020), https://www.gov.uk/government/news/cma-clears-amazons-16-investment-in-deliveroo.

26 James Bloodworth, *Hired: Six Months Undercover in Low-Wage Britain* (London: Atlantic, 2018).

27 Quoted in Ellie O'Hagan, 'Class inequality: "Rise with your class, not out of it"', Green World [website] (8 October 2015), https://greenworld.org.uk/article/class-inequality-rise-your-class-not-out-it.

28 Public sector pension liability, about £2 trillion: Alex Janiaud, 'Public sector pension liabilities break £2tn with 16% surge', *Pensions Expert* (6 June 2022), https://www.pensions-expert.com/Defined-Benefit/Public-sector-pension-liabilities-break-2tn-with-16-surge?ct=true. State pension 'commitment', about £5 trillion: 'Pensions in the national accounts, a fuller picture of the UK's funded and unfunded pension obligations: 2018', Office for National Statistics [website], https://www.ons.gov.uk/economy/nationalaccounts/uksectoraccounts/articles/pensionsinthenationalaccountsafullerpictureoftheuksfundedandunfundedpensionobligations/2018.

29 See 'Table 1A' (2020 figures), column 10 ('Number of employees'), line 154 ('United Kingdom') at 'SOI tax stats – country by country report'.

30 Sarah Butler, 'Morrisons shareholders wave through £7bn takeover', *Guardian* (19 October 2021), https://www.theguardian.com/business/2021/oct/19/morrisons-shareholders-wave-through-7bn-takeover.

31 'The gig economy: what does it really look like?' [PDF], Chartered Institute of Personnel and Development [website] (September 2023), https://www.cipd.org/globalassets/media/knowledge/knowledge-hub/reports/2023-pdfs/2023-cipd-gig-economy-report-8453.pdf.

32 Andrew Brem, 'The impact of Uber in the UK', Uber [website] (20 September 2023), https://www.uber.com/en-GB/newsroom/the-impact-of-uber-in-the-uk-2/.

33 See 'Table 1A' (2020 figures), column 10 ('Number of employees'), lines 123 (for France, with 322,000), 124 (for Germany, with 569,000), 132 (for Italy, with 208,000) and 149 (for Spain, with 203,000) at 'SOI tax stats – country by country report', IRS [website], https://www.irs.gov/statistics/soi-tax-stats-country-by-country-report.

34 See colour-coded map headed 'Net average monthly salary (adjusted for living costs in PPP)', at 'List of European countries by average wage', Wikipedia [website], https://en.wikipedia.org/wiki/List_of_European_countries_by_average_wage.

11. The American Way

1 Quoted in Ellen Terrell, 'When a quote is not (exactly) a quote: the business of America is business edition', Library of Congress [website] (17 January 2019), https://blogs.loc.gov/inside_adams/2019/01/when-a-quote-is-not-exactly-a-quote-the-business-of-america-is-business-edition/.

2 For whisky, see '£29 million boost for bioscience', Gov.uk [website] (11 April 2017), https://www.gov.uk/government/news/29-million-boost-for-bioscience. For Scotch beef and lamb, see 'Alister Jack calls on all Scottish MPs to back UK–EU trade deal', Gov.uk [website] (27 December 2020), https://www.gov.uk/government/news/alister-jack-calls-on-all-scottish-mps-to-back-uk-eu-trade-deal. For 'Test and Trace', see 'UK PM Johnson vows "world-beating" track and trace COVID system by June 1', Reuters [website] (20 May 2020), https://www.reuters.com/article/us-health-coronavirus-britain-track-idUSKBN22W1MW.

3 With thanks to Iain Overton to pointing this out. See Iain Overton, 'The UK's "world-beating" rhetoric: a distraction from reality?', *Byline Times* (28 April 2023), https://bylinetimes.com/2023/04/28/the-uks-world-beating-rhetoric-a-distraction-from-reality/. For Labour's proposals, see 'A new Britain: renewing our democracy and rebuilding our economy' [PDF], Labour [website] (5 December 2022), https://labour.org.uk/wp-content/uploads/2022/12/Commission-on-the-UKs-Future.pdf. The words 'world-beating innovators and entrepreneurs' are those of Conservative politician Nicky Morgan, speaking in her former capacity as Secretary of State for Digital, Culture, Media and Sport in January 2020. See 'Baroness Morgan speaking on how we can make technology work for everyone' [transcript of speech delivered at the Talent Charter Annual Event held at the Gherkin in the City of London on 15 January

2020], Gov.uk [website] (15 January 2020), https://www.gov.uk/government/speeches/baroness-morgan-speaking-on-how-we-can-make-technology-work-for-everyone.

4 Quoted in 'Mayor Bloomberg: "Make sure you are the first one in there every day & the last one to leave"', TechCrunch [website] (30 November 2011), https://techcrunch.com/2011/11/30/founder-stories-mayor-bloomberg-make-sure-you-are-the-first-one-in-there-every-day-the-last-one-to-leave/.

5 Quoted in 'Why Jeff Bezos should care more for Amazon's employees', *New York Times* (21 August 2015), https://www.nytimes.com/2015/08/22/business/dealbook/why-jeff-bezos-should-care-more-for-amazons-employees.html.

6 Quoted in Catherine Clifford, 'Elon Musk on working 120 hours in a week: "However hard it was for [the team], I would make it worse for me"', CNBC Make It [website] (10 December 2018), https://www.cnbc.com/2018/12/10/elon-musk-says-working-120-hours-in-a-week-was-a-show-of-leadership.html.

7 Quoted in Wilfred Chan, 'Elon Musk praises Chinese workers for "burning the 3am oil" – here's what that really looks like', *Guardian* (12 May 2022), https://www.theguardian.com/technology/2022/may/12/elon-musk-praises-chinese-workers-for-extreme-work-culture.

8 'Hours worked', OECD [website], https://data.oecd.org/emp/hours-worked.htm.

9 Sarah Green Carmichael, 'The research is clear: long hours backfire for people and for companies', *Harvard Business Review* (19 August 2015), https://hbr.org/2015/08/the-research-is-clear-long-hours-backfire-for-people-and-for-companies.

10 Alexis de Tocqueville, *Democracy in America*, trans. Henry Reeve, ii (London: Saunder & Otley, 1835), §1, ch. 8. Available at https://www.gutenberg.org/files/816/816-h/816-h.htm.

11 Quoted in Mark Thompson, 'Some GOP candidates seem to prefer howitzers to humiliation', *Time* (15 January 2016), https://time.com/4182006/republican-debate-iran-sailors/.

12 For the figure of $8–12 trillion, see '"There's a better way to do it – find it": a Thomas Edison TED talk by John Keegan' [video], Edison Innovation Foundation [website], https://www.edisonmuckers.org/ted-talk-on-thomas-edison/.

13 'Grants & funding', National Institutes of Health [website], https://www.nih.gov/grants-funding.

14 For solar cells, see 'This month in physics history: April 25, 1954: Bell Labs demonstrates the first practical silicon solar cell', American Physical Society [website] (April 2009), https://www.aps.org/publications/apsnews/200904/physicshistory.cfm.

15 For $717 billion, see Alexander Rhodes, 'United States exceeds $700 billion in gross domestic expenditures on R&D in 2020', National Center for Science and Engineering Statistics [website] (22 June 2023), https://ncses.nsf.gov/pubs/nsf23346.

16 Einar H. Dyvik, 'Annual expenditure per student on educational institutions in OECD countries for primary, secondary and tertiary education in 2020, by country', Statista [website] (7 November 2023), https://www.statista.com/statistics/238733/expenditure-on-education-by-country/.

17 'Top 200 universities in the world: 2023 uniRank world university ranking', uniRank [website], https://www.4icu.org/top-universities-world/.

18 'Leland Stanford Jr.', Wikipedia [website], https://en.wikipedia.org/wiki/Leland_Stanford_Jr.

19 For the figure of 85,000, see 'H1B visa (specialty workers)', Immigration Advice Service [website], https://iasservices.org.uk/us/work/h1b-visa/.

20 'H-1B visa', Wikipedia [website], https://en.wikipedia.org/wiki/H-1B_visa.

21 Quoted in Erica R. Hendry, '7 epic fails brought to you by the genius mind of Thomas Edison', *Smithsonian Magazine* (20 November 2013), https://www.smithsonianmag.com/innovation/7-epic-fails-brought-to-you-by-the-genius-mind-of-thomas-edison-180947786/.

22 'Billionaires by country', Wisevoter [website], https://wisevoter.com/country-rankings/billionaires-by-country/.

23 Quoted in George Ticknor Curtis, *A Treatise on the Law of Patents for Useful Inventions: As Enacted and Administered in the United States of America* (Boston, MA: Little, Brown, 1849), p. 502.

24 'World intellectual property indicators 2022' [PDF], WIPO [website] (2022), https://www.wipo.int/edocs/pubdocs/en/wipo-pub-941-2022-en-world-intellectual-property-indicators-2022.pdf.

25 For the US figure, see 'Patent practitioner home page', United States Patent and Trademark Office [website], https://oedci.uspto.gov/OEDCI/#:~:text=Find%20a%20patent%20agent%20or,current%20information%20available%20to%20OED. For the UK figure, see 'About us', Chartered Institute of Patent Attorneys [website], https://www.cipa.org.uk/.

26 'IBM builds a smarter planet', IBM [website], https://www.ibm.com/smarterplanet/us/en/; 'Policies & practices', P&G [website], https://www.pg.co.uk/policies-and-practices/purpose-values-and-principles/; 'Disneyland Resort – the happiest place on earth', Disney Parks [website], https://disneyparks.disney.go.com/au/disneyland/your-happiest-place-disney/.

27 Interview with the author, September 2020.

28 'Coke and McDonald's, growing together since 1955', *New York Times* (15 May 2014), https://www.nytimes.com/2014/05/16/business/coke-and-mcdonalds-working-hand-in-hand-since-1955.html.

29 'MediaTalk; Disney buys the rights to Winnie the Pooh', *New York Times* (5 March 2001), https://www.nytimes.com/2001/03/05/business/mediatalk-disney-buys-the-rights-to-winnie-the-pooh.html.

30 'Operation Creative blocks £6 million of UK advertising revenue from funding illegal websites', City of London Police [website] (6 February 2023), https://www.cityoflondon.police.uk/news/city-of-london/news/2023/january/operation-creative-blocks-6-million-of-uk-advertising-revenue-from-funding-illegal-websites/.

31 Frederick Winslow Taylor, *Principles of Scientific Management* (New York: Harper & Brothers, 1911).

32 Peter F. Drucker, 'The rise of the knowledge society' [PDF], *Wilson Quarterly* 17/2 (1993), http://archive.wilsonquarterly.com/sites/default/files/articles/WQ_VOL17_SP_1993_Article_02_1.pdf.

33 'Hawthorne effect', Wikipedia [website], https://en.wikipedia.org/wiki/Hawthorne_effect.

34 See, for instance, 'Lean manufacturing', Wikipedia [website], https://en.wikipedia.org/wiki/Lean_manufacturing; 'Six Sigma', Wikipedia [website], https://en.wikipedia.org/wiki/Six_Sigma; 'What are performance metrics?', Sage [website], http://tinyurl.com/3zfxv9zb.

35 See, for instance, Helen Gray, 'What is continuous improvement? (And how to include it in your company culture)', eLearning Industry [website] (19 January 2021), http://tinyurl.com/4vwuht4z; Sarah Laoyan, 'What is agile methodology? (A beginner's guide)', Asana [website] (15 October 2022), https://asana.com/resources/agile-methodology.

36 See, for instance, 'JIT just-in-time manufacturing', University of Cambridge [website], https://www.ifm.eng.cam.ac.uk/research/dstools/jit-just-in-time-manufacturing/.

37 'Marshall Field (1834–1906)', *American Experience* [website], https://www. pbs.org/wgbh/americanexperience/features/chicago-marshall-field-1834-1906/.

38 Quoted in Charles Arthur, 'Walled gardens look rosy for Facebook, Apple – and would-be censors', *Guardian* (17 April 2012), https://www.theguardian. com/technology/2012/apr/17/walled-gardens-facebook-apple-censors.

39 Keshav Thakur, 'Gillette's razor-sharp success: how a simple strategy built a business empire', LinkedIn [website] (22 November 2023), https://www. linkedin.com/pulse/gillettes-razor-sharp-success-how-simple-strategy-built-keshav-thakur-z1yyf/.

40 'EG Group reaches deal to buy Tesla Superchargers for its forecourts', *Car* (14 November 2023), https://www.carmagazine.co.uk/electric/charging-network/tesla-supercharger/.

41 'Market share held by mobile operating systems in the United Kingdom (UK) from January 2018 to July 2023', Statista [website] (4 September 2023), https://www.statista.com/statistics/934440/market-share-held-by-mobile-operating-systems-in-the-united-kingdom/.

42 Denny Ludwell, *America Conquers Britain: A Record of Economic War* (New York: A. A. Knopf, 1930).

12. Puppet Masters

1 Quoted in the fifth episode of *An Ocean Apart* (1988), a BBC documentary series presented by David Dimbleby and produced by Adam Curtis (9 minutes, 20 seconds in).

2 'Edward Colin Cherry', MacTutor History of Mathematics Archive [website], https://mathshistory.st-andrews.ac.uk/Biographies/Cherry_Colin/.

3 E. C. Cherry, 'Some experiments on the recognition of speech, with one and two ears', *Journal of the Acoustical Society of America* 25 (1953), pp. 975–9, doi: 10.1121/1.1907229.

4 Maegan Vazquez and Nikki Carvajal, 'Trump ponders tariffs on French wines in retaliation for tech company tax', CNN [website] (26 July 2019), https:// edition.cnn.com/2019/07/26/politics/donald-trump-france-wine-tariff/index. html.

5 Quoted in Sam Coates, 'Brexit: Joe Biden's ties to Ireland "could see him intervene if talks turn acrimonious"', Sky News [website] (2 November 2020), https://news.sky.com/story/brexit-joe-bidens-ties-to-ireland-could-see-him-intervene-if-talks-turn-acrimonious-12120863.

6 'Embassy of the United States of America, London', LinkedIn [website], https://www.linkedin.com/company/us-embassy-london/about/.

7 Arnaud Bertrand, 'Incredible, and maybe even unprecedented, answer by Arnaud Montebourg […] But for Americans it is the law to do so!' [Twitter post] (4 June 2023), https://twitter.com/RnaudBertrand/status/1665370246126125060.

8 Ibid.

9 'Arnaud Montebourg demande au gouvernement d'"interdire" le rachat d'une PME par un groupe américain', Capital [website] (11 April 2023), http://tinyurl.com/u5m97k39.

10 Ibid.

11 Quoted in Jack Maidment, 'Boris Johnson promises not to "jeopardise" UK national security ahead of crunch decision on whether to allow Huawei to help build Britain's 5G network as PM hints at compromise', *Daily Mail* (27 January 2020), https://www.dailymail.co.uk/news/article-7933473/Justice-Secretary-Robert-Buckland-warns-against-trying-bully-Britain-Huawei.html.

12 Quoted in Adam Payne, Thomas Colson and Adam Bienkov, 'Boris Johnson defies Trump and gives Huawei the green light to develop Britain's 5G network', Business Insider [website] (28 January 2020), http://tinyurl.com/mst4494p.

13 Quoted in James Pearce, 'UK government approves limited 5G role for Huawei', IBC [website] (28 January 2020), https://www.ibc.org/trends/uk-government-approves-limited-5g-role-for-huawei/5394.article.

14 Quoted in 'Reaction to UK allowing Huawei a role in 5G network', Reuters [website] (28 January 2020), https://www.reuters.com/article/idUSKBN1ZR1FU/.

15 'Trump "apoplectic" in phone call with Johnson over Huawei decision, report claims', *Independent* (7 February 2020), https://www.independent.co.uk/news/uk/politics/trump-boris-johnson-huawei-phone-call-angry-5g-a9322826.html.

16 Newt Gingrich, 'British decision to accept Huawei for 5G is a major defeat for the United Statees [*sic*] […]' [Twitter post] (28 January 2020), https://twitter.com/RnaudBertrand/status/1665370246126125060.

17 Quoted in Ashley Cowburn, 'Donald Trump official issues veiled threat to Boris Johnson over Huawei 5G decision', *Independent* (17 February 2020), https://www.independent.co.uk/news/uk/politics/trump-boris-johnson-huawei-5g-china-brexit-phone-call-a9338791.html.

18 Quoted in Leo Kelion, 'Huawei set for limited role in UK 5G networks', BBC News [website] (28 January 2020), https://www.bbc.co.uk/news/technology-51283059.

19 Quoted in Anna Mikhailova and Mike Wright, 'Boris Johnson fails to stave off Huawei rebellion as Tory MPs call for tougher measures', *Daily Telegraph* (14 July 2020), https://www.telegraph.co.uk/politics/2020/07/14/boris-johnson-fails-stave-huawei-rebellion-tory-mps-call-tougher/.

20 Quoted in 'Defence sub-committee oral evidence: the security of 5G, HC 201', House of Commons [website] (16 June 2020), https://committees.parliament.uk/oralevidence/534/html/.

21 Quoted in 'Huawei to be removed from UK 5G networks by 2027', Gov.uk [website] (14 July 2020), https://www.gov.uk/government/news/huawei-to-be-removed-from-uk-5g-networks-by-2027.

22 Quoted in Lily Kuo, 'Chinese media calls for "pain" over UK Huawei ban as Trump claims credit', *Guardian* (15 July 2020), https://www.theguardian.com/technology/2020/jul/15/huawei-china-state-media-calls-for-painful-retaliation-over-uk-ban.

23 Quoted in Harriet Brewis, 'Mike Pompeo claims WHO chief was "bought" by China leading to "dead Britons"', *Evening Standard* (22 July 2020), https://www.standard.co.uk/news/uk/mike-pompeo-who-bought-china-a4505081.html.

24 'Banning TikTok would boost Alphabet, Meta and Snap – here's how much their stocks could jump', Forbes [website] (23 March 2023), https://www.forbes.com/sites/dereksaul/2023/03/23/banning-tiktok-would-boost-alphabet-meta-and-snap-heres-how-much-their-stocks-could-jump/.

25 'UK chancellor welcomes Huawei's investment', Fibre Systems [website], https://www.fibre-systems.com/news/uk-chancellor-welcomes-huaweis-investment.

26 Patrick Wintour, 'David Cameron's appointment to investment fund "part engineered by China"', *Guardian* (14 July 2023), https://www.theguardian.com/politics/2023/jul/14/david-camerons-appointment-to-investment-fund-part-engineered-by-china.

27 'Inflation Reduction Act', Wikipedia [website], https://en.wikipedia.org/wiki/Inflation_Reduction_Act.

28 Victoria Waldersee, 'Tesla scales back German battery plans, won over by US incentives', Reuters [website] (22 February 2023), https://www.reuters.com/technology/tesla-scales-back-german-battery-plans-won-over-by-us-incentives-2023-02-21/; Richard Milne, Patricia Nilsson and Peter Campbell, 'VW puts European battery plant on hold as it seeks €10bn from US', *Financial Times* [website] (8 March 2023), https://www.ft.com/content/6ac390f5-df35-4e39-a572-2c01a12f666a.

29 Ibid.

30 Quoted in 'Extradition Act 2003: David Davis excerpts', Parallel Parliament [website] (21 January 2021), https://www.parallelparliament.co.uk/mp/david-davis/debate/2021-01-21/commons/commons-chamber/extradition-act-2003.

31 David Davis MP, 'David Davis MP holds adjournment debate on the operation of the Extradition Act 2003' [video], YouTube [website] (21 January 2021), https://www.youtube.com/watch?v=5hDyAjvSqjk&ab_channel=DavidDavisMP.

32 Clark Neily, 'A distant mirror: American-style plea bargaining through the eyes of a foreign tribunal', *George Mason Law Review* 27/3 (2020), pp. 719–48, https://lawreview.gmu.edu/print__issues/27gmlr719/.

33 Quoted in Henry Martin, 'Harry Dunn protestors demonstrate outside US base demanding spy's wife be returned to UK to face questions over road crash that killed the British teen', *Dail Mail* (4 January 2020), https://www.dailymail.co.uk/news/article-7851451/Harry-Dunn-protestors-demonstrate-outside-base-demanding-spys-wife-returned-UK.html.

34 Ali Bracken, 'Joe Biden's April visit to Ireland: massive security detail will involve welding the manholes shut', *Irish Independent* (19 March 2023), https://www.independent.ie/irish-news/joe-bidens-april-visit-to-ireland-massive-security-detail-will-involve-welding-the-manholes-shut/42393830.html.

35 'Scrapping HS2 will damage trust in Britain, warn US buyers of Birmingham City', *Financial Times* (25 September 2023), https://www.ft.com/content/c4d68338-fa60-43c8-b9db-de4edc9cb520.

36 Tom Hamilton, 'Tom Brady becomes minority owner at Birmingham City', ESPN [website] (3 August 2023), https://www.espn.co.uk/football/story/_/id/38125429/tom-brady-becomes-minority-owner-birmingham-city.

37 Eddy Wax, 'Trump vowed he'd "never" help Europe if it's attacked, top EU official says', Politico [website] (10 January 2024), https://www.politico.eu/article/donald-trump-vow-never-help-europe-attack-thierry-breton/.

13. The Ultimate Challenge

1 J.-J. Servan-Schreiber, *The American Challenge*, trans. Ronald Steel (New York: Atheneum, 1968).

2 Joanna Partridge, 'UK arm of EDF returns to profit as household electricity prices soar', *Guardian* (17 February 2023), https://www.theguardian.com/

business/2023/feb/17/uk-arm-of-edf-returns-to-profit-as-household-electricity-prices-soar.

3   Quoted in Leila Abboud, 'France's state-backed BPI raises "lake of cash" for stakes in domestic companies', *Financial Times* (26 May 2020), https://www.ft.com/content/e66fb49d-1ab9-4442-8677-3d283bb5de60.

4   'Gross domestic spending on R&D', OECD [website], https://data.oecd.org/rd/gross-domestic-spending-on-r-d.htm.

5   Noor Al-Sibai, 'It turns out SpaceX and Tesla get way more government money than NPR', Futurism [website] (15 April 2023), https://futurism.com/the-byte/spacex-tesla-government-money-npr.

6   John B. Horrigan, 'Lifelong learning and technology', Pew Research Center [website] (22 March 2016), https://www.pewresearch.org/internet/2016/03/22/lifelong-learning-and-technology/.

7   Omri Wallach, 'The top 100 companies of the world: the U.S. vs everyone else', Visual Capitalist [website] (19 July 2021), https://www.visualcapitalist.com/the-top-100-companies-of-the-world-the-u-s-vs-everyone-else/.

8   'Ownership of UK quoted shares: 2020', Office for National Statistics [website] (3 March 2022), https://www.ons.gov.uk/economy/investmentspensionsandtrusts/bulletins/ownershipofukquotedshares/2020.

9   See especially Figure 3 in Mike Brewer and Tom Wernham, 'Income and wealth inequality explained in 5 charts', Institute for Fiscal Studies [website] (9 November 2022), https://ifs.org.uk/articles/income-and-wealth-inequality-explained-5-charts.

10   18.6 per cent of people in Britain and 15.4 per cent of people in Poland are below the poverty line, according to CIA statistics. See 'Population below poverty line', under 'Economy', at 'Explore all countries – United Kingdom', The World Factbook [CIA website], https://www.cia.gov/the-world-factbook/countries/united-kingdom/ and 'Explore all countries – Poland', The World Factbook [CIA website], https://www.cia.gov/the-world-factbook/countries/poland/#people-and-society.

11   'The heart of the German economy', Federation of German Industries (BDI) [website] (24 April 2020), https://english.bdi.eu/article/news/the-heart-of-the-german-economy.

12   Quoted in 'Buffett dons biker gear with German deal', *Financial Times* (20 February 2015), https://www.ft.com/content/f8faf4f6-b6f1-11e4-95dc-00144feab7de. See also 'Warren Buffett to acquire Detlev Louis Motor-

radvertriebs in Europe push', ValueWalk [website] (2 February 2020), https://www.valuewalk.com/warren-buffett-detlev-louis/.

13 'Wealth inequality', London Datastore [website], https://data.london.gov.uk/economic-fairness/equal-opportunities/wealth-inequality/.

14 'Roger B. Chaffee quotes', Inspiring Quotes [website], https://www.inspiringquotes.us/author/1325-roger-b-chaffee.

15 Servan-Schreiber, *The American Challenge*.

Index